The Returns of Alwin Nikolais

BODIES, BOUNDARIES

AND THE DANCE CANON

EDITED BY

CLAUDIA GITELMAN

AND RANDY MARTIN

Wesleyan University Press Middletown, Connecticut

THE RETURNS OF
Alwin Nikolais

© *Tom Caravaglia* 2007

Published by

Wesleyan University Press, Middletown, CT 06459

www.wesleyan.edu/wespress

© 2007 by Wesleyan University Press

Printed in United States of America

5 4 3 2 1

Material from "Critical Reception of the Choreography of Alwin Nikolais" originally
appeared as:

Clive Barnes, "Dance 'Imago' or 'The City Curious,'" *New York Times*, 21 February 1967.
Copyright © 1967 by The New York Times Co. Reprinted with Permisson.

Arlene Croce, "The Case of Alwin Nikolais," *The Dancing Times*, December 1969, reprinted
in *Afterimages* (New York, 1978) © Arlene Croce.

Marcia B. Siegel, "New Dance: Nikolais 'Scenario,'" *Boston Herald Traveler*, 29 March 1971.
Reprinted with permission of the Boston Herald.

Alan M. Kriegsman, "Nikolais: Spells and Marvels," *The Washington Post*, 9 November
1974. © 1974, The Washington Post. Reprinted with Permission.

Deborah Jowitt, "How Do You Tell If It's Human?," *Village Voice*, 14 July 1975. Reprinted
with permission.

Continued on page 297

Library of Congress Cataloging-in-Publication Data

The returns of Alwin Nikolais : bodies, boundaries and the dance canon / edited by
Claudia Gitelman and Randy Martin.

    p.   cm.

Includes bibliographical references and index.

ISBN-13: 978-0-8195-6575-4 (cloth : alk. paper)

ISBN-10: 0-8195-6575-X (cloth : alk. paper)

ISBN-13: 978-0-8195-6576-1 (pbk. : alk. paper)

ISBN-10: 0-8195-6576-8 (pbk. : alk. paper)

1. Nikolais, Alwin.   2. Choreographers—United States—Biography.
I. Gitelman, Claudia.   II. Martin, Randy.

GV1785.N62G58 2007

792.8'2092—dc22

[B]   2006101275

Contents

Editors' Preface

Alwin Nikolais, choreographer, designer, composer, was born in Southington Connecticut, on November 25, 1910, and died in New York City on May 8, 1993. Creator of 118 choreographic works, in a career that spanned seven decades, he pioneered a form of multimedia dance and a novel approach to dance training that gave him access to the creative and improvisational abilities of dancers. Through his company, he sustained many long-term collaborations, none more significant than the one with his partner of forty-three years, dancer and choreographer Murray Louis. He himself studied with some of the seminal figures in American modern dance, among them Martha Graham, musician Louis Horst, and critic John Martin, as well as the German émigré Hanya Holm, whose teaching he assisted after his discharge from the U.S. Army in 1945. In 1948, Holm recommended him for a position as director of dance at the Playhouse of the Henry Street Settlement in New York City, where Nikolais formed the Playhouse Dance Company. He subsequently became the Playhouse's co-director with business manager Betty Young.

He achieved his first critical acclaim and national prominence with *Masks — Props — Mobiles* (1955) and *Kaleidoscope* (1956), which premiered at the American Dance Festival at Connecticut College. In the decade that followed he mounted eleven large-scale dances at Henry Street, where he elaborated on his innovative approach to light projections on dancers and cyclorama. He embraced the medium of television early and beginning with the popular *Steve Allen Show* in 1959 he pioneered technology that would take the medium beyond mere reportage of stage works. His company undertook increasingly extensive national and international tours from the sixties through the eighties, and continued as the amalgamated Murray Louis and Nikolais Dance. Among his signature works are *Allegory* (1959), *Totem* (1960), *Imago* (1963), *Sanctum* (1964), *Vaudeville of the Elements* (1965), *Tent* (1968), *Scenario* (1971), *Crossfade* (1974), *Guignol* (1977), *Gallery* (1978), *Mechanical Organ* (1980 reworded in 1982), and *Crucible* (1985). These works are characterized by an intense interest in the poetic attributes of abstract movement and the theater as a transformational space of illusion, imagery, and surprising kinesthetic effects.

Nikolais was the recipient of every major dance award given in the

United States, the Dance Magazine Award (1967), the Capezio Award (1982), and the Samuel H. Scripps American Dance Festival Award (1985), as well as the National Medal of Arts (1987). In France, where the Ministry of Culture invited him to found a school in Angers, he was made a commander of the Order of Arts and Letters (1982) and a knight of the Legion of Honor (1984). He was recognized with special citations and awards from over thirty cities around the world. He was an early recipient of support from the National Endowment for the Arts, as well as from private patrons and foundations, such as Guggenheim and Mellon. His mastery of the institutional means for disseminating dance rank him among the pioneers in making modern dance available to a wide audience and in rendering it a sustainable career.

Despite his accomplishments and influence, Nikolais has garnered relatively little scholarly attention. This collection of ten essays, followed by a compendium of documents and images, posits that looking at Alwin Nikolais is a fruitful intervention in broad cultural and theoretical conversations. The volume aims to do several things at once. Certainly it is an effort to fill a lacunae in dance history, to both document some of Nikolais' work and his approaches to creating it, and situate that work in an esthetic context of twentieth-century America. It is, at the same time, a reflection on what makes dance history, on the significance of its inclusions and exclusions, and on the terms of its ongoing revisions. Finally it is an effort to intervene in current thinking on the status of the body in performance, the politics of silence and invisibility, and the uses of art to imagine social possibilities. Given these concerns, the book hopes to appeal to readers with a particular interest in Nikolais, those who possess a more general attraction to dance history, and those drawn to performance studies and cultural studies.

The contributors are from diverse disciplinary backgrounds—American studies, dance, literary studies, music, performance studies, sociology. Some have worked directly with Nikolais, others have long been students of his work from the outside, and still others are coming to his work for the first time via this volume. The authors present a mix of those steeped in the traditions of dance criticism and history and those exploring the boundaries of new dance studies. By bringing together these epistemological and generational differences, this volume on Nikolais seeks to integrate a readership on dance that rarely shares the same archive.

The broad themes of the collection are laid out in the introduction by Randy Martin. The book starts with investigations in dance history and criticism, such as Claudia Gitelman's account of Nikolais' dance training method and Marcia B. Siegel's essays on *Somniloquy* (1967) and his European esthetic roots. Yvonne Hardt offers a European perspective on transatlantic influences, and Rebekah Kowal examines the tacit sexual politics legible in Nikolais' work. Leading performance theorist Hebert Blau treats some of the resonances between Nikolais and the future of theater, while musicologist Bob Gilmore evaluates compositional endeavors. The question of formalism in Nikolais' choreography and in abstract expressionism is explored by Philip Auslander, and a conceptual framework for understanding how the dance canon operates is provided by Mark Franko. For a documents section that concludes the volume, Naima Prevots has compiled a selection of some of the more perceptive critical responses to Nikolais, and Jana Feinman has shaped a chronology of his choreographic output. Other materials document his company's professional trajectory and reflect on the man in his own hand and that of his companion, Murray Louis.

We most gratefully acknowledge the generous access to documents and visual materials that Mr. Louis has provided as well as the assistance of Alberto del Saz, co-director of the Nikolais/Louis Foundation for Dance. Tom Caravaglia has opened the doors of his photographic studio to us. The Jerome Robbins Dance Division, the New York Public Library, and Judith Connick, curator of the Alwin Nikolais and Murray Louis Papers at the Robert E. and Jean R. Mahn Center for Archives and Special Collections, Ohio University, Athens, have been essential resources. We gratefully acknowledge the generous support of New York University and its assistance in the publication of this book. We also extend our gratitude to Suzanna Tamminen at Wesleyan University Press, whose editorial expertise and support have made this project possible. Readers to whom she submitted a manuscript draft proved extraordinarily generous and insightful in their reports to us. Finally, we thank all of the collaborators to this volume, who have been a pleasure to work with and who have confirmed our premise that the returns of Alwin Nikolais are many.

New York City   C.G. and R.M.
March 2006

A Guide to Color Plates

. . . .

CLAUDIA GITELMAN

"You have to remember, we did all this before computers," says photographer Tom Caravaglia, who not only documented Nikolais' work for over two decades, but aided him in the creation of scenic effects and also extended his work into the graphics that the choreographer employed for promotional purposes. A photo essay displays examples of Caravaglia's contribution to Nikolais' legacy as a visual artist.

Caravaglia provided images for slides Nikolais projected onto cyclorama, sets, and dancers. "Nik knew what he wanted. He would tell me what to shoot and then he'd put my negatives through all kinds of processes." Nikolais spliced, overlaid, filtered, and sometimes burned and glued as he meticulously fashioned the two-by-two inch glass slides he used in specially built projectors. Occasionally Caravaglia photographed individual dancers in precise positions so that their images could be projected onto them at points during a ballet.

Photographing during performances frustrated Caravaglia. Film was slow in the 1970s, and side light, which works so well to three-dimensionalize dancers, presents difficulties in producing a sharp focus. Nonetheless, Caravaglia's are among the best documents of Nikolais' company at work. When he brought performers into his studio where he could control light and add special effects, results were stunning. Caravaglia's work represents the fusion of kinetic and visual art that match Nikolais' esthetic ideals.

Color plates begin after page 114.
All photographs © Tom Caravaglia 2007.

Plate 1. *Temple* (1974), with studio lighting and special effects.
Plate 2. *Tent* (1968), in performance in the mid-1980s.
Plate 3. Raul Trujillo and Lynn Lesniak in *Liturgies* (1983). Light patterns projected from the wings "costume" them.
Plate 4. Composite of images and special effects for a poster.
Plate 5. Multiple exposures of a dancer costumed for *Temple*.

The Returns of Alwin Nikolais

CHAPTER 1

Nikolais Returns

. . . .

RANDY MARTIN

To peer at the work of Alwin Nikolais is to see paradox in both its methods and reception. His dance education came from disciples of German pioneer Mary Wigman (whom he saw perform in 1933) like Truda Kaschmann and Hanya Holm. He also studied at the quintessentially American summer enclave at Bennington College with formidable dancers Martha Graham, Holm, and Doris Humphrey, as well as critic John Martin and musician Louis Horst, who also taught composition. These commingled streams of influence place his formation at the epicenter of a transatlantic (rather than strictly American) modern dance. His first choreographic credit at age twenty-six was not for dance but for the movement he arranged for a 1936 production of Leonid Andreyev's 1911 pessimistic political satire *The Pretty Sabine Women* for the Connecticut Federal Negro Theatre. His last dance came in the penultimate year of his life, 1992, with *Aurora*, at a New York dance showcase, the *Joyce Theater*. In all, he created 118 works. He availed himself of every institution available for the dissemination of his work; he made an early use of television, government and foundation grants, and college residencies, but also founded his own independent school and foundation, persistently theorized his work, and took an interest in its documentation on film. He was the technical master of all the dimensions of the theatrical experience he achieved— a composer who purchased the first Moog synthesizer, a lighting designer who could wire his dancers as well as the stage to intricate visual effect, a costumer who treated textiles as a scenic sculptural form.

Yet his career success was shadowed by critical doubt that generated questions that recurred over five decades. Yes, he pushed boundaries, but was what he did still really dance? By stretching his dancers beyond what it appeared human bodies could achieve, did he leave them, perhaps, without their own humanity intact? Like other avant-gardists of his day he broke with the conventions of his own formative traditions, but did his knack for filling a large theater, his populist sensibility, also betray his roots? These, of course, are not simply questions for Alwin Nikolais. They lie at the heart of any critical reflection on what dance is. If the work that Nikolais himself yielded offers a dense thicket, by contrast the scholarly terrain occasioned by his work has been relatively sparse. This circumstance needs to be treated as an opportunity and not as a bitter lament. If Nikolais' life was a paradox whose sensibilities and valences require careful scrutiny, his critical afterlife can serve as a challenge to the orthodoxies by which we come to know what dance is and how it operates. This collection of essays and documents is dedicated to both.

In the formative years of modern dance, before the advent of a university-based scholarly discipline, the work of critics performed the double operation of evaluating an individual performance and establishing the conceptual boundaries for what constituted the art form. John Martin, Walter Sorrell, Edwin Denby, and Arlene Croce wrote major books of history and criticism while employed by newspapers and magazines such as the *New York Times* and the *New Yorker*. Deborah Jowitt and Marcia B. Siegel wrote significant dance criticism and also took up university positions. Ann Daly, Susan Leigh Foster, Mark Franko, Felicia McCarren, and Marta Savigliano represent the turn to dance studies that emerged within the university setting starting in the 1980s. While critics of journalistic affiliation abound, the formation of a scholarly field of dance theory has complicated without canceling the earlier dual function of critics to define and evaluate. Any contemporary consideration of a major choreographic figure such as Nikolais needs to reckon with both kinds and sites of critical authority.

While he is the subject of a number of well-researched but unpublished dissertations, the first written in 1967 and the most recent in 1993, the critical controversy Nikolais attracted has not been carried forth by the very interdisciplinary approaches that could readily have found resonances in his work for their own conceptual issues and interests. Dance studies from earlier approaches are changed by the analytic emphasis from one of dance's definition (when can something be considered dance?) to one of its effects and operations (how does dance work, what does it do and make legible in the world?). If, like the name for his foundation, Nikolais is something of a chimera, whose confusion of boundaries points out how boundaries are formed and maintained, his past points us towards ways of thinking about dance's future.

Potentially, the dimensions of what dance does are without limit. Here, however, we will focus on three that were posed by Nikolais' contemporaries, but that have become especially pressing for how we think dance today—bodies, boundaries, and the canon. Canons are made of judgements about what should be seen and institutions for making those judgements visible. In literature, this means looking at the weave that joins professors and publishers, disciplines and readerships. In dance, we look to the spaces between critics and presenters, producers and audiences. The translation between artistic fields, all of which purportedly have canons, are not precise, however, leaving somewhat open the question of how well an idea divined from biblical interpretation (which books continue to be worth reading) applies to a more ephemeral form. If Nikolais' relationship to the dance canon is at best an unstable and uneasy one, it may help us understand as much about the dynamics and foibles of canonization as it does about his work and its reception.

Clearly, the dance canon is predicated upon considering something inside dance. Such definitional and epistemological considerations describe but one approach.[1] While there were critics who questioned whether Nikolais' work was dance, he himself made crossing boundaries part of his art. He was interdisciplinary, and his work moved across esthetic boundaries of abstract expressionism and pop art, the painterly and the televisual, popular and esoteric. The larger question begged by the definitional boundary of dance is what a given archive should be read in relation to. The modernist convention in dance—movement for itself—is to put dance in conversation with its own history. Nikolais' work suggests that dance is not simply made out of itself, but from a larger repertoire of social and even cosmic kinesthetics. It is not simply his stagings that are abstract, but his training of dancers is also based upon analytics of how any set of motional relations can be grasped. Nikolais generates a kind of social physics that can be read in relation to other cultural phenomenon, especially the emergence of what was called systems analysis, which was developed in the forties, fifties, and sixties when he too was formulating his oeuvre. Systems approaches took elemental aspects of an observed environment and developed generalized methods for understanding how human affairs could be organized. Returning to Nikolais offers a provocative way not only of considering dance's questions, but also of making legible some key cultural expressions of his day.

Placing Nikolais

Like other modernists of his cohort, especially Merce Cunningham, Nikolais celebrated pure motional esthetics against a previous emphasis on narrative or emotional characterization. Unlike the pioneers of modern dance who were his own teachers, and his fellow experimentalists with improvisation and movement *concrète* who first performed at Judson Church and came to be known as dance's postmodernists, Nikolais' choreography and training was not centered around his own involvement as a dancer. Throughout his career, this separation between Nikolais and his dancers was not lost on critics, who

1. *Alwin Nikolais studying his notes during a rehearsal at Fredrick Lowe Theatre, New York City, in 1975. Photograph © Johan Elbers 2007.*

characterized it as a form of dehumanization—a term he himself would at one point come to embrace, albeit uneasily.[2] The critical concern was not with the separation per se, but with the sense that the dancers were subordinated to serving as instruments of visual effects; they became indistinguishable from props, and pure motion was achieved at the expense of the dancing person. Who this person was, how dance should properly disclose humanity, was not discussed. It was asserted that modern dance was a vehicle for the pure presence of the body, the humanity of which was taken to be axiomatic. Overconfidence about what it means to be human presents its own problems, not the least of which have been foreclosure of the humanity of colonized others or pre-emption of the rights of the living in the name of the unborn. Dance critics are certainly not the authors of such hubris. But the criticism of dehumanization provides an opportunity to explore what cannot be taken for granted in dance: namely, an understanding of what a body is. Nikolais' practical esthetics, decentralization, is suggestive in this regard.

More needs to be said about canon, boundaries, and bodies, and how they tie together the contributions that compose this book. First, however, it is important to see how Nikolais' own work helps lend these problematics a certain legibility. Before coming to dance, Nikolais (whose first job in the theater came in 1927 as an organist and manager) was a puppeteer. He had his own marionette theater in 1934 and by 1936 received government arts support when he created work for the Federal Theater Project in Hartford, Connecticut.[3] After his Bennington experience, he choreographed a series of pieces in the late thirties for the Avery Memorial Theatre and the theater at Hartt College, where he was an instructor. After his military service (1942–45) he assisted Hanya Holm in Colorado, and in 1948, she suggested him for a job at the Henry Street Settlement that she was unavailable for. Nikolais began his work there with the nucleus of a company (including Murray Louis, Gladys Bailin, Phyllis Lamhut, Beverly Schmidt [Blossom], Bill Frank, Coral Martindale, and Dorothy Vislocky) that would stay with him for over a decade.

He depended heavily on the distinctive movement qualities and creative capacities of his dancers to achieve his kinesthetic vision, and precise ensemble work was key to his theatrical esthetic. But it was not until 1953 that he produced a concert—a collection of dances by him and his students called *Etudes II: Masks, Props, and Mobiles*—that bore the distinctive features of his work. Up until then he could be considered to be working in the tradition of expressive dance—a tradition that he would subsequently reject. This would mark what Louis Althusser called an "epistemological break," the point at which a person's work turns against its own foundations and marks its decisive trajectory.[4] A dozen years later in 1965, when Minneapolis's Walker Arts Center commissioned *Vaudeville of the Elements,* the esthetic and stage sensibility was firmly established. When the piece played in New York the following spring, the terms of Nikolais' critical reception were clearly articulated. Clive Barnes, writing for the *New York Times* complained that Nikolais seemed "as content to work with tinsel as with diamonds, and to find his satisfaction too easily in the cute and the slick." *Time* magazine observed that "as vaudeville shows go, it might have been conjured up by Ed Sullivan on an LSD binge."[5]

Vaudeville opens in darkness. Small lights appear across the transom, a sparkling like stars unmoored from their galactic sockets. Rods of chromatic color, as if the Northern Lights had been shredded and set in adagio, form prismic intersections. The eye is drawn into a scenic field and relinquishes all orientation of scale. What seemed cosmic now looks microscopic, as the lights conjure Brownian motion that no heavenly bodies could abide. No sooner do the dancing lights suggest an eternity, than the discernible contours of human forms appear, now attached to the sticks whose animation could only have

2. Premiere performance of Vaudeville of the Elements, *1965. From left: Ray Brousard, Carolyn Carlson, Susan Buirge (rear), Bill Frank, Phyllis Lamhut, Murray Louis, Ann Carlson, Ray Johnson, Mimi Garrard. Photographer Eric Sutherland for Walker Art Center, Minneapolis.*

been incandescent. The moving forms flit about as if a Rorschach silhouette had become a Matisse cut-out, or a Balinese shadow dance had ditched its shadow. As the sticks had been, dancers in multicolored unitards are now the recipients of light and treat the sticks like sources for their own movement memories. But the light is promiscuous. It shifts its attraction now to dancers suspended in elastic grids, geometric strips with shimmering animism. The twists in the grid, with the dancer serene and arachnid-like at the center, imagines a magmatic screen-saver with the stage its cathode ray tube. But if the lines on a computer screen are passive, these cross-wires of space have an interior energic flow. Sound, abstract as light, percolates evanescently. In one instant, the score seems to be made by the movement; in another, the sound seems to come from outside the dance. A next wave of dancers appears clothed in white net couture with red tassels that trail behind them on the floor. Their feet caress the floor with the resilience of pizza dough spun downward. Lateral glides imply the locomotive apparatus of centipedes. The feet do what the light once did, focus attention on the capacity to insinuate movement where blank stillness reigned. The dancers achieve an absolute unison that is years of training in the making and dispersed in an instant. A costume change later fills the stage with light-catching silver buckets that encircle dancers arms and legs until detached, when they are subordinated to the dancers own geometric effects. The parade of elements produces a riot of images, each sealed by the performers' stillness, absorbed by all that went into one cadence so that another might issue forth. This kinesthetic grammar maintains an active anticipation. The lights become stroboscopic and cast the dancers into oscillation between the projected surfaces and the projectors of surface. A solo by Phyllis Lamhut in full light takes all of the intelligent effects into swirls of exquisitely commanded concentricity of arms and legs. Upstage, vertically hanging strips of cloth occlude the dancers but allow them to emerge incessantly, only to conceal themselves again. A new act, and dancers comport themselves with lumbering elegance in soft bags. They conjure molluscs in full evolutionary throttle with a whimsy that opts for Dr. Seuss. Again life's artifice to animate is disclosed in the fully apparent motional effects the dancers achieve. Murray Louis solos, but his body is driven by dual drives of motional power in his chest and pelvis, allowing the space between to float free. The company returns in chess piece caterpillar forms that look to have fallen from the ball at Alice's Wonderland. The strips of the first act agglomerate the bodies into bas reliefs that melt back behind the slivered curtains. The dancers come to inhabit the stage, and then, in an instant, they are gone, having disappeared back into the darkness.

This is an account of some of what can be seen in the first two acts of the piece. The third, called "Tower," shatters the dancers' own silence that has prevailed to this point and has the dancers break from the sublime corporeality that characterizes the archetypal figures of modern dance, who appear but cannot speak for themselves. *Vaudeville of the Elements*, on this reading, complicates what is commonly said about Nikolais' work. Dancers are not statically entombed and encased, but enact a constant veiling and unveiling by which they alternate between appearing as the prime movers and the moved, in which they serve sculptural effects and disclose what the body itself can sculpt. The massive assemblage of elements—images, effects, dance vocabulary, deployments of ensemble and solo, props, costumes, lights, music— operate inductively and deductively. Like the later work *Gallery* (1978), which offers dancers as targets who wind up losing their heads at the end, audiences are enticed by comic scenes that in turn elicit reflection on their complicity as spectators to the slaughter. This is the telos of classic Greek tragedy, spectatorial complicity in the death of the protagonist is meant to generate catharsis and adhere the public to civic norms. *Vaudeville* is brash, even opulent in its assemblage, its cornucopia of scenic offerings as abundant as the utopian promises of sixties consumer excess. It is also rigorous in its inventory of what can be done by dancers and by theatrical illusion. *Vaudeville* is systematic in its approach to materials, turning images inside out, exploring their genesis, pushing the limits of the subject-object/dancer-dance relationship. The careful engineering of these elements suggest a science of observation and experiment where parts are exquisitely honed to add to a total machinery. Yet the confidence required to stage a total event of this sort, to affect a world, a gestalt, implies a system that generates the elements in the first place.

Between Structure and System

This play of part and whole, of assemblage of elements from what is found to hand in the kinetic world and what can be imagined from abstract reflection, was famously set into juxtaposition by the anthropologist Claude Levi-Strauss in his book *The Savage Mind*. Levi-Strauss was concerned with confronting the ethnocentrism of his day, which threatened to obliterate cultural difference in the name of a homogenizing modernity. The savage or primitive mind acts as a *bricoleur*, who assembles the stuff of ritual out of what is found in the immediate environment, a diversity of elements that are used to enact an event that yields a more general explanation. The modern mind, by con-

3. *The opening of Act III of* Vaudeville *at its premiere in 1965. Dancers babbled as they built their tower, which eventually exploded and collapsed. Carolyn Carlson and Phyllis Lamhut are front. Photographer Eric Sutherland for Walker Art Center, Minneapolis.*

trast, acts as an engineer and begins with the conceptual structure, the total design, which explains, instructs, and constructs the individual event. It is worth thinking about Levi-Strauss with Nikolais in mind. The anthropologist discloses that a web of deployable dualisms or structures underwrites both the engineer's and *bricoleur*'s modes of cultural practice, but is not content to show an equivalent complexity in the activity of the two. After dozens upon dozens of examples of how the primitive and the modern mind operate, he undercuts the very dualism he had used to craft his edifice by arguing that the two are but moments of the present situation. "The entire process of human knowledge thus assumes the character of a closed system."[6]

Nikolais' intellectual interlocutors were many, and among those of a more theoretical cast, Marshall McLuhan, Rudolph Arnheim, Carl Jung, and Suzanne Langer would be counted. Although Levi-Strauss' book came out in 1966, when *Vaudeville* had its New York debut, the choreographer did not seem aware of the work of the anthropologist or other French thinkers like Jacques Lacan, Roland Barthes, Louis Althusser, or Michel Foucault, who came to be known as structuralists. It is difficult to look at Nikolais' work and not see it as a structuralism, precisely because of the systematic play between underlying principles of association and manifest, tangible elements. The variety theater referenced by the title of the dance certainly pertains to Nikolais own roots, and also to his methods and his attentions. No instance of human expression was outside the structuralists' interests. Theirs too was an analytic that could be applied across the disciplined boundaries that were being institutionalized in the academy after the Second World War. The question of what made expression human was not to be taken for granted, since that led to all manner of cultural exclusion. As Levi-Strauss put it, "The ultimate goal of the human sciences is not to constitute, but to dissolve man."[7] By calling into question the particular cultural and historical entailments of human form as generalized from a particular instance (modern Western bourgeois male), structuralism itself was cast as "anti-humanist."[8] As we can see from Nikolais and Levi-Strauss, opening up how the human form should appear, dissolving its unitary situation into a multiplicity of locations, and extending the human into the webs of artifice generated by cultural creativity are more properly understood as "posthuman," or the process by which humans make themselves by their own history rather than being naturalized in historical givens.[9]

Nikolais' work enables this dance between people and things, agents and structures, contingency and determination, the animate and the inanimate. His means for achieving these ends he termed decentralization, an approach that informed both his teaching and his scenic compositions. Decentralization is a "practice" meant to "contrive methods of releasing the body from the limiting vortex of the ego, the self." This can be achieved by "focusing one's dynamic force away from the self and allowing it to reach out and bring other concerns under control." Consequently, dancers can "merge into an environment" where each is a "contributing member rather than a dominating dweller."[10] To his critics, it is precisely his critique of the ego and ethnocentric self as a form of domination that is turned against him and used to assert that his work lies outside the boundaries of dance. Writing in 1956, Walter Sorrell stated that Nikolais "dehumanizes his dancers and makes them part of the external material he chooses for the development of an idea. His ideas are those of a sculptor, or painter, not primarily of a dancer." Over twenty years later, Clive Barnes would claim that his concerts "bear as much resemblance to dance as the motto in a fortune cookie bears to literature."[11] Here Sorrell and Barnes disclose most directly the nexus between their authority to evaluate individual works and the authority to arbiter the boundaries of the dance field. The assertion that an idea belongs to a fixed disciplinary domain, that there is a given relationship between expressive form or media and ideational content, is foundational to the modernist enterprise. It is as if the specialization upon which the expertise required to make informed judgements resided in the nature of art and not in the history of its division of labor. Ironically, the appeal to expertise upon which such critical authority rests not only delimits one disciplinary domain from another, but also cuts across them. As Nikolais himself understood so well with respect to his motional esthetics, to assert a set of boundaries within a given environment introduces techniques not simply to police but also to transgress the elements of time and space that they form.

The commitment to boundaries sealing off discrete systems describes the very Cold War environment from which Nikolais' work emerged. Paul Edwards has described the dominant trope of the era as the "closed world," where containment becomes a value tantamount to the preservation of life itself.[12] By this reckoning, human affairs were to be modeled on a machine, specifically a thinking machine or computer, which treated the mind as an instrument for processing information. The resulting systems sciences that emerged from military applications to anticipate the location of enemy targets were applied across diverse fields of business, technology, and the explanation of human behavior. The spread of systems theories—which appeared at the same time as formal professional and academic specialization — legitimated the ideals of political mastery through technological advancement that characterized the post-war era. The closed world meant to construct a universe where each element of the system had a specific purpose for the whole and a connection to each other. Ideologically it intended a closure of the imagination where what was given within the system stood as the horizon of human possibility, such that some other social system, like communism, would appear entirely alien, even pathological to humanity.

But the capacity to imagine such a world itself required a technology. The geometry of four-celled tables and binary number systems, even of multivariate statistical plots and graphs, offered up a minimal visual field. Science fiction, Westerns, and war movies provided cinematic parables of what happened when enclosures were violated by baleful others. The fullest visualization of the systems imaginary could be found in the abstract arts, where materials were gathered forcibly on a surface to command their planes of display. The year of Nikolais' death, Tobi Tobias characterized the visual experience of his theater as akin to "being mesmerized by a lush, sophisticated screen saver."[13] Nikolais articulated the look of the digital esthetic with analog means. He used live theater to achieve the visual enclosure that the computer screen would render iconic. Nikolais' training was based upon an analytic, like that of Rudolph von Laban before him, that treated the motional capacities of the body in systemic terms. Motion, the privileged domain of dance, affected a translation and equivalence between the physiology and the physics. The master grammar of the training—time, space, shape, and motional quality—was to operate as a kind of kinesthetic machinery capable of inscribing any conceivable or observable motion as dance. While Laban's movement system was treated as applicable to domains of work and life, Nikolais' dialectic with the enclosure of the theater was far richer and more sustained than that of his German predecessor, but also far more confined in its application to the universe of art.

Unlike structuralism, which rested upon the same trope, systems sciences meant to be dehumanizing in their means and ends, even if this was mandated by the very human ambitions of progress. Destruction would be mutually assured, minds would be modeled on machines. With all expression transcribable as information, technological advancement would yield total control. The significance of locating Nikolais in relation to these two major intellectual currents of his day is to move beyond a simple refutation of the epithet of dehumanization to discern what in social and historical terms it might be a symptom of. Nikolais then becomes a site for this broader cultural decoding. He offers a critique of humanism's unwitting dehumanization, its reductive and exclusionary judgement, unburdening people of the dull wit of mastery. At the same time, he provides a visual and kinesthetic realization of what a digital world would look like. In his theater, abstraction was a kind of literalization and the rationalization of what could be expected from the output of minds and bodies when rendered into a total design. Dance is certainly a place to mine the limits of the human body, a project and a prospect that may make its participants seem as if they are doing so from beyond those limits. Deborah Jowitt grasps this irony well when she connects the purportedly dehumanizing absence of Nikolais' own body in his dances to the unconscious effects that the dances create:

Nikolais has never danced in his own works, and his presence in the theater reinforces his persona as a puppetmaker or magician—sitting, as likely as not, in the light booth calling cues for the lighting and sound that he has created, while on the stage below the dancers swim into existence, merge with each other or the backdrop, now sentient creatures, now quivering shapes. Ironically, these dancers, highly trained, often contributors to the choreography, by the very nature of the work often appear will-less onstage—performing their fluid actions as if they were unconsciously, or instinctively, fulfilling their part of a large pattern, whether it be carnival show or mechanical organ or the life cycle of an amoeba.[14]

Another way of understanding structuralism, precisely as Jowitt does for these dancers, is as the language of the unconscious, and here the visible and the unseen meet without resolving the antinomies of dehumanization that Nikolais makes legible. It should be evident by now as well that bodies and boundaries intersect around the problematic of dehumanization, the limits of the body becoming the limits of dance. Dance can fix what a human is or it can map what the sentient inhabitation of the world might yield. Such matters are not decided arbitrarily. The work of the canon is no less than the economy by which certain embodiments are privileged and boundaries achieved. Nikolais' relationship to the dance canon is as unstable as the object itself. More productively, his relationship helps us to understand its very instability.

Dance Circuits

The canon itself is always fragile, tugged between its migration from ecclesiastical texts in the fourth century to individual authors in the eighteenth, and its translation from literature to music, dance, and visual arts, late in the nineteenth century.[15] Beth Genné has observed that the designation of a cluster of ballets as "classic" early in the twentieth century is coterminous with the rise of modern dance.[16] According to Wolfgang Iser, the process of canonization, of selection of objects for interpretation, bases its authority on the censorship of others.[17] The power to decide what is seen is not merely an interpretive act, but also an institutional means by which publics are created and sustained. The symbolic struggle over inclusion of books in syllabi on college campuses that has made headlines in the context of the culture wars of the past two decades can leave the impression that a few sites and commentaries stand for the general condition of what is thought and known. John Guillory asserts that it is the institutional reproduction of what gets read, the accumulation of cultural capital, that is more salient than the interpretive acts of evaluation and exclusion, which after all assume that a text has already been placed in circulation.[18]

Since so much of the deliberations concerning the canon derive from the example of literature, and the literary debates have moved into the realm of sociology, the question of what the canon means and how it operates in dance requires some consideration. While certainly not all critics of literature are or were academics, literary criticism as a specialized mode of understanding could mark those texts that would be placed in circulation within the university. In dance, while college departments were formed earlier in the twentieth century when professional criticism was also emerging (John Martin's tenure at the *New York Times* was 1927–1962), criticism precedes the creation of a stable institutional edifice for placing dance in sustained and continuous performing circuits and the academization of dance criticism. Federal aid, starting with the G.I. Bill, which funded college attendance; the National Security legislation of the late fifties, which underwrote new disciplines like area studies; and the 1965 National Education Act supported and directed the expansion of higher education. State aid also made the national circulation of dance possible. While the Federal Theater Project of the 1930s exposed many communities to live performance, the National Endowment of the Arts (NEA) was oriented toward both professionalization and institutionalization. Martha Graham, who hadn't had a national tour in fifteen years, used her first NEA grant in 1966 to do so.[19] Nikolais as well received his first NEA grant in 1966. The Federal Theater Project commissioned his first works in 1936 and 1937, and the NEA was a continuous supporter in the years that his work was established as part of a national and international repertoire of modern dance. Eleven of twenty works he created between 1970 and 1980 were supported by the NEA. His first fifteen years at Henry Street yielded forty-one works, most of them self-produced and locally performed (mostly at the Playhouse itself).[20] In 1957, Nikolais received his first of three major university commissions (from University of Illinois for *The Bewitched*, with music by Harry Partch), and his first commission from a dance presenter, the tenth American Dance Festival at Connecticut College. The key terms for evaluating Nikolais' work were already in place when he was self-producing and supporting himself through teaching at Henry Street—before his work became widely accessible through national and international touring and patronage.

In addition to funding work and providing occasions for live performance, television was perhaps the key predicate for the more general circulation of dance. When the venerable public television series *Dance in America* aired five programs on George Balanchine and the New York City Ballet in 1978 and 1979, the company subsequently sold out its live performances. Twenty years before, Nikolais made eight appearances on the *Steve Allen Show*, followed by a series of stints in Europe and another show for CBS in 1968. Dance historians Nancy Reynolds and Malcolm McCormick see Nikolais' ease with the medium as launching his national tours and enabling him to reach a larger and more diversified audience than any of his contemporaries. Reynolds and McCormick also argue that it was middle-class acceptance of high culture that fueled the dance boom.[21] One might just as easily argue the same for middle-class acceptance of popular culture. Certainly, television, from *American Bandstand* to MTV, was a significant agent of the dissemination of dance forms.

The notion that Nikolais would be at home in a medium that both delineated and confounded high and popular forms suggests a different approximation of the idea of postmodernism than the one that typically appears in dance periodization. Periodization, the notion that prevailing esthetic expressions follow a successive temporal logic, is one of the integuments of canonization. The innovative performances that took place at Judson Church between 1962 and 1964, from which contact improvisation, release technique, and a quotidian esthetic issued, are presented as a unique rupture from which a modernist like Nikolais is excluded.[22] At issue is neither the influence nor the ingenuity of these seminal performances, but rather an appreciation of how the dance canon is formed retrospectively as a purely interpretive act. That Nikolais also erased boundaries between art forms as between art and daily life, and used improvisationally generated experimentation as a form of making the familiar strange (defamiliarization), does not mean that his esthetic is one with that of his contemporaries. But when we add the institutional to the interpretive dimensions of canonicity, we see that the strictly stylistic basis for proclaiming a postmodern break becomes more fragile and difficult to sustain.

While dance was subjected to the protocols of the culture wars in the late 1980s, when choreographers had to sign anti-obscenity pledges in order to receive their NEA awards, the most public brush dance had with the climate of making art a stage for cultural division came in the notorious nonreview of Bill T. Jones by Arlene Croce in the *New Yorker*. Croce refused to review Jones' *Still/Here* (1994) on the grounds that it employed terminally ill people, transgressing the boundary between art and life and making criticism impossible. But she did write a polemic called "Discussing the Undiscussable."[23] The loss of expert authority, the questioning of all-encompassing explanations or metanarratives, serves as another boundary-blurring aspect of the postmodern. To this we need to add that the consequent decentering of authority for the cultural position from which one could speak for others was expressed as multiculturalism, which makes legible the not-always-subtle encodings of race and sexuality in the whole victim-art affair. Nikolais' decentralization anticipated multiculturalism's critical procedure, but its universalizing systems approach would keep the cultural critique unmarked in all but its most general formulation as a refusal of western egocentricity. Croce was absolutely correct that this function of criticism to speak for art was a victim of art that took up the authority to speak for itself. The affair, coming in the year after Nikolais' death, also announced the culmination of the assault on the institutional devices that had made the canonization of dance possible: the funding streams that allowed presenters and university dance programs to flourish.

The relationship between the university and the professional dance worlds is a final leg upon which the institutional edifice of dance canonization stands. Dance history and criticism is largely an adjunct to the undergraduate dancer's curriculum. The most influential syllabi in a dance department will likely describe the steps most worthy of undertaking rather than the choreographic works that must be placed in memory. Many dance departments around the country operate with a generic grammar of ballet and modern technique, which both allow particular influences to flourish while denying the authorship that canonization assumes. Nikolais did a five-week residency at the University of Wisconsin in 1978, which along with the NEA and the local PBS affiliate, funded the creation of *Aviary*. A dissertation written on the residency by Sue Ann Straits found that university dance students viewed the residency at different times as "an interference with, a supplement to, or an integrated part of the Wisconsin Program."[24] At the time of the residency, all but four of twelve faculty were trained at Wisconsin. Today college faculty are likely to have terminal academic degrees (whether M.F.A. or Ph.D.) and increasingly to have come from professional careers of their own. Nikolais, who both maintained his own school and taught at others around the world, traversed the professional and university domains at the hour of their mutual emergence.

The dance boom and the university boom were of a piece. The number of students who received degrees in art and the number of people employed as artists both doubled from the beginning of the seventies to the end of the nineties; annual rates of arts baccalaureates increased to 66,000 and employment topped 2 million. During this twenty-five-year period, the proportion of liberal-arts degrees was in decline and growth in artist employment was outpacing the creation of all new jobs.[25] Artist employment had increased at an annual rate of 2.7 percent, as opposed to a 2.4 percent increase for professional specialists and 1.3 percent increase in the total civilian workforce. At the same time, unemployment, defined as those actively seeking work but un-

4. *An electronic event for television, CBS-TV, 1968. Archives, the Nikolais/Louis*
Foundation for Dance

able to find it, tends to be higher for artists than for the population as a
whole.[26] While the strains on becoming and maintaining oneself as an artist
are palpable, the decentralization of dance preparation and presentation may
continue to limit the reach of canonization in dance. Nikolais' own career
suggests that this may be part of dance's own history.

Bodies, Boundaries, and the Dance Canon

The decentralization that was a signal achievement of Nikolais' work
could also describe the state of scholarly attention devoted to it. Nikolais has
figured in many compendiums on modern dance. He was, for example, one
of the choreographers featured in Selma Jeanne Cohen's seminal *The Modern
Dance: Seven Statements of Belief* with the symptomatically titled contribution,
"No Man From Mars." His representation there situated him as a major figure in American dance. Yet, at least in English, there has been no single volume dedicated to a critical assessment of his work.[27] The perspective of this

volume is that the relative paucity of material presents an opportunity rather than an occasion to lament.

How does dance devoted to inventing itself come to be? If motional innovation is the ends of modern dance, by what means or instrumentality is this to be achieved? The body is the medium of this instrumentality, but Nikolais acknowledged that what complicates the ability to separate subject and object in dance is the fact that the "instrument and the artist are one and the same."[28] While technique is typically associated with codified movement, Nikolais attempts to realign critical reflection and the corporeal capacity to break from motional routinization and to deinstrumentalize the body so that the mind and body are rescripted as part of a "fragile linkage."[29] In the end, however, the idea of a modern dance technique may be overly freighted by the broader modernist demands to instrumentalize the body and discipline it to the prescribed ends of labor, political consensus, and social control. For this reason, Claudia Gitelman prefers the term *training* to *technique* and *pedagogy* to *instruction*. Gitelman was a senior faculty member for many years at the school founded by Nikolais and Murray Louis, and she is still sought as an exemplary teacher of the tradition. Her chapter "Sense Your Mass Increasing with Your Velocity: Alwin Nikolais' Pedagogy of Unified Decentralization" relies on commentary from Nikolais and a number of those who danced with him, but is also informed by extensive direct experience. By placing the training in a cultural and esthetic context, Gitelman is able to avoid the very technical approach that appears to sunder the preparation of dancers from the choreographic imaginary. At the same time, Gitelman recognizes that even the most complex pedagogy does not cancel the modernist assumptions of authorship, and she leaves us with some of the antinomies of a self-generated creative process in the service of a singular choreographic authority.

Dance is notoriously difficult to document. Old black-and-white films can provide a tantalizing sketch that leaves one to imagine the absent kinesthetic detail—to say nothing of the stage effects—that audiences would have found so arresting. The standard review format—for those dailies that even assigned a critic to regularly cover dance—forces critics to conjure the dance in a parsimonious handful of piquant images. But specialized dance journals and literary magazines allow the dance to be embodied in the essay and the writer's voice to offer a landscape upon which the choreographer's images can be made tangible in memory. Marcia Siegel is among the most accomplished of these writers, and two of her essays, "The Omniloquence of Alwin Nikolais" (1968) and "Artisans of Space" (1981) have been specially edited and adapted for publication here. Siegel provides us with a glimpse of Nikolais at the height of his international renown. The first essay, on *Somniloquy* (1967), commissioned for a performance at the Guggenheim Museum, is a study in how technical limitations are reinvented for and as artistic vision. By reflecting on the dancers training and Nikolais' assemblage of music and other theatrical elements, she provides a picture of the subtle incarnation of a finished work. With "Artisans," she establishes an esthetic genealogy of his formation in the roots of movement engineer Rudolph Laban and the spatial formalist Oskar Schlemmer. Siegel reminds us that nationalist claims for American dance modernism need to be complicated by its transatlantic crossings, so amply synthesized in Nikolais' approach.

Dance has certainly not been immune to the larger narratives of American cultural exceptionalism. Yvonne Hardt establishes a framework for looking at contemporary arts practices across borders by comparing Nikolais with German expressionists Sasha Waltz and Laban. She reads them all as seeking to transcend the limitations of the centered self. They share a formal approach to transgressing and challenging fixed boundaries and disclose a more nuanced interconnection among seemingly disparate or dichotomized elements such as image/dance, body/technique, figurative/abstract. This esthetic-analytic operation she terms "debordering" (*Entgrenzung*). Hardt offers a reading of how choreographic devices make perceptible social and political forces. At the same time, in a move away from the simple binary between political and apolitical dances, she allows us to see the limits to dance's politics. Nikolais, for example, makes the conformist impulses and sexual prudery of his day evident without proposing alternatives. His politics, which can be activated by a critical approach to his work, lie more in the choreographic means to reveal how the world is ordered, than in the visions of a reordered world that had characterized the avowedly political work of those who preceded and followed.

The 1950s in the United States, the decade in which Nikolais came to prominence, has proven as challenging to dance historiography as to that of Cold War America. Both artistic and cultural contexts are conventionally seen as moments of quiescence. By this reckoning, innovation and ferment somehow run in thirty-year cycles, and dance at the beginning of the twentieth century, the thirties, and the sixties articulated with an explosion of corresponding populist, labor, and identitarian social movements. Such strict periodization certainly effaces lines of influence and overlap that run through art and politics. But it also leaves the activism of the silent eras—be it esthetic or organizational—inexplicable and illegible. Like Hardt, Rebekah Kowal refuses a simple either-or position and wants to understand Nikolais and his times as both maintaining and challenging convention, as normalizing the body at the same time that it is marked as different. Her essay "Being Motion:

Alwin Nikolais' Queerness at Mid-Century" examines sexual politics that do not get named as such. Kowal shows the ways in which Nikolais' scientific approach to the body and his concern with objectivity had a cognate in the indeterminate, aleatory methods of John Cage and Merce Cunningham, which provided an alternative to the prevailing masculinist esthetic of the day. But in contrast, the partnership of Nikolais and Murray Louis was itself unnamed but visibly staged, and Louis embodied in another the artistry of principle that defied mere objectification.

In critical and cultural terms, Nikolais was treated as a futurist at a time when utopian aspirations for the future and a conviction that models for these possible worlds could be made visible were very much alive. As a process and an esthetic, digitization has certainly confounded the boundaries between actual and possible, present and future. Imaginary worlds can be conjured and crafted with all the searing effects of reality, and even unforeseen catastrophes, like the Twin Towers collapsing in flame, can seem as if already experienced on the screen before they transpire on the world stage. If Nikolais anticipated the look of the digital world, he did it through the medium of theater. Yet the appearance of cinema and television had prompted anxiety over the future of theater long before digitization came to reign in visual culture. Director and performance theorist Herbert Blau could count Nikolais' experimentations as contemporary with his own. Blau had shared Nikolais' 1960s and 1970s, and had seen the choreographer's work back in the Henry Street days. In the early 1980s, Blau wrote an essay entitled "Flights of Angels, Scattered Seeds." It examines the relationship between the future of theater and the theater of the future in conversation with questions of technology and the body that Nikolais' work provokes. Blau's piece appears in a somewhat condensed version here, intercalated with new reflections on Nikolais, thereby restaging in writing a practical exchange of the times, as well as providing a shuttle between the concerns and interpretive frameworks of theater and dance.

Theater should certainly not be taken in the singular. It is a performance genre, but also an assemblage of elements for public presentation. Nikolais comes out of the former and assumes the mantle of the latter. He is as much a director as a choreographer, but also an auteur whose mastery of all scenic elements is part of his presentation. His emergence as an auteur comes at the same time as in film there emerged a form of criticism, marked by a Francois Truffaut essay in 1954, that looks at the director-writer-producer as an author casting a distinctive signature upon a body of work.[30] The equivalent trinity in dance—altogether more rare—is choreographer-designer-composer. Of these, the role of Nikolais as composer has received the least scholarly attention. Musicologist Bob Gilmore offers what he considers a provisional study of Nikolais' music. In method, these scores pose problems similar to choreographic studies. Few of the compositions were notated; many involved sampling, collective creation, and uncited appropriation of the work of others. In his interest in sampling, sonic capture technologies, and non-Western music, Nikolais shared pursuits with other experimentalists of the 1950s, like Henry Cowell, Lou Harrison, and Harry Partch. His development over the course of the decade sees him move from basic sampling to more accomplished collage, and from program attribution to his first LP release, *Choreosonics*, under his own name—a progression consistent with a assumption of a fully auteurist artistic profile.

As we have seen already, Nikolais' prowess with and attention to scenic design were a source of confusion for some critics, who took this as *prima facie* evidence that he was doing something other than making dances. From a less circumscribed critical optic, it is possible to consider Nikolais' sculptural and painterly scenic sensibility in conversation with modernist visual esthetics. Philip Auslander provides a reading of Nikolais' modernist formalism in relation to its best-known avatar in the visual arts, Clement Greenberg. Greenberg eschewed representational paintings for nonfigural abstractionists like Jackson Pollack, and sought the medium specificity of painting in its two-dimensionality or flatness, which emphasizes the purity of form as a reference only to itself. Auslander gives an account of how Nikolais achieves similar ends by taking the human form, which seems replete with representational reference, and defamiliarizing it, so that only the motional attributes of the dance are in evidence. While his theater may liberate a surfeit of imagery in the audience's imagination, the dance is the surface upon which these images become legible. The dancers contribute to this scenic presence rather than the dance establishing them as an originary source. Auslander allows us to see that there are two roads to defamiliarization available at the conjuncture that will come to be called the postmodern, potentially pluralizing the concept itself. One road entails the suppression of the body as reference, the other suppresses its reference as ordinary movement in daily life. In neither case, it turns out, is the defamiliarization wholly sustainable, but the designation of only one route to the postmodern suggests a kind of master narrative of succession shared with the modernism from which it had presumably broken.

The question of how we narrate succession, progress, and movement is key to how we understand canon formation. Mark Franko provides us with a conceptual approach to understanding how the canon operates in modern dance, which helps us make sense of Nikolais' uneasy relationship to it. For Franko, the canon regulates far more than what gets seen and what is forgotten; it provides the interpretive framework, a plot, by which modernism itself is sustained, along with its attendant assumptions of the autonomy of the work and the progressive nature of formal innovation. To demonstrate the uniqueness of their contribution, modern dancers have been expected to generate a distinctive technique, which can travel more readily than company-bound choreography. Nikolais was at odds with this horizon of expectation. Franko then looks at the 1980s, when new ways to historicize dance and bring it into the present were being devised under the sign of dance studies, and a renewed and more sophisticated interest in reconstruction opened the question of what esthetic milestones we might use to locate ourselves. The eighties were the culmination of a proliferation of dance styles that the singularizing tale of modernist succession could not accommodate. The culture wars and the attack on the National Endowment for the Arts were part of a broader backlash that the newly ascendent authority found ungovernable. All manner of interest, value, and affiliation can be found when the canon becomes unmoored. Revisiting those pasts augurs what may lie ahead. Here we look to the returns of Alwin Nikolais.

NOTES

1. For an authoritative collection of this sort, see Roger Copeland and Marshall Cohen, eds., *What is Dance? Readings in Theory and Criticism* (Oxford: Oxford University Press, 1983). For a sustained philosophical reflections, see Francis Sparshott, *A Measured Pace: Toward a Philosophical Understanding of the Arts of Dance* (Toronto: University of Toronto Press, 1995).

2. "Beneath it all however I have a preference—one I suppose in which my major distinction rests. This is in so-called 'dehumanization.' I go psychotic every time I hear the word. To most it means no sex come-on—to others it means no Nureyev (or maybe those mean the same). I recall one critic who wrote in an early review (he later overcame his difficulty), 'When I attend a Nikolais concert I need a warm friend beside me to feel human presence.' I thought . . . Oh shit!!" Marcia B. Siegel, ed., "Nik: A Documentary," *Dance Perspectives*, Vol. 48 (Winter, 1971), 10.

3. See Claudia Gitelman, "The Puppet Theater of Alwin Nikolais," *Ballet Review* Vol. 29, No. 1 (Spring, 2001), 84–91.

4. Louis Althusser and Etienne Balibar, *Reading Capital* (London: New Left Books, 1970).

5. Both quotes from Grant Winston Gray, "The Dance Theater of Alwin Nikolais," Ph.D. dissertation, University of Utah, 1967, 150–51.

6. Claude Levi-Strauss, *The Savage Mind* (Chicago: University of Chicago Press, 1966), 269.

7. Ibid., 247.

8. This was in part a debate with Althusser. See E. P. Thompson, *The Poverty of Theory* (London: New Left Review, 1978).

9. For a useful discussion of these currents, see Patricia Clough, *Autoaffection: Unconscious Thought in the Age of Teletechnology* (Minneapolis: University of Minnesota Press, 2000).

10. Alwin Nikolais and Murray Louis, *The Nikolais/Louis Dance Technique: A Philosophy and Method of Modern Dance* (New York: Routledge, 2005). The book was assembled by Murray Louis. These comments were part of a manuscript, "The Unique Gesture," written by Nikolais and incorporated into the book. Quotes are from pp. 9 and 11.

11. Both quotes are taken from Jana Feinman, "Alwin Nikolais: A New Philosophy of Dance, The Process and the Product." Ed.D. thesis, Temple University, 1994, 7. Even in the mid-1950s, *dehumanization* was a contested term. For example the philospher and critic George Beiswanger wrote, "Now one may take this in two ways, as dehumanizing the dancer or as animizing the thing. I am inclined, perhaps perversely, to the latter view, remembering how man through sheer rhythm ties himself back into the ecstasy or terror of a moving universe." "New London: Residues and Reflections." *Dance Observer* (January, 1957).

12. As Edwards explains, "The extension of mathematical formalization into the realm of business and social problems brought with it a newfound sense of power, the hope of a technical control of social processes to equal that achieved in mechanical and electronic systems. In the systems discourses of the 1950s and 1960s, the formal techniques and tools of the 'systems sciences' went hand in hand with a language and ideology of technical control." Paul N. Edwards, *The Closed World: Computers and the Politics of Discourse in Cold War America* (Cambridge, MA: The MIT Press, 1996), 114.

13. Cited in Feinman, Op. Cit., 6.

14. Deborah Jowitt, *Time and the Dancing Image* (Berkeley: University of California Press, 1988), 358.

15. For a very useful collection of essays on the roots and conditions of the canon controversy see Jan Gorak, ed., *Canon vs. Culture: Reflections on the Current Debate* (New York: Garland Publishing, Inc., 2001).

16. Beth Genné, "Creating a Canon, Creating the 'Classics' in Twentieth-Century British Ballet," *Dance Research: The Journal of the Society for Dance Research*, Vol. 18, No. 2 (Winter, 2000), 132–162.

17. See Wolfgang Iser, "The Authority of the Canon," *The Range of Interpretation* (New York: Columbia University Press, 2000), 13–40.

18. John Guillory, *Cultural Capital: The Problem of Literary Canon Formation* (Chicago: University of Chicago Press, 1993), viii. Guillory borrows his title from the

work of Pierre Bourdieu and calls for a sociology of the canon to address the crisis in the literary form as such.

19. See Jan Van Dyke, *Modern Dance in a Postmodern World: An Analysis of Federal Arts Funding and Its Impact on the Field of Modern Dance* (Reston, VA: National Dance Association, 1992).

20. A list of the Nikolais repertoire, which includes location, date, and source of commission, is available at the Nikolais/Louis Foundation Web site, www.nikolais louis.org/NikolaisChronology.pdf. Accessed August 2005.

21. Nancy Reynolds and Malcolm McCormick, *No Fixed Points: Dance in the Twentieth Century* (New Haven, CT: Yale University Press, 2003). Balanchine reference on p. 495, Steve Allen and effect of television on touring on p. 378; claim for middle class on pp. xiii and 493. It should be observed that the idea of a boom is not especially stable, particularly if it leaves an aftermath in which we have all gone bust. There is some empirical information gathered on what might be entailed. See Leila Sussman, "Anatomy of the Dance Company Boom, 1958–1980." *Dance Research Journal* Vol. 16, No. 2 (Autumn 1984); 23–38.

22. See, for example, the recent collection on the sixties edited by Sally Banes, *Reinventing Dance in the 1960s: Everything Was Possible* (Madison: University of Wisconsin Press, 2003).

23. Arlene Croce, "Discussing the Undiscussable," *The New Yorker* (December 26, 1994–January 2, 1995), 54–60. For a critical appraisal of the affair, see Carol Martin, "High Critics/Low Arts," in Gay Morris, ed., *Moving Words: Re-writing Dance* (London: Routledge, 1996), 320–33.

24. Sue Ann Straits, "The Alwin Nikolais Artist-in-Residence Program at the University of Wisconsin Madison: an Ethnography of Dance Curriculum in Use." Ed.D. thesis, University of Wisconsin, Madison, 1980, p. iii.

25. Figures on education taken from, "Table 297. Earned degrees in visual and performing arts conferred by degree-granting institutions, by level of degree and sex of student: Selected years, 1970–71 to 2001–02," *Digest of Education Statistics Tables and Figures 2003*. Available online at: http://nces.ed.gov/programs/digest/d03/tables/dt297.asp. Accessed August 2005.

26. The data is taken from the Bureau of Labor Statistics and is reported by the National Endowment for the Arts in its *Research Division Note #61: Artist Employment in America—1997* (Washington, DC: 1998), 1.

27. Selma Jeanne Cohen, ed., *The Modern Dance Seven Statements of Belief* (Middletown, CT: Wesleyan University Press, 1966). A dissertation by Estelle Nikolich, "Nikolais Dance Theater: A Total Work of Art" was submitted in 1979, but was not subsequently published. The same is true for a 1978 Ed.D. thesis by Nancy Thornhill Zupp, a 1967 dissertation by Winston Grant Gray, and a 1994 Ed.D. thesis by Jana Feinman, as well as Sue Ann Straits' study of the 1978 Madison residency.

There has been a monograph, "Nik: A Documentary," edited by Marcia B. Siegel and published in 1971 by Dance Perspectives Foundation (*Dance Perspectives 48*), which excerpted some unpublished Nikolais manuscripts. More recently, a study, *Alwin Nikolais*, was published in Italian by Francesca Pedroni (Palermo, L'Epos, 2000), but has not been translated.

28. Nikolais/Louis, Op Cit., 24.

29. Ibid., 8.

30. The auteur school of criticism had great importance for a period of time. The school was first suggested by François Truffaut in his essay "A Certain Tendency in French Cinema," which appeared in *Cahiers du cinéma* in January 1954. The translated essay appears in Bill Nichols, *Movies and Methods*, vol 1. Berkeley: University of California Press, 1976. The school was given substance by Truffaut and other critics who wrote for *Cahiers*. It was popularized in English by Andrew Sarris in his essay "Notes on the Auteur Theory in 1962" first published in Gerald Mast and Marshall Cohen, eds. *Film Theory and Criticism* New York: Oxford University Press, 1974. See Michael Groden and Martin Krieswirth, eds., *John Hopkins Guide to Literary Theory and Criticism* Baltimore: Johns Hopkins University Press, 1994.

CHAPTER 2

Sense Your Mass Increasing with Your Velocity

· ·

ALWIN NIKOLAIS' PEDAGOGY OF UNIFIED DECENTRALIZATION

CLAUDIA GITELMAN

Nowhere is it recorded that Alwin Nikolais uttered the words famously spoken by George Balanchine: "But first a school!" The notion must have resided in Nikolais' consciousness, however. Like the great ballet neoclassicist, Nikolais developed a training program as the foundation to the dance company he created. Again, like Balanchine's, Nikolais' pedagogy helped to define him as a choreographer and provided syntax for his participation in ongoing esthetic dialogues. Looking at Nikolais' teaching helps to clarify the ways in which he both broke with and honored his heritage in dance modernism and elucidates how the specificity of his method of training dancers was indispensable to the creation of his oeuvre.

Both Balanchine and Nikolais relied on a European dance heritage with which they juxtaposed an American culture of ingenuity in order to generate ideas that ballet and modern dance had not considered to that time. Balanchine's artistry was rooted in the Imperial Ballet School in St. Petersburg. Still a teenager while Russia was disrupted by political upheaval and experiencing a window of artistic openness, he showed an apparently natural talent for choreography and leadership. Leaving Russia in 1924, he was soon choreographing for Serge Diaghilev's Ballets Russes. After Diaghilev's death and a brief period directing his own company, he was enticed to the United States and in the next decades transformed the language of ballet.[1]

Nikolais, Balanchine's junior by six years, was the son of middle-class Russian and German immigrants to the United States and did not visit Europe until he served in World War II. His artistic epiphany occurred earlier, when he saw the German modern dancer Mary Wigman perform in the early 1930s. He then studied with Wigman-educated Truda Kaschmann in Hartford, Connecticut, and at Bennington Summer School of the Dance with American modern-dance masters Martha Graham, Charles Weidman, Doris Humphrey, and Wigman's representative in the United States, Hanya Holm. On his return from war service he concentrated his study with Holm and became her assistant. Both respecting and modifying pedagogic praxis and theory rooted in Europe, he began developing a training program for dancers at the Henry

Street Playhouse in Manhattan in 1948. In the next several years he embarked on experiments with his students that ultimately led to a new form of dance staging.

While it would be possible to tease out further similarities between Balanchine and Nikolais—such as a preference for nonliteral narrative and extrapsychological themes, respect for theater's ability to amaze, and an interest in popular as well as elite culture—my purpose here is to concentrate on descriptions of Nikolais' pedagogy and explore its relationship to his total esthetic. My essay stays close to teacher-student interaction, with an eye toward examining how a dance technique develops in the dance studio, is applied in the rehearsal workplace, and born witness to on stage. In the case of Nikolais, whose training method and choreographic style developed in tandem, a look at the dicta of his pedagogy helps to understand his artistic vision and its relationship to the cultural economy of his era.

I base my examination on direct observation during the 1970s and the first half of the 1980s, a period during which Nikolais choreographed prolifically and had his largest pool of students. For an earlier period I rely on interviews with dancers who studied with him in the late 1940s and danced in his company as he attracted national and international attention in the 1950s and 1960s.[2] Hampered by cancer treatment after 1986, Nikolais' choreographic output suffered, and the amount of time he devoted to studio teaching declined. Videotape records of lectures he gave from 1984 until 1990 are valuable documents of the crystallization of his pedagogic theory, as well as of practicalities of the curricular progression he favored. I also had access to files of undated handwritten notes discovered after Nikolais' death.[3]

The European-derived, theoretically based pedagogical method of which Nikolais was the inheritor through Holm and Kaschmann discouraged formation of a systematized dance vocabulary. In destabilizing that convention of dance technique as it is usually understood in ballet and modern-dance practice, the choreographer challenged a craving for order implied in codified movement systems of other dance masters in the 1950s. His students gained physical mastery in technique classes of nonrepeating movement material. They also trained in skills of improvisation. Requiring selection of constraints of choice in the nanosecond of delivery, improvisation encourages spontaneity and can be viewed as a generalized critique of the conformity required in the Cold War economy.

Burgeoning enrollments in dance schools in the 1960s and the 1970s coincided with a liberalized youth ethic embracing physicality and group interaction. Many students, attracted to Nikolais' classes because they offered an alternative to the rigid aristocracy of systematized dance languages, valued the opportunity for spontaneous problem solving that improvisation offers. Dancers who were, or would become, drawn to contact improvisation, as well as others who participated in happenings, registered for semesters of training along with those who aspired to traditionally configured dance careers. In 1971 Nikolais and his partner Murray Louis produced the first public performance of the decidedly nontraditional four-man group calling itself Pilobolus; Jessica Sayre, who had been excited by happenings she participated in at Oberlin College in the 1960s, studied with Nikolais, ultimately becoming a member of his company; some members of the all-male contact-improvisation group Mangrove studied with Nikolais. During this period, as improvisation became a popular performance practice, Nikolais resisted prevailing ideas by insisting that improvisation remain in the studio as a pedagogic and creative tool. Improvisation was, for him, a skill neither open ended nor constrained by limited goals, such as contact improvisation's concern with weight sharing and bodily contact.

Positioned between late modern and postmodern periods in dance, Nikolais' methods of generating and staging movement are, in some respects, iconoclastic with regard to both. In other respects they show interesting traits common to each. If, as he proposed, any practiced invention, notwithstanding its absence from a grammar of codified movement, could qualify as dance, could not any quotidian action also qualify? The validity of singular and self-referential gesture is a logical way station toward the rethinking the nature of dance that occurred in the 1960s and has become known as a gateway to post-modern dance. In breaking through barriers of authoritized modern dance, he gave others virtual permission to do so.

Dedicated to the proscenium theater, Nikolais did not countenance the practice of those early postmodernists who beckoned spectators to nontheatrical settings to witness pedestrian movement. Sally Banes notes, "In effect, the post-modern choreographers proposed that a dance was a dance not because of its content but because of its context—i.e., simply because it was framed as a dance."[4] Vernacular movement becomes art when an audience convenes to observe it as such. Instead of stripping dance of theatrical accoutrements, however, Nikolais mobilized technologies of sound production, stage lighting, shadowing and mirroring effects, and prototypes of other production techniques that would come into wide use in the last decades of the twentieth century.

With pedagogic convictions challenging the historicized purity of dance language, Nikolais identified methods for altering spectator/performer relationships. Without regard for "correct" dance behaviorism, he sent dancers running up the theater's back wall to leap out and down onto the stage. Low front light projected onto them distorted scale and time as magnified shadows sped toward the audience ahead of their "real" doubles (*Prism*, 1957). In 1968 the postmodern choreographer Trisha Brown let performers find their way in slow motion across a giant vertical pegboard (*Planes*). She projected aerial film footage to create the illusion of figures in free fall. There is no direct influence between the two works, but coincidental results are striking. Both *Prism* and *Planes* honor art's inherent artificiality by manipulating audience perceptions.

Decentralized Performing

Nikolais was one of several choreographers in the immediate postwar period to reject the dominant prewar modern-dance esthetic, which although innovative in style, was representational and psycho-socially configured. He and some other dance artists jettisoned characterization and literary and musical motivation to explore communication inherent to movement itself. Movement research and pedagogy took up concerns of the body's material properties, rejecting dance that was expressional in terms of human relationships, whether individual or epic. These postwar artists discarded heroic, emotional, and gender displays, both as they appeared in staged characterization and as they seeped into dancers' presentations of themselves. Nikolais used the word *decentralization* to describe the state to which dancers should aspire in class and on stage.

Invoking Marshall McLuhan, he often told students, "The medium is the message," assigning to *medium* and *message* the spatial, temporal, sculptural, and motional constructions he invented for each training session. In the McLuhan sense that the nature of technology effects meaning, it can be said that the nature of bodily performance affects what is communicated—self or motion [5] Ego involvement, Nikolais noted, inhibits transfer of the body's materiality and its motional properties. "Motion predicates itself," students heard him say. Nikolais' choreographic and pedagogic principles required dancers to transcend personal fixations in order to let motion explain itself.

Decentralization signifies several of Nikolais' esthetic convictions. Dramatic dance centers a heroic—or antiheroic—figure with which audiences can identify. Nikolais rejected that convention. Traditional modern dance finds virtue in moving from the center, where *center* means both the inner resources of the person dancing and the core of the body. For a decentralized dancer there is no single point of initiation. She/he attends to articulating joints; peripheral designs of body parts, points, lines, and volumes in space; dynamic textures; and qualifiers of motion identified by physics. Centered motivation tends toward the emotional; decentralized execution is intellectually commanded.

Decentralization, then, is an ideological formation that constituted Nikolais' response to esthetic and socio-cultural conditions of his time. But decentralization is also a pedagogic strategy he used to overcome limitations of movement vocabularies that derive from the instincts of a single teacher/choreographer. Demanding the body's absolute attention to a simple action—such as tracing a circle on the floor with a foot—he challenged both novice and experienced dancers. Instead of keeping the body centered and gazing forward while inscribing a circle, students softened the supporting leg and shifted the position of torso and head to focus—or *grain* in Nikolais parlance—toward the linear structure. Arms and hands, too, repositioned themselves to help focus attention to the spatial design. The resulting proficient attention to specific bodily mechanisms and empirical forms substituted for named coordinations that dance systems traditionally rely on for perfecting execution. By providing nonhabitual structures for their mediation, Nikolais imposed an obligation of availability to choreographic need but not a prescribed vocabulary.

Unification of focus is a paradoxical requisite for decentralized performing. If a student tilted her/his head during a reach of the arm or change of footing, as do ballet dancers to whom *épaulement* (shouldering) is natural and automatic, the guilty student might have heard, "Don't give me that kiss-my-neck look!" Oppositional pulls of the body, such as a twist of the spine so that a shoulder or hip resists a gaze in the opposite direction, had no place in Nikolais' esthetic. Such behaviorisms smack of psychological states of longing, say, or defiance. Banning isometric tension was another departure from traditional modern dance and a significant element in shaping bodies to postwar dance values. Agreement of energy expenditure and physical task keeps bodies available for detailed articulation, unifying execution and motional intent. The paradox of decentralized unification also emerges in Nikolais' theatrical creation. Assuming ultimate responsibility for disparate elements of his productions—sound, costuming, lighting, and sets—he aimed for unified productions, proposing an alternative to an esthetic of fragmentation and irony identified with Merce Cunningham and some other artists of his generation.

As I will chronicle later, Nikolais' decentralized esthetic led to deliberate depersonalization of dancers in his choreography and that of his students by 1955. His work troubled assumptions of an earlier generation of modern-dance audiences about the traditional function of dance. Reviewing the 1957 premiere of *Runic Canto,* a prominent dance critic accepted that the dance is devoid of literary base and finds that it "throbbed with energy of primitive ritual." She hoped that it was "a step toward a communication of feeling," and away from "cold and clinically applied devices."[6] The critic seemed to express anxiety about choreography that pursues invention over the natural, spectacle over sentiment, and the new over a mythologized past. Deperson-alization, by seeming to render identity unstable, challenged an entrenched dance esthetic, and, more broadly, can be seen as a form of social critique aimed against the age of the so-called Organization Man, an age when social mechanisms vaunted predictability and consistency.

Curriculum

A visitor to Nikolais' school would have noticed first that his studios lacked mirrors, which typically cover the wall that dancers face during class. If he or a surrogate teacher found him/herself teaching in a studio equipped with mirrors, as was often the case during master classes in colleges and universities, he took a position against a nonmirrored wall, denying students the opportunity to check their "line" and compare themselves to other dancers. DON'T INDULGE.[7] A visitor might also remark that during the most important segment of the lesson students were organized to travel across the floor in a path that put them in profile to their teacher. Negotiating the pattern built for them, dancers changed facing, direction, and floor pattern, but opportunity for frontal presentation was denied them. FOCUS ON THE THING DONE.

Another break with convention was the absence of an accompanist. Nikolais and members of his teaching staff seated themselves behind drums of varying size, timber, and pitch, sounding them with softheaded mallets. The rationale was to eliminate the emotional overlay that tends to habitually infect music emanating from pianos and other melodic instruments. DON'T BE MAD, SAD, OR GLAD. The absence of mirrors, direction of travel, and type of accompaniment is at odds with the usual dance studio training in modern dance and ballet, as is the absence of a demonstrator on whom students are invited to model themselves.

Class began with a rigorous series of stretches and strengthening exercises, during which dancers worked on the floor in various reclining and sitting positions. The warm up, like other aspects of Nikolais' training, had European roots. At Mary Wigman schools, the actual dancing activity was preceded by an hour of *gymnastik* taught by a member of her staff. Hanya Holm, upon establishing the Wigman School in New York, modified the preparatory work and connected it to the main class. Nikolais' warm up in the 1950s had gymnastic characteristics, remember students. Gymnastic elements remained as the warm up became streamlined and more extreme in its demands for unrestrained motional responsiveness. Careful attention to joints and muscles in the first exercises gave way to whorls of swings, rolls, coils, and stretches.

Once on their feet, students were subjected to scrutiny in order to establish immediacy, or "realness." CLEAR THE EYE. Tensions in the lower back or between the shoulders draw attention to an anxious self; hips not aligned, thighs not lengthened, arches not lifted, impede clarity and readiness to move. Nikolais did not deal with these problems by "hammering out the kinks." To release tensions and energize recalcitrant muscles he coaxed students to invent and inhabit a spatial aura. First stressing height dimension to establish verticality, he then asked dancers to psychically impress themselves on their surroundings in order to demonstrate the body's other dimensions and directional interest. As dancers learn to project themselves onto their surroundings, they take on a frankly presentational attitude. "Never allow action without awareness," Nikolais cautioned novice teachers in a lecture on pedagogy in 1990. "Dancers must want to perform. They must sense life. Your job as teachers is to make that come through." Nikolais' insistence that students project aliveness runs counter to the claims of dancers who profess to move naturally. If we allow that dance is culturally constructed, it follows that movement systems to which any group is trained will seem natural to those practitioners. Moving before an audience is presentational no matter how natural dancers wish to be.

For knee bends (the *plié* in ballet), which prepare dancers for locomotion and aerial work, Nikolais employed geometry favored by Holm—six positions of the feet and arms instead of the five ballet positions appropriated by most modern-dance training systems. Third and fourth positions place the feet in a diagonal relationship to the trunk, bisecting frontal and sideward orientation to space. Sixth position—the crossed fourth in the ballet lexicon— is accompanied by arms reaching parallel and upward rather than curved to surround the head. When changing positions of the arms and legs the dancer quickly bends her/his knee to lift a foot and bends the elbows slightly so that direction toward the center of mass is suggested before a new position is achieved. This contrasts with the practice of dancers trained in ballet, who, when changing from the first position (heels touching, legs rotated outward with lowered arms framing the body) to the second position, raise the arms in front of their bodies before opening them, while simultaneously sliding one foot to the side and exhibiting the crescent of its high arch before lowering the heel. WE DON'T GO THROUGH DENVER TO REACH BOSTON.

The important lesson, the "across-the-floor" section of each two-hour class, began after roughly forty-five minutes of preparation in floor and standing exercises. LET'S COME ACROSS. JESSIE, ROB, LYNN, GERALD—YOU LEAD. A theme or subject was established, "Today we'll work on rebound quality." Nikolais directed verbally. When he did occasionally demonstrate, it was at the beginning of the lesson to ensure that students were sufficiently prepared to work in a decentralized, unified manner. For example, he might spend minutes demonstrating and observing dancers bringing the fingertips of their upstage hand into contact with their downstage elbow during four walking steps, insisting that the elbow lift from the side and the hand travel across the front of the body so that the different paths of each were traversed to achieve contact in the same time interval. The chest and head changed position to focus attention to the action; thigh, knee, and step were qualified as well. Nikolais criticized impediments to perfection by teasing and scolding his students, but he never manipulated a recalcitrant arm, head, or back. Students' failings, he charged, were caused by conditions they placed on movement because of habit or psychological interference. DIVORCE YOURSELF FROM YOURSELF.

He might follow this lengthy preamble with a series of other points of bodily contact, requiring full attention to each. DON'T STAY IN THE SAME STATE OF MIND. Then, in a class on rebounding energy like the one I am hypothesizing, he incrementally altered dynamics until body parts exploded away from each other, sending dancers into the air, spinning, and recovering in tricky rhythms that challenged coordination. Students had not encountered the same movement phrase before and would not encounter it again. I DON'T TEACH STEPS.

In some classes, dancers were called upon to demonstrate unified attention to points that journeyed through the body's interior space. GOING INWARD IS NOT WITHDRAWING. Such would be necessary, for example, when interest slid from the left shoulder to the right side of the lower ribcage, and then to the back surface of both shoulders. With a fluid core, a decentralized dancer executing a series of rapid changes of focus to inner and outer space can suggest the quality of a puppet—a quality that Nikolais occasionally used in his choreography. The French dance historian Laurence Louppe observes that perceiving dancers as puppetlike beings poses a threat to the authority we believe ourselves to have over our identity and free will. The delicate na-

1. Nikolais giving a master class at the University of New Hampshire in 1969.
© University of New Hampshire. Photograph by Jack Adams.

ture of a puppet also suggests innocence and a lost state of grace. Such double inferencing, she suggests, can cause a troubling loss of orientation in the viewer. Imposing puppetlike movement on dancers in some of his ballets is one of several devices Nikolais used to contest the modernist narrative of human perfectibility.[8]

As a curriculum became routinized, the "big four" of time, shape, space, and motion emerged as overarching categories of movement that teachers and students investigated properties and employed in discussions and evaluations. Refining and expanding upon ideas of dance scientist Rudolf Laban, Nikolais suggested myriad opportunities to stimulate invention. Dancers might study momentum as one of many ingredients of motion. SENSE YOUR MASS INCREASING WITH YOUR VELOCITY. Creating linear boundaries was one of many ways to consider space. IDENTIFY THE STRUCTURE. Dancers could study the sensation of time. WEIGH THE DURATION. A shape was not a heroic (or bashful or alluring) pose, but a sculptural form requiring awareness of mass and body surface. DANCE IS NOT DECORATION OF SELF.

The daily two-hour technique class was followed by an hour-long theory class four days a week. Theory class usually, though not invariably, included improvisation. New students were led through exercises to introduce them to the requirements of improvisation. One was to facilitate unpremeditated, immediate response to stimuli. TOO SLOW. TRY AGAIN. Another was to encourage critical decisions about assuming leadership and following the lead of others. DON'T BE BOSSY. Another necessary skill was to determine appropriateness of changing course or continuing a line of investigation. STAY WITH IT. DEVELOP THAT IDEA.

After the demands of improvisation were mastered, following sessions began with verbal amplification of the premise of the technique class just given. Students' individual exploration in starts and stops interspersed with criticisms and suggestions followed. Typically, dancers were then paired or grouped in ensembles to interact while vivifying the principle under study. An overarching aim of improvisation as a pedagogical tool was development of performing ability. Tuned to a dynamic environment shared with other bodies, students simultaneously created and performed a kinetic event.

Another primary purpose of improvisation as studio practice was informed spectatorship. Experiencing autonomy as they assumed responsibility for unpremeditated decision making, students submitted to the authority of an audience of teacher and fellow students. Measured against their skill in making a performance "work," students became objects to be judged by their teacher and peers. However, because the specific mandate of students at Nikolais' school was to enliven a bodily action or motional property, dancers' identities remained intact. Liberated from play acting a character or embodying an emotional relationship, they preserved their subjectivity.[9]

Dancers in Nikolais' company improvised on stage during lecture demonstrations, a frequent component of residency packages. The choreographer selected one or several dancers to demonstrate an aspect of the technique— usually one of the big four. Dancers had no forewarning about topics they would be asked to demonstrate. Working in a community of trust, they built a coherent structure and brought attention to the principle under discussion. A panel of former company members convened in 1992 to talk about their careers hinted that opportunities to improvise in lecture demonstrations and during the creation of dances so thrilled them that improvisation may have been the primary reason they freely donated their bodies to Nikolais' vision.[10] Opportunities for improvisation in staged performances were constrained, restricted to decisions in the timing of prescribed gestures in predetermined places on stage.

Composition class held a hallowed position at the beginning or end of each week. On their own time students prepared a study to satisfy an assignment given them the preceding week. Studies were in solo format and without musical accompaniment. Assignments early in the semester were practical and relevant to topics under study in technique and theory. "Rotary action of the joints," "volumes of space," "fast and slow," are examples. By the end of a semester students confronted assignments such as "texture of heavy and light," "thick and thin," "soft and hard," which they were to choreograph without mimesis. Nikolais insisted that skillful design of motion, space, shape, and time made it possible to sentiently communicate an abstraction, that is, a quality divorced from any object. When he was eyeing students for replacement in his company, Nikolais evaluated them on the basis of their skills as improvisers and choreographers. He looked for noneccentric, courageous decision making in the former, and in the latter, invention and ability to sustain a gestalt.

Workplace and the Stage

Moving on to an analysis of how Nikolais' pedagogy enabled his choreography and informed its process, it is instructive to observe briefly the pedagogic challenges both he and George Balanchine turned to their respective advantages as they built training programs and organized dance companies. Balanchine's first classes in the United States attracted women trained by various teachers in a variety of ballet styles. Neither body type nor work ethic was uniform. With his iconic neoclassical ballet *Serenade* (official premiere March 1935) he brilliantly exploited these differences and at the same time made his first move toward training a corps of dancers to a style that wedded the Imperial Russian ballet language, modified by his exposure to Soviet and émigré modernism, to the temperament of his adopted homeland.

Nikolais faced a variegated class of professional and amateur dancers in 1948—a few teenage women with ballet classes behind them and a group of World War II veterans with prewar careers who were retraining under the G.I. Bill. Using a strategy that seems counterintuitive to the task of unifying a company, he designed a system of esthetic barter that encouraged diverse responses to ideas he posed and gave dancers ownership of material they created. Phyllis Lamhut, an original student and company member, recollects that teacher and students stimulated each other: "In improvisation and composition he could lean back and see what was happening. He had an enthusiastic, dare-devil group of people. Now that's a lucky man! Improv was where we explored, we went beyond technique."[11] A dialogue emerged that acti-

In the Playhouse at 466 Grand Street, neighbors see and participate in producing fine plays. And in our Schools of Drama and Dance, young people have an opportunity to express themselves in many forms of the theatre arts such as the above Technique Class for Dance Major Students.

2. Nikolais' first class at the Henry Street Playhouse in 1948. From left: Jack Spencer, Luke Bragg, Gladys Bailin, Gino Mortenghi, Phyllis Lamhut, Sheldon Ossosky, Anita Lynn. Settlement House calendar for 1949, courtesy of the Nikolais/Louis Foundation for Dance.

vated both parties, as students, stimulated by their teacher, produced results that helped Nikolais to develop choreographic ideas.

One more analogy between the artistry of Balanchine and Nikolais is worth pursuing. While they were instituting training programs that would help to define their mature work, each choreographer took several seasons to break with models of dance production with which they had worked previously—Balanchine in Europe from 1925 to 1933, and Nikolais in pre–World War II America. Balanchine gradually transformed Serge Diaghilev's ballet-making process as a collaboration of composers, designers, choreographers, and librettists into his signature expression of pure and intricate relationships of dance and music. The first dances Nikolais choreographed for his new company relied on themes similar to those used by choreographers with whom he had studied at Bennington in the late 1930s. *Extrados* (1949) was in three sections: "Focus Toward Faith"; "Submission to Faith"; "Focus Toward Self." As late as 1951 he made a subject- and character-driven piece. A program note situates the dance within the dominant prewar modern dance esthetic: "In *Vortex* a persecution existing in the mind of the central figure achieves brief nightmarish reality." Twenty years later, Nikolais admitted that these works were "inappropriate" for the cultural climate of the late 1940s. "*Extrados* was terrible."[12]

While he was creating dances using themes of traditional modern dance, his unusual training methods were attracting the attention of the modern-dance community. In 1950 the journal *Dance Observer* published a lengthy interview with Nikolais about teaching choreography. Although he paid respect to his Bennington teacher Louis Horst, who based choreography instruction on theme and manipulation of movement material in relation to musical forms, Nikolais rejected stimulation from musical or other art sources. His interviewer asked Nikolais about the inclusion of improvisation in his curriculum, showing that that aspect of his training method was a topic of interest. When questioned about the use of stage properties, he said: "Props should be avoided in early composition. I do find, though, that in improvisation (as training), a prop will often bring about the students' transcending their 'self consciousness.'"[13] Although he was not yet using the term "decentralization," his reply shows that he was working in that vein.

Engaged in a pedagogic process that discouraged them from projecting personae, novice dancers nonetheless report experiencing personal enlargement. Lamhut recalls: "I always felt the training was about *me*. It made me part of a greater event. It was not 'Look at us,' but 'look at the result.' We were making it happen."[14]

From the inception of their study, Nikolais' first students gained performing experience. They danced Nikolais' self-described "inappropriate" modern dance pieces at the Henry Street Playhouse and other venues and performed in children's dance plays he created for his community constituents and that toured throughout the region. *Lobster Quadrille, Merry-Go-Elsewhere,* and other concoctions used fanciful costumes—in one, a cylindrical fish had toilet-tank floats for eyes—and tangled plots that often needed the "help" of young audiences for resolution. Dancers also had opportunities to perform work they developed in composition classes.

With a concert in January 1953, teacher and students turned away from past esthetics in a program titled *Etudes II: Masks, Props, and Mobiles.* Students performed seven works they had choreographed, and Nikolais contributed two numbers. A joint concert in early 1955 titled *Village of Whispers* clarified his vision of dance that broke with past motivation. "It was the birth of de-centralization—the idea of abstraction took hold. I saw that motion contains its own intelligence."[15] These ideas were fully realized in December of that year. Different student choreography was shown, and Nikolais repeated two pieces from 1953 and created two new dances. A program note introduces the 1955 concert *Masks — Props — Mobiles* as "an experimental program in which the dancers are depersonalized or in which their motions are extended into external materials."

Nikolais used the words *masks, props,* and *mobiles* to gesture toward his pedagogical aim of transcending students' temptation to exhibit themselves. Dancers did not wear facemasks in any of the three concerts, although in some numbers faces were painted to give performers a surreal aspect and to help shield personal identity. In one number, which Nikolais choreographed and which remains in repertory in the twenty-first century, entire bodies are masked by stretch fabric. The material performs along with the "mobiles" (dancers) who animate it to create a narrative of evolving shape. Empathizing with the strength required to keep the fabric taut, the magnified scale of the forms, and a few phalliclike thrusts into the fabric, many spectators as-sign male character to the figures. Both female and male dancers perform *Noumenon.* With masking in this and other works and with his habitual use of unisex costuming, Nikolais challenged a binary model of gender.

Louppe observes that masks relieve dancers of the role of "psycho-analytical commentator," rendering the body the double service of freedom from naturalism and increased responsibility for expression.[16] The service rendered by masking is also provided by engagement with objects. Whether simply positioned in proximity to material objects or animating them, per-formers give those objects a performative function. More to the point, in doing so they acknowledge the body's own materiality.[17] Whether they did or did not use masks or props in studies programmed on the three concerts, dancers masked themselves with decentralization. "Murray [Louis] is not danc-ing in a dark corner. He *is* a dark corner," observed a member of the audience watching *Village of Whispers.* Throughout his years of teaching Nikolais often repeated the comment he had overheard. To him it affirmed that dancers could embody what he called "a state of space." Dance could be nonliteral and also communicate subject.

Sympathetic dance critic John Martin, reviewing *Masks — Props — Mobiles* for the *New York Times,* acknowledged the importance of pedagogic process:

"[F]rom his patient and concentrated teaching, a performance company has actually begun to develop." Martin allowed that theoretically based training permitted dancers to move "by their own musculature, instead of in terms of other dancer's 'technique!'"[18] More validation came from *Village Voice* critic Marianne Preger: "It would seem that the identification with objects opens up new and exciting sources of movement." Intuiting the concept of decentralization, she lauds dancers who were "totally involved in Theatre rather than in Self."[19]

Nikolais made use of the improvisational craft to which he trained his students when he began choreographing lengthy works, and he perfected the use of objects, which became texts to give dancers options for movement. Lamhut describes the rehearsal process: "Nik would say, 'See what you can do with this [a wooden disk strapped to one foot].' We'd all get excited about discovering things. He'd see something interesting: 'Watch Bill [Frank]. Everybody work on that. . . . Okay, now try some other ideas,' and so on. By the next rehearsal he'd have improved the prop. We'd work again and eventually he'd start setting sequences."[20] The give-and-take between dancer, choreographer, and object led, in this instance, to the opening segment of the 1956 ballet *Kaleidoscope*.

As Nikolais added more texts to his productions—side lighting in saturated colors, slide projections, surreal set pieces, and other stage technologies that he pioneered—performers' responsibilities increased. Suzanne McDermaid, a prominent company member in the 1970s, says, "You have to be an extremely strong performer to make the environment around you respond to your vibrancy."[21] A loyal cadre of students accepted decentralization as empowerment. In granting performative function to objects, sets, and lighting effects, dancers became responsible not only for their own activity, but also for total scenic coherence. The choreographer asked dancers to place themselves "in skilled conversation with the environment and the things and happenings within it." His aim, he explained in 1971, was to establish man as "a fellow traveler within the total universal mechanism rather than the god from which all things flowed. . . . He lost his domination but instead became kinsman to the universe."[22]

Reacting to dramatic and emotional narrative that he thought was suffocating modern dance in postwar America, and disturbed by dancers' assumptions about self-expression, Nikolais developed strategies that overcame hindrances to the inherent expressivity of motion. The use of objects and maskings worked well. Success in that area led him to devise technical training methods that enabled decentralized receptivity to movement opportunity. What is interesting here is how the artist's esthetic development is inextricably bound to his pedagogy. As choreographer he came to rely on the skills in which he trained students: one was conversance with a theoretical language; a second was an appetite for experimentation; and a third was the ability to give the body immediacy. A corollary to the third was the ability to grant performative function to objects and atmosphere.

In the twenty-first century few dancers train exclusively with the choreographer(s) for whom they work. Dancers prepare themselves in many styles of dance as well as with gym workouts and body therapies. Choreographers encourage eclectic training that produces a high level of competency and is not marked by a single esthetic. Susan Leigh Foster contrasts what she calls "hired" bodies with bodies formed by earlier dance techniques, among which Nikolais' can be numbered: "Not only did each mark the body so deeply that a dancer could not adequately perform another technique, but each aesthetic project was conceived as mutually exclusive of, if not hostile to, the others."[23] Such was the case during the era when choreographers maintained schools and assembled companies from among students who, aspiring to carry their teacher's esthetic concerns to the public, undertook what was often a lengthy tutelage leading to tightly rationed performance outlets. George Balanchine and Alwin Nikolais were two in the last generation of dance artists to closely supervise the training of dancers who performed their work and whose choreographic visions were enabled by their pedagogy.

The Modernist Narrative

Whether Laban-derived, as was Nikolais', or with genealogies that include other late nineteenth- and early twentieth-century theorists such as François Delsarte and Emile Jaques-Dalcroze, modern-dance pedagogy assumes that properties of human movement are knowable and subject to categorization. European originators of modern dance used pedagogic tactics based in intellectual investigation, but did not codify movement vocabularies. American modern dancers systematized personal dance languages and defended them as anatomically truthful. Dance modernism joins this faith in reason with humanist values and nineteenth-century Romantic ideas about intuitive hero-artists. Supported by faith in Western science and belief in unified humanity, dance professionals of the modern period assumed that people geographically, ethnically, and generationally distinct respond similarly to image and allusion. Neither European nor American dance modernists rejected the notion of hero-artist or escaped the myth of universality.

Use of an elaborate theory of motion to guide instruction at his school, and his embrace of technology in stage works, keeps Nikolais within the larger modernist project of scientific invention. He was an abstractionist in the tradition of the industrial transformation that broke down machine and human tasks into abstract units of force.[24] A kinetic calculus helped him to train decentralized performers. He defied Newtonian mechanics, however, by rejecting training methods that inscribe bodies with a movement language perfected through machinelike repetition.

Nikolais also embraced abstraction in another sense by abandoning literal reference and illustration in his dances. However, he is not an exemplar of what Norman Bryson calls dance criticism's "grand narratives of modernity" leading from abstraction to the formalist esthetic.[25] After breaking down components of motion for the purpose of training dancers, Nikolais put those components back together in order to investigate subject. His student Murray Louis was a dark corner (but not a man dancing in a dark corner); advanced students struggled with composition assignments like "haunted house" and "carnival," succeeding if they created a state of space without resorting to mimicry. Dance critic Anna Kisselgoff writes, "As decorative as it may seem, Mr. Nikolais' dance theater is also intended to convey a philosophical idea." "The secret of Mr. Nikolais' appeal," she writes, "is in our recognition of his subject—the human condition." She points to human evolution and human folly as recurrent themes in his dances.[26] Nikolais' dances managed, without plot lines or specificity of character and situation, to remind audiences of the human predicament. This could be as innocent as the anxiety of disappearance and surprise reappearance engineered with the age-old sliding panel trick, or as lethal as the self-knowledge of sadistic pleasure in mayhem and destruction.[27]

Although Nikolais' program of decentralizing dancers challenged post–World War II craving for stability, he shared in the post–World War II culture of abundance. His lavish use of color, sound, light, and every theatrical device he could dream up speaks to an appetite for sensory profusion. His pedagogy registers other inconsistencies. Humanist goals are apparent in a curriculum that guided students' discoveries and preserved their subjectivity. However, students were granted agency in an environment of restraint. Nikolais set strict limits on improvisation; inviting dancers' choices, he retained the authority to reject or accept them. An absent leader who did not appear on stage, he nonetheless preserved the sanctity of modernism's self-contained genius, accepting accolades as a heroic creator of total theater that mobilized costuming, material objects, stage lighting, and sound, all of which he considered inseparable ingredients of his choreography.

The value Nikolais placed on spontaneity in schooling dancers matched the intuition he claimed for developing his own choreography and suggests his view of himself as creator. Speaking about his choreographic process in 1987, he described rehearsals more complex but similar in outline to the 1956 rehearsal described by Lamhut. He then claimed to work from instinct when choosing movement material that dancers offered him: "It [the dance] dictates where it wants to go." While some choreographers of his generation used scores, game rules, and other predetermined structures, whether contrived or aleatory, Nikolais claimed spontaneous decision making. He complained: "Students in comp[osition] can obscure an idea." He advised: "Don't rationalize the means. Work from intent. Develop a feeling for it." In the same interview he expressed admiration for the "orderly German theory taught by Hanya Holm" and "the precise concepts" she used in teaching.[28] Two roots of Nikolais' pedagogy and choreography—an intellectually determined calculus of motion, and trust in the unpremeditated—suggest an apparent paradox inherent to modernism. His works and the pedagogy that enabled them expose tension between reason and instinct harboring within art making in its broadest context.

NOTES

1. There exists a vast amount of published material on George Balanchine. I rely on three sources: Bernard Taper's 1984 biography *Balanchine* (Berkeley: University of California Press), *Thirty Years: The New York City Ballet* by Lincoln Kirstein (New York: Alfred A. Knopf, 1978), and Tim Scholl's *From Petipa to Balanchine* (London: Routledge, 1994).

2. I am grateful for conversations with Murray Louis, Phyllis Lamhut, and Dorothy Vislocky. Ruth Grauert, Nikolais' long-time assistant and sometimes stage manager, technical director, and tour manager, was especially helpful to me in understanding the workings of the early school.

3. In these years, Nikolais gave pedagogy workshops as a component of Christmas courses at his school. Videotapes of the lectures are in the archives of the Nikolais/Louis Foundation for Dance, New York City. Written material relevant to pedagogy is in the Alwin Nikolais and Murray Louis Papers, Robert E. and Jean R. Mahn Center for Archives and Special Collections, University Libraries at Ohio University, Athens, Ohio. Nikolais abandoned plans to publish a book about his philosophy of dance. After his death, Murray Louis selected parts of Nikolais' notes, augmented them, and added a class manual with accompanying DVD. Nikolais, Alwin and Murray Louis, *Nikolais/Louis Dance Technique: A Philosophy and Method of Modern Dance* (New York: Routledge, 2005).

4. See Banes' introduction to the 1987 paperback edition (Middletown: Wesleyan University Press), xix, of her iconic *Terpsichore in Sneakers* (New York: Houghton Mifflin Company, 1977).

5. McLuhan introduced the statement in 1964 in *Understanding Media: The Extensions of Man,* which "made of its author the foremost oracle of his age." (See Lewis H. Lapham, introduction to the MIT Press edition of the book, 1994). Nikolais, always sensitive to the zeitgeist of his age, soon began appropriating the phrase.

6. Cohen, Selma Jeanne, "The Dance Festival," *New York Times,* August 25, 1957.

7. I inject Nikolais' words to vivify his presence and emphasize fundamental precepts of his teaching.

8. Louppe's insights arise in the context of her analysis of Oskar Schlemmer's productions as director of the Theater Workshop at the Bauhaus from 1925 to 1929. "Les Danses du Bauhaus: une Généalogie de la Modernité," in *Oskar Schlemmer* (Paris: Réunion des Musées Nationaux, 1999), 188–189. Nikolais also challenged Modernist notions of progress with ballets that ridiculed human folly, and with others that showed dancers overpowered by a universe they themselves had created. *Tower* (1965) and *Tent* (1968) are examples. He reveals a contradictory utopianism when he contends that his total theater represented a new humanism by showing men and women interacting with universal mechanisms, rather than in domination of them. (See Nikolais, Alwin, "Dance Semantics," *New York Times,* August 19, 1956.)

9. Virginia Spivey observes that a dancer's subjectivity is maintained when she/he resists transformation into a character. See "Sites of Subjectivity: Robert Morris, Minimalism, and Dance," *Dance Research Journal* Vol. 35, No. 2 (Winter 2003), 112–130 and Vol. 36, no. 2 (Summer 2004), Drawing on scholarship that treats the work of postmodern theorist and performer Yvonne Rainer, Spivey unknowingly expresses agreement with Nikolais' decentralizing purpose: "She downplayed the dancer's personality, neutralizing the dramatic appeal of the performer and focusing instead on the body's movement alone."

10. See "Dancers Roundtable" in Conference Proceedings, *Dance Reconstructed* (New Brunswick, NJ: Mason Gross School of the Arts, 1993), 151–166. Beverly Blossom, Karen Sing, Suzanne McDermaid-Friedell, Jessica Sayre, James Teeters, and Sara Pearson represent the Nikolais Company during various periods from 1950 through the early 1980s.

11. Audiotape and transcript of my interview with Lamhut on January 21, 2000, are in Jerome Robbins Dance Division, the New York Public Library.

12. Nikolais admitted this during a pedagogy lecture, December 18, 1984.

13. "On the Teaching of Choreography: Interview with Alwin Nikolais" is the second of three interviews conducted by Martha Coleman (*Dance Observer,* De-

cember 1950). The first interview is with Louis Horst (*Dance Observer,* November 1949), and the third with Jean Erdman (*Dance Observer,* April 1952).

14. Lamhut, personal interview, September 17, 2004.

15. Videotaped pedagogy lecture, December 19, 1984.

16. Louppe, 186.

17. Spivey extends my observation with the argument that encounters with objects in a theatrical or gallery setting force viewers, too, to recognize their materiality, "to acknowledge their mutual existence in real space and time." Spivey, 125.

18. Martin, "The Dance: New Life," *New York Times,* February 19, 1956.

19. Preger, "Dance: Masks, Props, Mobiles," *Village Voice,* January 4, 1956.

20. Lamhut, personal interview, February 18, 2004.

21. Barbara Estelle Nickolich, in her Ph.D. dissertation *Nikolais Dance Theater: a Total Art Work* (New York University, 1979), quotes an interview McDermaid gave journalist Jackie Farnam for the *Rochester Democrat and Chronicle,* December 5, 1976.

22. Marcia B. Siegel, ed., "Nik: A Documentary," *Dance Perspectives* Vol. 48 (Winter 1971), 11.

23. Susan Leigh Foster, "Dancing Bodies," in *Incorporations,* edited by Jonathan Crary and Sanford Kwinter (New York: Zone Books, 1992), 493. Foster pursues discourses of instruction with descriptions of ballet technique, Isadora Duncan technique, Martha Graham technique, Merce Cunningham technique, and contact improvisation technique.

24. Norman Bryson points to entries in the eighteenth-century *Encyclopédie* of applications to human bodies of mechanical processes performed by machines. Bryson, "Cultural Studies and Dance History," in *Meaning in Motion,* edited by Jane C. Desmond (Durham: Duke University Press, 1997), 55–77.

25. Bryson, 70.

26. Kisselgoff, "In a Nikolais Work, There's Always Depth with the Dazzle," *New York Times,* January 24, 1993.

27. One example is the pop-art ballet *Gallery* (1978), which ends with the disturbing image of heads being blown apart. For other examples see my essay "The Puppet Theater of Alwin Nikolais," *Ballet Review Vol. 29, no. 1* (Spring 2001).

28. Nikolais, Videotaped interview with Jana Feinman, March 9, 1989, collected in *Alwin Nikolais: Philosophy, Process, Product 1948–1969* (private collection).

CHAPTER 3

The Omniloquence of Alwin Nikolais

. . . .

MARCIA B. SIEGEL

In his first job Alwin Nikolais accompanied silent films on the piano and organ. That job was remarkably prophetic even though it had nothing to do with dance, for he was working in a new performing medium made possible by technology, where he used his musical skill and kinetic sensitivity to amplify the actions of human bodies. Dance was to be the filter through which the far-reaching interests of this man would flow, and dance is still the indispensable factor in his striking theater innovations.

It was the German modern dance, with its emphasis on rhythm, form, and dynamics, that first attracted Nikolais. His dance teachers were Mary Wigman's disciples, Truda Kaschmann in Hartford and later Hanya Holm. He studied briefly with the American giants too—Martha Graham, Doris Humphrey, Charles Weidman—but their subjective, psychological explorations were less congenial to him. As Hanya Holm's assistant in the 1940s, he followed Holm's teaching practice of developing the dynamic and spatial properties of movement rather than building up a specific technique. Instead of patterns of action, he taught the principles of motion, which could later become the basis for his choreography.

He took these ideas with him to Henry Street Playhouse in 1948, where he found his students unwilling to part with their "treasured self-expression." He began to give them props and other devices to help them "transcend themselves and become another thing." As his company developed at Henry Street during the 1950s, the use of external devices seemed a logical way to achieve a dance form that would go beyond the dramatic, personal choreography of the period. Nikolais thinks most modern dancers were preoccupied by the "foetal, phallic and fertile drive," and he felt sexuality should be kept in balance with other life forces. He does not see man struggling heroically against the universe, but as a creature that fits into a larger cosmos. Beginning with *Masks, Props and Mobiles* in 1953, the company embarked on a series of experiments that let the dancers work in environments created by extensions of the

This article first appeared in *Dance Magazine*, April 1968. It is reprinted here in slightly edited form.

1. The Playhouse Dance company performing Somniloquy *at the Solomon R. Guggenheim Museum in New York City, February, 2, 1967. © Chimera Photo. Courtesy Jerome Robbins Dance Division, The New York Public Library, Astor, Lenox and Tilden Foundations.*

body, such as costumes, props, unusual lighting effects, nonliteral sound, films, projections, and other elements of design. What has evolved is a hybrid theater form whose spectacular visual effect has never been questioned, but whose integration of visual, aural, technological, and kinetic elements is so successful that audiences and critics sometimes find it hard to evaluate. "I like to mix my magics," Nikolais has written, and *Somniloquy,* his latest major work, is an evocative, highly inventive example of his genius.

Somniloquy was commissioned by the Contemporary Music Society for a performance at New York's Guggenheim Museum in February 1967. Two concerns, one practical and one aesthetic, directed Nikolais' thinking as he undertook that commission. It is characteristic of him that a year later he was unable to say which consideration had the greater influence on the piece.

The stage space at the Guggenheim is an enclosed chamber with an apron of equal size. It has white walls, no space offstage for entrances and exits, no provision for hanging or moving lights and scenery, and no permanent switchboard. The piece, then, would have to utilize a minimum of lighting equipment; scenic possibilities would be restricted, and the options as to use of the playing area would be reduced. Instead of being a liability, however, these drastic physical handicaps were used in the design of the piece. A scrim was hung between the enclosed space and the forestage, creating in effect three playing areas—the spaces in front of and behind the scrim, and the entire space when the scrim was withdrawn. These spaces were varied still further by lighting that could define small sub-areas and show one area superimposed on the other through the scrim.

The lighting limitations at the Guggenheim seemed to lend themselves to a design idea Nikolais had been wanting to explore. In his 1956 work *Prism*, he had played with op art techniques, isolating parts of the dancers' bodies with sharply defined beams of colored light. He decided to work with this concept in *Somniloquy*, using slide projections, conventional leko spotlights, and flashlights held by the dancers. The flashlights were equipped with rheostats and special plastic globes, devised by Nikolais, to which designs made of gelatine could be attached. The actual lighting set up was primitive: two slide projectors, four lekos and twelve flashlights. Instruments were added when the piece was revived at Henry Street last fall, but only to clarify the original idea.

Nikolais says the purpose of *Somniloquy* was to explore the imaginative fantasy area that can be created by a low-key luminosity. In this indistinct environment, man is chameleonlike; his appearance can change, and the viewer is never quite sure whether he is seeing an illusion or a reality. The choreographer wanted to present a succession of abstract sensations, to which the audience could apply its own imagery, but there was no thematic material carried through the whole piece. Nikolais says this would lead the audience to find stories; he believes that art should be nonnarrative although highly suggestive. In the rather ponderous language he sometimes uses to describe his ideas, Nikolais calls *Somniloquy* "a musicality of theatrical design."

The lighting sequences and the group movement were choreographed simultaneously, since they were closely interdependent. Not only the light cues, but also the colors and the projected designs were worked out at the same time as the choreography. "The dancers don't work to counts," he explains. "The illusions worked best at a particular space speed, and the dancers had to learn what that was. In the final scene, where white dots were projected onto the entire stage, and the dancers moved through the dots, I had them come out in the audience one at a time to see the effect that was being created. Once they knew the illusions they were creating, they could perform it better. They had to develop a kind of tactile sense of the design on them."

The smaller sections, a quartet, two duets, and a solo for Murray Louis, were choreographed separately. The solo and the duets, one for Carolyn Carlson and Bill Frank and one for Louis and Phyllis Lamhut, took place in front of the scrim, with designs projected on the dancers from two slide machines. Nikolais is interested in finding a way to throw moving patterns onto moving bodies, but so far even film projectors are not powerful enough to do the job effectively. "I always seem to be looking for something that hasn't been invented yet," he said. Frequently he has improvised something without waiting for the engineers to catch up with him. In this case, he had to be content with stationary designs, which nevertheless had their own effectiveness. If a dancer hit the projection in just the right spot, he appeared to be sliced down the middle and could use the two sides of his body in isolation, making himself into a kind of dynamically split personality.

Perhaps because they are less dependent on the total theatrical effect, these small group sections give the best demonstration of Nikolais' dance technique. He regards technique as a means to gather skills together, not as a set of patterned actions. Its object is "to get the body to respond to any kind of dynamic that the mind dictates." Dynamics and space are its raw material, and Henry Street dancers can handle these elements with virtuosity.

A Nikolais technique class starts with a series of formidable stretches, but after that there are no set drills or combinations. On a recent morning he was exploring the contrast between controlled and relaxed movement. He asked his students to walk quickly and correctly across the stage, and then, on a given beat, to turn and release the tension throughout the body, then to resume the walk. Inventing each variation as he went along, he built up the exercise with jumps, changes in direction and level, and rhythmic complexity. His comments to the students never deal with specific errors of placement or counting; instead he tries to evoke the movement qualities: "Make a softer environment for the body." "Play with textures—see if you can play on the whole body surface." "Try to get your timing as a breath thing, you don't have to count." "Get more contrast between the two so that your environmental shape in space changes." "Be more positive with your space." He uses all kinds of imagery to illustrate his points: "You can't have fog in the eye and clear weather in the foot." "Take the starch out of it a little bit and then put it back." "Get your motor going."

In the theory class that followed, the students experimented with releasing tension from various joints: the wrist, elbow, shoulder, neck, hip, knee. They then did a series of group improvisations on the theme of encounter, in which they responded to each other by using one of the two dynamics they had been practicing.

After several years of such training, Nikolais' dancers seem able to accomplish almost any kind of technical feat, but they have also developed an acute sense of time and space. Their dancing is not a response to an inner emotion, and it is not representational. That is, they do not dance *about* anything, they simply dance. Nikolais' critics often object to this cool approach. They seem unable to react emotionally because his dances never spell out any emotional attitudes, never take sides. Nikolais says: "We haven't yet established what we mean by emotional. You could say the same thing about Bach. I don't deal with sad, mad or gladness ever, I deal with change—of color, sound, motion. Change is the basis of a sentient disturbance, which is the beginning of emotionalism. If you're in an all-red room for a long time, it will become colorless, and it will drive you nuts after a while because your need for change has been frustrated. But there can still be communication even if it isn't the extreme kind—one is consonance, the other dissonance. The dancers communicate this sentience through metakinesis. Their bodies undergo changes of balance, shape, pulse, and the audience has to feel this too. Dance is an abstract art. I can no more explain the emotionalism of what I do than Margot Fonteyn can explain an arabesque."

Nikolais' objective, environmental approach underlies all his choreography, which is inseparably linked with the human experience even when it seems most dehumanized. He never makes dances about specific issues or problems, but he feels his audience can find a great deal in his work that relates to contemporary life if they allow their imagination free play. "We're drastically concerned about our existence in space. For fifty years we explored psychological relationships. Now we're concerned with environmental relationships, and this leads to an even more primal sense. We don't trust any one sense any more. We want to understand by having all our senses coordinated to find a truth. This is why we have multi-media theater. Your specific references will come out of your own Rorschach. Though I'm probably as neurotic as the next one, I have a free access to associations. Inner visions come easily. Many people have the capacity for this and have long since failed to use it." Nikolais is one of a growing number of people in dance who can use the word "beautiful" without self-consciousness. "Man is beautiful when he's part of an environment, but when he stands aside, he loses part of his humanism. He might even offend himself."

Although he sounds somewhat cerebral when asked to explain his work, Nikolais' approach is usually instinctive. "I don't trust conscious reasoning," he said. "I let an idea reflect in and out of my mind for a long time before I start a new piece" When he composes a new score he maintains the same open approach. He long ago discarded conventional musical sounds in favor of the purely rhythmic impulse of percussion. Then tape recorders came along, and he could reshape instrumental, vocal, and percussive sounds to remove their traditional connotations. With the invention of the synthesizer, he could create almost any kind of sound he wanted. Nikolais' sound studio occupies a floor of the building where he lives, a few blocks from Henry Street Playhouse. An impressive collection of percussion instruments stands around in a forlorn group across the room from the newer electronic gadgetry—several tape recorders, amplifiers, speakers, and the synthesizer, a five-foot long panel of knobs, dials, switches, and meters in challenging array.

When the choreography for sections of *Somniloquy* was completed, and the dancers had developed the ensemble phrasing that would work best, Nikolais had them dance through an entire section while he ran a blank tape through a recorder. He marked cues on the tape by hitting the microphone with a pencil at intervals of ten seconds to a minute and a half, wherever a change in mood, tempo, or specific action occurred. The dance was repeated again, with the cued tape, to check the accuracy of the timing. The structure of the score would be determined by the information on this tape.

By manipulation of its many controls, the synthesizer can produce any conceivable kind of sound, from low rumblings to an oscillating hum to rhythmic plinks. Nikolais can program it for a "random" sequence of tones, which he can then modify in duration, tempo, volume, and timbre. Or he can insert sounds deliberately. He can orchestrate the sounds by taping a section and playing it back while the synthesizer creates another set of sounds. As in his choreography, he never works with specific thematic ideas, and he will include "accidents" if they work. The completed score for the 40-minute *Somniloquy* took about 150 hours to make, Nikolais estimates, about the same amount of time as the choreography.

Making the slides to be projected was another enormous task. There were 200 of them, all handmade by Nikolais. Mounted between two-inch-square sheets of glass, they could cover an area twenty by twenty feet when projected by specially adapted carousel projectors with zoom, wide-angle, and regular lenses. The slides were made in a variety of ways: some were painted with ani-line dye; some were collages of bits of gelatine; some had designs scratched into opaque paint; some had layers of different color gel that were laminated together by baking. Some individual slides required up to half an hour to make. Nikolais had to make sure the tiny designs would work when they were blown up and the colors would not fade under the strong light of the projec-tor bulbs. "It was a monk's job," he says.

Since he plays so many other roles, it is not inappropriate to see him cast as painstaking artisan and tinkerer. In fact, he probably would have it no other way. "It is impossible for me to be a purist," he wrote in *The Modern Dance: Seven Statements of Belief;* "my loves are too many for that. I am excited by things very old and also very new, and by so many things in between as well. Thus, I cannot be content as only a choreographer."

CHAPTER 4

Artisans of Space

. . . .

MARCIA B. SIEGEL

World War II put an end to the fruitful and popular strain of modern dance that had grown up in Germany and Eastern Europe over two decades. The anti-German feeling that accompanied the war, and the pains of dispersion, destruction, and economic recovery that followed it, have blurred whatever traces remained of that period's dance discoveries. Now they all come under the label of German Expressionism, which was never very accurate in the first place. Although the Germans have a term for the modern dance, *Ausdruckstanz*— dance of expression—even its practitioners couldn't agree on it. When I started studying the 1920s and 1930s intensively, I realized that at least two approaches to dance prevailed, approaches related by their common cultural environment but quite different in other respects.

While the dancers we think of as Expressionists—like Mary Wigman, Kurt Jooss, Harald Kreutzberg—were trying to devise dance forms to project the feelings arising out of the political and psychic struggles of the time, others were working more theoretically, trying to define how the human body works within its physical element, space. Both Rudolf Laban, the chief teacher of Wigman and many others, and Oskar Schlemmer, head of the Theater of the Bauhaus, tried to understand the properties of movement and extend its imagery.

The nineteenth century's discoveries in science and technology had torn Europe from its rural, Christian-monarchist moorings. By virtue of his presumed relationship to an all-powerful God, man had imagined himself at the top of the evolutionary heap. But Darwin, Freud, and Einstein took away this confidence in man's ultimate control. World War I, according to theater director Erwin Piscator, proved that "bourgeois individualism was finally buried. . . . Those who returned no longer had any relationship to the great-

This article is based on the third of eight lectures on twentieth-century dance that were given by Marcia B. Siegel during the fall of 1980 as part of a three-year program on "The Meaning of Modernism" at the Walker Art Center, Minneapolis. It was published in the Spring 1981 issue of *The Hudson Review* and has been revised and expanded by the author for this volume.

ness of man which had served as the symbol of the eternity of divine order in the parlors of pre-war society." While the artists of the early twentieth century had been casting about for new connections or further disrupting order with their futuristic rages, by the 1920s art was beginning to come to terms with the machine. The question no longer was how to hang on to the rusty anchorages of the past, or how to find substitute gods, but how to habituate oneself to an industrialized world.

Walter Gropius chose to make peace with this world now forever beyond man's domination: "The old dualistic world-concept which envisaged the ego in opposition to the universe is rapidly losing ground. In its place is rising the idea of a universal unity in which all opposing forces exist in a state of absolute balance." The Bauhaus school, which Gropius founded in 1919, attempted to unify technology with the arts and crafts, to create new symbols for a new consciousness, and to see what activity was possible within a fabricated environment. The Bauhaus artists, like the Cubists and the Constructivists who were working elsewhere in Europe, rejected aestheticism as a premise; they didn't want to flee this world even if it defied their previous perceptions of motion, velocity, time, distance, continuity. They wanted to incorporate their product into what was clearly an inescapable set of new realities.

If we look at the Cubist paintings of Picasso, at the exploded theater designs of the Russians, at the mosaic patterns of art deco objects, we see how visual artists were wrestling with these new dislocations of accepted order. Form is fractured, splintered, and blown into scattered fragments. The certitudes of the horizon line and its perpendicular coordinates have been shaken loose, tilted, sprung out of plumb. The representational figure against a landscape is no longer the subject of modern painting; the artist is working with manipulations of line, composition, and color, unencumbered by ornament. The color harmonies of Kandinsky, the floating shapes of Calder and Arp, the optical studies of Albers, the severe, formal graphics of Mondrian, the disassembled but meticulously placed forms of Malevich, Lissitsky, and Léger, all represent a hunger for basics, for truths that are deep enough not to give way. By carefully placing the human figure within these geometries, the artist might make reason out of a confusing universe.

Working in the theater, the Constructivists made intricate, nonliteral environments that would force actors and dancers to move in unaccustomed ways, and that could be manipulated by the performers into new configurations. It was literally a theater of structure, where the audience was encouraged to see the inner mechanisms of the stage as well as its magical outer appearances. Some of the Constructivist designs actually look overbuilt, as if the artists were saying that a universe increasingly complicated, multiplied, or blasted apart could still be real, could still be substantial enough to support activity. The fact that this period saw the widespread use of aircraft, automobiles, elevators, photography, and motion pictures, all of which cause us to perceive the properties of space in new ways, probably explains, at least in part, how the actor came to placed in such strangely altered theatrical spaces.

Pavel Tchelitchev's *Ode,* produced in 1928 for Diaghilev's Ballets Russes, with Léonide Massine as choreographer, employed several real and illusionary devices to create unusual spatial relationships. The basic set was a web of tapes radiating from a central vertical support, and a row of dolls constructed in false perspective, which were later to be joined by live dancers dressed the same way. In one section of the ballet, dancers plied the tapes to make what the English critic A.V. Coton called "a geometric succession of moving, Euclidean forms about which the figures wove a complementary notation of space-images." At this period Tchelitchev was especially interested in light, and *Ode* had many effects created by shadows, colors, projections, and even a dance on a blacked-out stage (a nonspace) where the dancers wore tiny flashlights on their heads. Film was also a part of this production, including blown-up images of flowers. To enhance the clarity of these designs, Massine concentrated on uncluttered, linear movement for the dancers. To the critic Cyril Beaumont, *Ode* "suggested a kind of visual 'laying bare' of the intelligence at work."

At the other end of this conceptual track were those who tried to clear the theater space of everything except the basic architecture to allow for a plastic flow of individuals and massed groups of performers. Having no stylistic or symbolic relationship to the play in themselves, these scenic elements simply offset the space, made it more visible, as a picture frame or a window does. The Berlin theater director Leopold Jessner's most notable of many such designs was the so-called Jessner Stairs, a graduated series of levels that could be placed anywhere on stage and on which the actors could be ranged in varied groupings. The stairs were well suited to the intentions of German choreographers, who used them to add height and depth to their group designs. An early use of the stairs in the United States was seen in Irene Lewisohn's 1930 production of Charles Martin Loeffler's *Pagan Poem,* with Martha Graham and Charles Weidman in the leading roles. A few years later, Weidman and Doris Humphrey adopted the idea of unadorned boxes and platforms as the scenic modules for all their company's dances.

Finally, there was an interest, particularly at the Bauhaus, in the theater as a space for the audience as well as the performers. Schlemmer's Bauhaus

Stage at Dessau was a flexible producing space, a modest, practical beginning to what the Bauhaus designers visualized as a total space—indoors and out— in which the play of space, body, line, point, color, light, and sound could be experienced in new perspectives by the audience. Schlemmer even saw the Dessau Bauhaus building, with its clean planes of masonry and glass, its flat roofs and projecting balconies, as a potential stage—anticipating the urban environmental dance that took place in the United States forty years later.

Schlemmer had been trained as a painter and sculptor, but even before he began his association with the Bauhaus in 1920, he had produced an early version of his most famous work, the *Triadic Ballet*. Schlemmer viewed the stage as a composition on canvas, and the dancer within it as a draftsmanlike arrangement of forms, colors, lines, and volumes, obedient to the laws of space as well as the internal laws of human functioning. He wanted to create abstraction from this tangible set of raw materials, and he suggested four basic ways in which natural laws could be applied to transforming the human body. Encased in boxlike constructions, it could become "ambulant architecture." If the body's basic shapes and divisions were emphasized, he imagined a marionette. The possibilities for motion in space, the body's capacity for rotation, direction, and cutting through space, could produce a "technical organism." And images could be developed from the symbolic associations he saw in the body's form, such as the star shape of the spread hand or the cross of shoulders on spine, creating "dematerialization."

Costumes that extended these properties couldn't completely free man from the laws of gravity, but Schlemmer advocated any technical means in the theater that would create the illusion of such freedom, including the use of mechanical figures. In his theater experiments he utilized both the concept of the *Übermarionette*, the mechanical doll, and of the *Kunstfigur*, the human figure used as art object.

He and the other theater workshop members at the Bauhaus put these theories into action first of all by the use of costume. The literal, personifying aspects of the performer were hidden under molded, twisted, padded and built-up materials that were fitted to the body so that the dancer, by moving, could create superhuman shapes and effects. Props and masks could further exaggerate the size and reach of the body's parts. Lighting and projections could change the mood and even the environment itself.

Mensch und Kunstfigur (*Man and Mask*), a remarkable film made in Germany in 1968, combines nine reconstructed, brief Schlemmer dances with some understated but apt cinematic devices that further his ideas of transcending mundane spatial experience. Although there is little conventional dancing here, the performer has to be acutely conscious of how he is surrounding, penetrating, and shaping himself in space and with relation to the other performers. The imagery has considerable range, even among these simple pieces. Some are directly satirical. In the *Gesture Dance*, three masked, padded personages enact minimal conversations, changing the emotional implications with variations in the tilt of the body or head, the extending or withdrawing of a hand. In *Game of Bricks*, a similarly dressed trio moves one-and-a-half-foot cubes into different formations, suggesting individuality, competition, and finally conformity. In *Form Dance*, the purpose seems more abstract, as the figures place various props—poles, a large white sphere, a small metal ball—into positions that resemble the paintings of another Bauhaus teacher and frequent collaborator at the theater workshop, Laszlo Moholy-Nagy. In other pieces, the body seems to disappear entirely. Clad in black against a black background, the dancer manipulates handfuls of white hoops in graduated sizes to create disembodied op art designs (*Hoop Dance*), or moves long poles attached to his limbs to make moving geometric designs in *Stick Dance*, which Schlemmer called "a song of the joints."

Looking at the Schlemmer work, with its percussion, prepared piano, and synthesized sounds, its eerie yet concrete interplay of forms and voids, one can indulge in fantasy or simply in sensory entertainment. A student of the Bauhaus stage, Alfredo Bortoluzzi, remembered it years later as having had the aim of "bringing movement and picture into a firm harmonic relationship."

Rudolf (von) Laban, the other great theorist of space, didn't think of pictures at all, even though he too had more of a background in the visual arts than in dance. Laban worked outward from inside the person. In a period when physical culture was widely practiced in Germany, he distinguished the lived experience of the body (*Erlebnis*) from mere body training (*Körperlich*). If space is a limitless something that surrounds us and that is filled with other people and objects related to us by their size, distance, and proportions, then space itself changes according to the way we move in it. "Space is a hidden feature of movement and movement is a visible aspect of space," Laban said in the introduction to his book on space theory, *The Language of Movement*.

Starting from the physical structure of the body as a vertical being with two sides, a front and a back, Laban defined the space around the body—an expandable envelope called the kinesphere—according to different sets of directional possibilities. The pure vertical, horizontal, and sagittal axes correspond to up-down, side-to-side, and forward-back motion. The diagonal inclinations between these pure dimensions could be schematized to form a cube, by connecting with straight lines the arms-reach terminus of each diagonal. Other directional systems could be plotted in the same way and formed into other imaginary geometric structures. Laban then worked out progressions of movement through these crystals—scales, swings, and spirals that formalize movement much as ballet exercises do, but that orient movement always to the space outside the dancer's body rather than retaining the ballet dancer's internal reference points of body axis, position of the limbs, placement of the head, and so on.

Laban was also concerned with the dynamics of movement—the source and variation of the energy flow that activates movement and that creates individual phrasing and patterns of action. He thought that certain dynamic tendencies were related to certain space tendencies—that, for example, advancing in space is more normally associated with the aggressive properties of force and speed, while retreating has an affinity with the indulgent qualities of slowness and spreading out of energy. Even if one doesn't agree with his theory of affinities, or with the specific values he associated with the space-weight-time factors, Laban's clarification of the movement process as a dialogue between the body and space makes a convincing presumption that the dancer is always in a communicative or expressive mode.

Laban spoke of spatial tension existing within the body as it moves off its vertical axis and into the more precarious sideward or backward diagonals, and he built into his scales and progressions different forms for easing or heightening these tensions. When people worked together, in pairs or groups, the spatial tension took on a collective dynamic; it could be strengthened if many bodies felt it together, or an element of contrast could be introduced with opposing movement tendencies. Rhythm could add another dramatic element. In other words, Laban worked for the same kinds of theatrical effects as theater directors always had, but he worked almost entirely from the moving body as a source of feeling and concerned himself less about what the audience would see.

Laban used these ideas most effectively in his movement choirs. These were groups of people, often laypersons or children, who moved together to develop a common theme. The aim was not to show a formal, uniform technique or design, but for each participant to reinforce the collective drive by expressing the motive or spirit with his own movement. The movement choirs grew out of a national passion for physical activity on a large social scale—gymnastics, sports, folk dancing and hiking groups also spread over Germany during the 1920s and 1930s. The Nazis turned this craze to their own account, politicizing any dance groups they found to have sympathetic leaders. By the early 1930s Laban had become a potent figure in dance, as a teacher, theoretician, and organizer of large civic pageants and festivals. He was ambitious, charismatic, and perhaps naïve enough to think he could preserve his autonomy while accommodating the new masters.

Scholars differ violently over Laban's relationship to the Nazis. Whether he sympathized with their ideology or shrewdly played politics in order to preserve the modern dance under the regime, he could not have been as gullible as his defenders argue. Born in Austro-Hungarian Bratislava, he obtained German citizenship well into the Hitler era, in 1935. With schools and theaters under his influence throughout the country, he became a kind of czar as director of Propaganda Minister Joseph Goebbels' *Reichstanzbühne*. At the end of his three-year contract as choreographer at the Berlin State Opera in 1934, he was chosen to organize a performance for the opening of the Dietrich Eckart Theater on the eve of the 1936 Berlin Olympics.

Vom Tauwind und der Neuen Freude, a huge piece for twenty-two movement choirs from all over Germany, seems to have straddled the line between celebrating peace, harmony, and the individual soul, and paying tribute to German nationalism and military power. When Goebbels saw a dress rehearsal, two months before the scheduled performance, he disapproved. Depending on which account is to be believed, Laban was either dismissed and effectively prevented from working in Germany again, or he hung on for another year as a consultant, with severely curtailed responsibilities, before he was able to emigrate. Probably he had become too prominent for the Nazis to ostracize, so he was shunted out of the public eye, with some absences due to ill health. He made his way to England in 1938.

Laban continued to work in exile, turning his attention more and more to researching movement patterns of factory workers, until his death in 1958. Fellow refugees and new followers in England and the United States transplanted his theories and developed them in the fields of dance education and movement analysis rather than theater.

Oskar Schlemmer also believed there could be a rapprochement between art and the state, that the artist could operate independently from the dictates of politics. For voicing these perceived heresies he was dismissed from his principal teaching job in 1933 and accused of Marxist-Jewish tendencies. He hesitated about leaving Germany, and he continued to protest the regime's many warning signals about the radicalism of his work, without understanding why the Nazis found it unacceptable. Exhibitions and critical recognition of his paintings in New York and London only drew more condemnation. Schlemmer was declared *Entartete* (degenerate) along with his colleagues from the Bauhaus in 1937, but still could not abandon his homeland. By then he was scrabbling together a living in Stuttgart and Wuppertal and persisting in his work as a painter and sculptor. He died in 1943 at Baden-Baden.

World War II swept away all of this creative activity, and many of its artifacts were either confiscated by the Nazis or destroyed in the fighting. After Europe had rebuilt its cities and its economy in the 1950s, dance gained a new but conservative foothold in the opera houses. The curiosity, the idealism, and the adventurousness that had prompted the *Ausdruckstanz* went dormant; it seems the Germans did not want to be reminded of the experiments of the recent past.

The most important legatee, paradoxically, of both Schlemmer and Laban, is Alwin Nikolais. Trained by Mary Wigman's disciple in America, Hanya Holm, he inherited his movement approach from Laban, but his theatrical methods come out of the same sensibility as Schlemmer's. There are many possible reasons why Nikolais never fully declared his debt to the two German masters. During the war and immediately afterward, public opinion turned against anything German, and the Marxist label, with which avant-gardists had been stigmatized, became increasingly provocative.

When Nikolais returned to civilian life after serving as an intelligence officer during the war, he began intensive dance studies with Holm, serving as her assistant for four years. Hanya Holm, who had come to New York in 1931 to start a Mary Wigman school, soon felt the effects of Wigman's failure to leave Germany. With Wigman's agreement, she changed the name of her school so as not to be tainted with Wigman's supposed Nazi sympathies. Holm's nationality also put her at a disadvantage with the American modern dancers, who were building their own careers in the 1930s. For professional as well as patriotic reasons, they wanted to be seen as creating an indigenous art form, absurd though it was to deny the many connections and influences that existed between them and the Laban-instigated *Ausdruckstanz*. Holm started out as one of the Bennington "Four Pioneers" of modern dance, but when Bennington's summer school ceased and America entered the war in 1941, Holm was offered the chance to start a summer course at Colorado College. She taught and choreographed there for the next four decades. In New York she maintained an active career as a teacher and choreographer of Broadway shows, but creatively she stood outside the modern-dance mainstream after dissolving her company in the early 1940s.

Holm's training was once removed from Laban. Mary Wigman had re-worked Laban's theories and pedagogy in order to assert her own claim on the dance field as an independent artist. Holm and then Nikolais continued to re-make the rhetoric. But essentially they all subscribed to Laban's conceptualizing of energy and space, and to the idea that the dancer moves from an inner impulse, rather than imitating a preconceived outer model such as the ballet vocabulary. The Laban-Wigman-Holm tradition also embraced the idea of improvisation as a compositional tool, and rejected setting dance to existing music in favor of percussive or vocalized sounds, often generated by the dancers themselves.

On Hanya Holm's recommendation, Nikolais took over the theater at the Henry Street Playhouse on the Lower East Side of New York. This served as a laboratory and showcase for his multifaceted work from 1949 to 1970. It was there that he was able to try out and perfect his lush theaterscapes made of color, sound, shapes, and phenomenally adaptive dancers.

Nikolais had even less direct contact with Schlemmer's theater work, although it is hard to imagine he knew nothing about the Bauhaus, whose principals, Gropius, Moholy-Nagy, Josef Albers, Lyonel Feininger, and Paul Klee, had emigrated and re-established their careers in the United States along with scores of other German modernists and intellectuals in the 1930s. Nikolais was an antiromantic in his approach to theater, an abstractionist in the modern-art sense. He condemned the use of the stage as a platform for stars, ego, sexuality, and the psychological revelations of his modern-dance mothers. Like Schlemmer he wanted to create a primarily visual theater in which the dancer was only one of many contributing elements.

Nikolais often spoke of his intention to show man as "kinsman to the universe" and his total-theater pieces, with their "dehumanized" dancers blending into fantasy environments created by lighting projections, props, and electronic sound, were a continuing journey into the territory laid out by Schlemmer. He was making what Schlemmer would have called "space dance." Spectacle "comes into existence through the movement of colors and shapes alone. Man's only role is that of 'spiritus rector' at the control of the panel from which he directs the entire mechanism," Schlemmer wrote in 1931. If either one of them was making use of mechanical devices and technology, their aim was to restore a balance to a stage too long dominated by human bodies alone. Movement for both of them was a painterly resource.

Like Schlemmer, Nikolais tried to depersonalize the dancers—Schlemmer might have called it dematerializing—by concealing their real bodies with costumes that gave them new shapes, extended their limbs, or limited their movement to selected body parts. Moving within these enclosures, they could create geometric stage pictures. In Nikolais' *Tensile Involvement* they played a proscenium-sized game of cat's cradle; in Schlemmer's *Stick Dance* and *Hoop Dance* they created moving crystal and spiral designs. Schlemmer further altered the dancers' appearance with concentrated lighting effects; Nikolais made them appear and disappear in dappled groves of projected color.

Both Schlemmer and Nikolais were interested in puppets and masks. These devices could further disguise the dancers' individual identities, freeing them to misbehave as perpetrators of clownish escapades, or transforming them as conduits into ritualistic and supernatural worlds. Both directors looked for symbolic associations that would transcend the audience's everyday expectations. They both referred to the dancer as "figure," a term belonging to the realm of sculpture and the iconography of cultural objects. And of course, both of them were fascinated with the possibilities that technology could bring into the theater.

Nikolais wanted more from the dancers than to act as figural space-controllers. Early in his investigations at Henry Street Playhouse, he encouraged their sensitivity to the effects they were creating under his lights and shadows. Later, he cleared out spaces in the web, the canopy, the dreamscape, where they would emerge, nearly naked, to dance highly articulate solo and small-group passages. Here a more personal style appeared, different from the skittering, tilting, locomotive camouflage they used in the design sections. Nikolais' dancers, beginning with the 1950s group that included Murray Louis, Phyllis Lamhut, Gladys Bailin, and Bill Frank, were acutely in control of an expressive, Laban-defined universe of dynamics and kinespheric space. They could modulate their timing and phrasing precisely, control their stopping and going, change the flow of energy through an arm or a torso, from successive to locked. They could switch from tense angularity to released floppiness. They were completely clear in shaping their movement. They could activate swings, bounces, and glides with their whole bodies engaged, or skim the floor on their insteps. They could isolate any part, focus their movement into the tightest corner or make it scan a distant horizon.

Nikolais has had many dance successors. Today, with the popular culture so saturated in technological effects, dancers have appropriated electronic sound, projections, lights, scrims, movable structures, and more sophisticated gadgets that weren't around in Nikolais' time: computers, motion capture, and animation techniques. Groups like Pilobolus and Momix have refined the language of the "dehumanized" body into a kind of collective acrobatic that provokes the imagination. But no one since Nikolais has fused the design impulse and the movement impulse so masterfully into a true total theater where the dance takes an essential place, no less and no more.

SOURCES CONSULTED

Barron, Stephanie, ed. *Degenerate Art: The Fate of the Avant-Garde in Nazi Germany.* Los Angeles County Museum of Modern Art, 1991.

Bayer, Herbert, Walter Gropius and Ise Gropius, eds. *Bauhaus 1919–1928* (1938). New York: The Museum of Modern Art, 1976.

Dörr, Evelyn. "Rudolf von Laban: The 'Founding Father' of Expressionist Dance" in *Dance Chronicle,* Vol. 26, No. 1, 2003, pp. 1–29.

Gropius, Walter, ed. *The Theater of the Bauhaus* (1925). Middletown, CT: Wesleyan University Press, 1971.

Karina, Lilian and Marion Kant. *Hitler's Dancers: German Modern Dance and the Third Reich.* New York: Berghahn Books. 2003.

Lehman, Arnold L. and Brenda Richardson, eds. *Oskar Schlemmer.* Baltimore: The Baltimore Museum of Art, 1986.

Nikolais, Alwin. "Growth of a Theme" in Walter Sorell, ed. *The Dance Has Many Faces.* New York: Columbia University Press, 1966.

Nikolais, Alwin. "No Man from Mars" in Selma Jeanne Cohen, ed. *The Modern Dance: Seven Statements of Belief.* Middletown, CT: Wesleyan University Press, 1966.

Nikolais, Alwin. "Hanya Holm" in "Hanya Holm—A Pioneer in American Dance." *Choreography and Dance,* Vol. 2, Part 2, 1992, pp. 53–61.

Preston-Dunlop, Valerie. *Rudolf Laban: An Extraordinary Life.* London: Dance Books, 1998.

Scheper, Dirk. *Oskar Schlemmer: The Triadic Ballet.* Berlin: Akademie der Künste, Documentation #5, 1985.

Schlemmer, Oskar. "Misunderstandings: a Reply to Kallai" in *Schrifttanz,* Vol. IV, No. 2, October 1931. Preston-Dunlop, Valerie and Susanne Lahusen, eds. *Schrifttanz: A View of German Dance in the Weimar Republic.* London: Dance Books, 1990.

Siegel, Marcia B., "Nik: A Documentary." *Dance Perspectives* 48. (Winter, 1971).

CHAPTER 5

Alwin Nikolais—Dancing Across Borders

YVONNE HARDT

Dancers come on stage in wooden cone-shaped costumes. At first their movements seem limited and stiff as they move like chess players across the stage, staggering about with little steps. When they begin to circle, using the stabilizing bottom surface of the cones to lean out into space, the potential of the costumes becomes apparent. They allow the dancers to tilt at an angle not possible without them. They also ensure a smooth circling action. Suddenly, the dancers disappear within the wooden shelters, again transforming our perception of the costumes. What seemed stiff is now lively and organic. While only the arms reach out, softly discovering the spacelike antennas, one is reminded of a snail in its shell. This illusion is enhanced when the cones lie on the floor, continuously hiding and revealing parts of the dancer's bodies. Later on, in another section of the piece, the dancers, now free of any hard surrounding, manipulate each other or stand as a very close group that sways like a plant in water. Swinging movements continue. Then the dead seem to move when one dancer, stuck into the pants of another and dangling from there seemingly lifeless, gives impulses back with every movement of his "living" partner. Throughout this dance piece, borders between what is animated and what is lifeless disappear.

Have you been pondering what piece of Alwin Nikolais' I am describing? While all the elements are here that remind one of his works, especially the importance of costumes and props, it is, however, a description of a few moments in a piece called *noBody* by the contemporary German choreographer Sasha Waltz. The similarities become even more striking if we know that Waltz explored the notion of transcendence in this last and final part of her trilogy about the body.[1] Transcending the individual dancer was an important feature of the works and writings of Nikolais. While notions of transcendence do not figure in writing about Nikolais, I think there are reasons that make this a good starting point to reflect on Nikolais and to develop an analytical viewpoint that shows how pertinent a reflection on the notion of transcendence can be for contemporary dance scholars looking at him.

First of all transcendence allows for various historical comparisons. For instance, perceiving dancing as transcending the individual shows a remarkable resemblance to early ideas of Rudolf von Laban, one of the founding figures of *Ausdruckstanz* (expressionistic dance) in Germany. Tracing these similarities and possible influences not only troubles the exceptionalist narrative that commonly underwrites discussions of modern dance in American dance historiography, but also raises interesting political questions about whether ideas of transcending the individual within a communal setting have similar ideological implications for all three choreographers—Waltz, Nikolais, and Laban. Second, similarities between these choreographers suggest that the notion of transcendence is not merely metaphysical, but is linked to a technique of the body that provokes recognizable choreographic elements. Accordingly, instead of situating this notion on a purely metaphorical or mystical level, I propose to conceive it also as a process of bodily interactions that erases stable contours and movements. The transgression of limitations and borders then becomes central to demystifying the notion of transcendence. It becomes possible to see Nikolais' work as exemplifying an art-historical discussion that looks at dissolving borders and challenging modes of perceiving as key components of contemporary arts practices.

Debordering (*Entgrenzung*) does not signify simply the act of dissolving or challenging borders/margins (although it can), and it does not necessarily indicate the total disappearance of them. The term keeps borders implicit as a point of reference to show how they might decompose and how new ones can be erected. Separations might be broken up by expansion, or by fusion so that no part can be taken as a separate entity.[2] Debordering points to the process by which dance makes legible the very connections constituted by communal and collaborative activity.

By focusing on the dissolving of borders, I also hope to reconceptualize the focus on abstract, esthetic "wizardry" that has been so prevalent in writing about Nikolais. I will suggest that Nikolais first sets clear boundaries and works with concrete means and symbolic images in order to dissolve them later on. More specifically, I propose that looking at Nikolais with this in mind helps to deconstruct dichotomies between image and dance, body and technique, and between the figurative and abstract. The idea of abstractness, often used ambiguously, seems to function more as a way to both situate and differentiate him in the context of the modern-dance scene of his time than as a descriptive term for his dances. By focusing on the notion of abstractness, I will argue that he creates new borders that implicitly allow one to raise questions about their function and also about the regulatory practices that create them.

This discussion of abstraction also places Nikolais in a specifically American context of the 1950s and 1960s that is more extensively discussed in other sections of this book. This context cannot be totally excluded here, however, because it explains some of the differences between Nikolais and the modern-dance tradition in Germany (by which he is influenced), as well as to the contemporary-dance scene at the turn of the twenty-first century. I want to suggest that these differences are due to changing body concepts. The body plays an ambivalent role in Nikolais' dances. There is tension between an individual transcending her/himself by being responsive to others and the environment on one side, and bound body movements and postures that show the dancer to be closed in on the other side. While Nikolais' work prefigured many avant-garde practices in regard to abandoning story line and explicit emotional expressivity in favour of perceiving dance as pure movement, there remain differences in the handling of the body. For example, although attention given to the interrelation between dancers resembles some of the important aspects of contact improvisation, it lacks a sensual composure. A climate of sexual prudery, a belief in rationalization and technical advances, and a social context in which the unifying tendencies of society were strictly enforced for the sake of political stability, are reflected and enacted in Nikolais' dances. He made these tensions explicit, but he did not revolt against them or propose an alternative. In this and other ways his work is an example of how the crossing of certain boundaries involves holding on to others.

Starting with the notion of transcendence in dance and focusing on dissolving borders I will do more than pursue a purely esthetic analysis, but suggest that debordering is socially significant and linked to issues of power. As such, this essay is not so much about Nikolais but rather geared toward issues of relationality in order to open dance-theoretical perspectives that are relevant for the analysis of dance today.

Transcendence, Techniques of Transformations,
and the Dissolving of Esthetic Borders
Nikolais explicitly sought to create an art that transcends the individual, merging dancers with the universe by focusing on the relationality between dancers and their environment.[3] His working method required dancers to focus on elements outside of themselves. This was accomplished through a working process based, in part, on improvisation.

Both the focus on improvisation and the focus on relationality can be traced back to German *Ausdruckstanz*, which directly influenced Nikolais through the work of Hanya Holm, a student of Mary Wigman. Nikolais repeatedly mentioned the important influence of Holm and her working style, which offered freedom to the individual through improvisation and guided dance composition. However, improvisation does not function outside the category of technique and does not generate a totally new dance form. A tendency to perceive improvisation outside the realm of technique has led to the presumption that Nikolais did not develop a dance technique as, for instance, did Martha Graham and Merce Cunningham. But dance technique is not only a codified movement vocabulary. Looking at the clearly recognizable traits in bodily action and shapes and at choreographic patterns shows how improvisation can generate a specific body and movement esthetic. Nikolais offered both an analytic approach to understanding the esthetic possibilities for creating movement and a means for training dancers toward these ends. Nikolais and his students considered themselves to be working within a dance technique. One might even want to argue that through his improvisation technique, Nikolais brought attention to the use of space and dynamics that shape much contemporary dance practice today in the United States. Even before the practice of Laban Movement Analysis became widely known, Nikolais took up its main principles.

In his ground-breaking books *Die Welt des Tänzer* (*World of a Dancer*) in 1920 and *Choreographie* in 1926, Laban articulated concepts that focused on the relationship of movement in a three-dimensional space. Dancers were asked to extend themselves into space and explore their "kinesphere," the personal space around them that was considered dynamic in the sense that it moved with the dancer. While the kinesphere was perceived as round, Laban's icosahedron (a polyhedron having twenty faces) marked in a geometric way this three-dimensional space around the dancer and was a tool for expanding his/her movement potential. In general, his movement conception was geared toward sensitizing the dancers to space. Reflection upon and analysis of movement were important tools in this process, "because our goal is the mastering of movement through its understanding."[4] In Laban's writing, choreography was no longer considered the precise setting of certain steps in a specific order or form, but a movement conception and analysis that was characterized by transformation.[5] Laban clearly privileged the "study of movement" (*Bewegungslehre*) over the "study of changing" forms (*Haltungslehre*).

The range of movement through space was best experienced by swinging through the most external points of the kinesphere in the so-called swinging scales. Swinging was more than just a physical exercise in this context. It was also emotionally and metaphorically charged. In German, to swing means both to move in a swinging manner and to radiate. This double meaning is a key to understanding how transcendence is conceived in Laban's writing and other writing of his time. Swinging (*Schwung* or *Mitschwingen*) was central to an idea of communication on a somatic level. It linked the dancer to the audiences and to the universe, which was also believed to be pulsating or swinging. For Laban, swinging marked the transformation between points of tension and relaxation that he considered the source of all movement.[6]

This interest in transcending the individual was most clearly articulated in Laban's theoretical reflections on community culture and movement choirs. Both were highly charged politically.[7] For Laban, communal culture and the transcending of the individual could most appropriately be reached through group improvisation in the form of movement choirs. According to him, this would sensitize each individual to the others and generate a communal movement of flow. Usually a group of people, often lay dancers, improvised along patterns that were structured by space, rhythm, or movement quality. With this they put Laban's movement analysis into action. Groups usually followed a lead dancer, trying to copy the movement. However, maintaining a relationship to each other, especially in regard to spatial orientation and dynamics, was more important than actual synchronization. For instance, as a group moved downward, the positions of hands and individual body parts stayed diverse. The group was guided by an outside structure, and resisting its flow it would handicap the whole group. A harmonious group appearance was central to Laban's movement choirs, which were characterized by fluid movements, especially swinging and constantly changing group formations. The relationship between movers was key to the process.

Both Nikolais' choreographic technique and his reflections on dance echo this sort of analytical as well as mystical understanding of movement. I suggest three specific ways of making that comparison. One is on grounds of esthetic and movement conceptualization with the focus on sensitizing the dancers to space and to the notion that transitions and interactions are more important than a codified movement vocabulary. Second, there is a similarity in the belief that dance can communicate directly through the body. Both Laban and Nikolais share a belief in a somatic communication based on an empathic feeling of movement recognition. Last but not least, they use these movement concepts as a means of transcending the individual. Both Laban and Nikolais see this transcendence as important, although their reasons differ. Laban wanted to create a new and harmonious group feeling and culture. Although Nikolais' notion of transcendence is also a protest against too much individualism, he does not aim to create a visionary new group. Rather, his deconstruction of individuality, influenced by a scientific, technical, and metaphoric understanding of the world, make it impossible to see the individual and his/her feelings at the center of the universe. At the heart of that difference lies a different understanding of the body and its relationship to technology.

Nikolais adapted the writing of Laban to his specific needs in the context of the post-war era in the United States. He asked his dancers, in the same way that Laban did, to perceive their movements as not ending within the limits of their own body but to image them prolonged in space. For that Nikolais did not only use the imagination (e.g., imagined lines and points in space) but also used objects external to the dancers, asking them to create a symbiotic way of moving with them. Everything that can be done with a costume or with a prop is explored through improvisation. The dancer is not simply a puppet manipulated into executing movements, as is sometimes suggested by the toylike appearance of his dancers. Rather, he or she creates a new movement vocabulary, although it is not independent movement. It is always relational movement, only possible through the process of interaction.

I prefer to describe this with the term "relationality" instead of "decentralization," the term used by Nikolais to refer to this outward-focused improvisation technique. Relationality seems to be more inclusive than the term "decentralization," which is problematic in regard to Nikolais because the body center remains quite important for his dances. This contrasts, for instance, with the dance style of William Forsythe, which is also described in terms of decentralization and is equally influenced by Laban's movement analysis. The American dance star and choreographer, who first danced for the Stuttgart Ballett and has been the long-standing director of the Frankfurt Ballett (now Forsythe Company), has also created a multimedia theater that exposes the means of its production. While both choreographers share an interest in exploring the configurations of the space of movement, Forsythe breaks the body into parts, seeing each joint as having its own kinesphere. Working from the classical base, he decentralizes the movement by giving each joint an individual life, which often seems to work against or at least independently of each other. Thus, Forsythe creates highly polymorphic figures and a movement vocabulary constantly challenging equilibrium.

In Nikolais' dances, decentralization cannot be understood in this sense. He and a few of his dancers had some training in Graham and other modern techniques, which emphasize a strong body center. This physical memory stayed apparent even when movements are extended into space. A good example of this is the solo of the "Artisan" in *Imago*.[8] It can be seen as a tribute to a historic modern-dance technique that works with a stable center and uses tools of suspension and relaxation, even when delineating and shaping space in a way that is very different from Graham's movement vocabulary. The "Artisan" stays grounded and uses a mode of tension and relaxation that is inherent to classical modern dance. The solo dancer enters describing clear squared floor paths, the arms parallel to each other, thus stylizing the running movement. Many movements are executed in grand plié in second position, requiring a strong dancer, especially when moving fast. Accordingly, the whole character seems strong, determined, and in control of his movement and space. While the arms move quickly to one side, and the head moves to the other, his movements are nonetheless closely bound to a stable center and equilibrium.

Nikolais' dances live the tension between a certain form of stability and its dissolving. "Artisan" is also a good example of how borders and physical contours can be challenged by an increasingly dynamic use of space. A shift of dynamics, repetition, and articulation of joints make the solo of the "Artisan" lose its original static feeling and transform it into remarkably contemporary movement material. This can be seen as paradigmatic for Nikolais' dances. Even if the movements sometimes seem stiff and limited, transgression and dissolvings can only take place because Nikolais first establishes clear borders by forcing limitations on the dancers or demanding a strict focus on space, tasks, and objects. Stasis and reduction can actually highlight motion, a central characteristic of Nikolais' work.

Nikolais' dance style was not arbitrary, and his technique of placing the dancers in relationality to their environment brought with it a certain recognizable esthetic effect that critics usually described in terms of flux, transformation, or play that resisted any stable movement shapes and possible symbolic meaning.[9] A dance based on relationality can disturb the sense of orientation and makes it difficult to anticipate movements to come, as is seen in the full-company version of Tensile Involvement (1968).[10] In this piece an indefinable assemblage of lines, colors, and bodies cannot be visually untangled. Dancers are involved with bands that link them to each other, creating a net that has no central perspective to lean on, to orientate the viewer in space. Then a memory of flux contrasts with clear squared forms that suddenly frame the dancers. Afterimages of dynamics linger in space when the strings are still. Something seems to trick perception; clear outlines of space and movements are lost. A symbiotic relationship creates something new through relationality that dancer, light, or costume could have done alone. When dancers lean onto discs or sticks in Nikolais' dances (as Sasha Waltz lets her dancers lean onto wooden cones) one cannot distinguish where the movement of the dancer ends; definitely, it is not with the surface of the skin. The movement extends, on a purely physical level, the boundaries of the dancer's body and its movement range. Simultaneously, this symbiotic interaction questions on a more metaphorical level the boundaries of the individual.

1. Tensile Involvement *as a full-company work created in 1968. From left:*
Gladys Roman, Janet Katzenberg, Gerald Otte, Bill Groves, and unidentified dancers.
Photograph © Tom Caravaglia 2007.

This debordering of the individual is paralleled by how the content or semantic function of Nikolais' dance is constructed, because the dancers are
not making themselves, their stories, or feeling the center points of the work.
The focus is geared on both the semantic and somatic level to the outside in
order to transcend the human body or rather to set it in relationship to others. Thus, the dissolving of esthetical borders is also created by a rejection of
emotionally charged subjectivity.

Abstraction, Emotion, and Empathy

The supposed absence of individuality and emotional subjectivity is usually explained by Nikolais and his critics with a reference to abstraction and
a discussion about how dances can have meaning. I will suggest here that the
use of the notion of abstractness needs to be defined and analyzed specifically

for Nikolais and that there is no universal understanding of what abstraction and the anti-emotional might mean. By not taking these terms for granted, one is able to see contradictory texts as starting points for the deconstruction of their fixed meanings, suggesting a corrective to dichotomies between emotion and non-emotion and abstract and figurative that are so dominant in the writing of North American dance historiography in differentiating between earlier modern dance and the dance avant-garde of the 1960s. Nikolais' notion of bodily communication is not so far away from the German and American modern-dance tradition as Nikolais wants to suggest with his emphasis on abstraction, non-narrative, and anti-emotion art.

Descriptions of Nikolais' work have centered on motion and transformation to the rigorous exclusion of what is linked to the literal and the emotional. This exclusion has been encouraged by Nikolais, who very early began to explain his dances in articles and program notes. He rejected certain types of emotionally charged movements and the stories around which they were generated, associating them with Freudian, sexually driven performance. Dancers are not agonizing over their fate or contemplating solutions, but rather, "they make the play of forces visible by their kinetic machinations within the environment."[11] The kinetic interplay is somehow understood as affectively neutral and regarded as an antipode to emotional communication. In this way, Nikolais is repeatedly measured with reference to the old school of modern dance, seen retrospectively as emotionally driven and narrative, with a strong correspondence between certain movements and their emotional connotation. One critic wrote: "Upon leaving the Henry Street Playhouse after this particular performance, we realized that we had for an hour or two been suspended in an esthetic world-of the-future—a word not of symbol but of essence, not of gesture but of impulse."[12] Detaching Nikolais' work from dance that relies on symbolic movements and meaning is based on clearly articulated oppositions. This differentiation is pertinent when one is familiar with modern dance that is believed to arouse images of archetypal movements pregnant with emotional significance.

In this process of distinguishing himself from the historic modern dance, however, a new form of emotion arises. Its creation and presentation work along the lines of a new raison d'etre that is no less emphatic than the beliefs of the early generation of modern dancers. Nikolais writes:

One of the major characteristics of our current dynamics is our capacity to transcend the literal, and to replace it with an abstract metaphoric language. . . . The dance artist, when he composes can subdue his literal character and invite attention to the motion, the shapes, and to the time and space in which these occur. He has found means to make a direct language of motion, and to use his literal figure as a sensitive instrument to delicately enact the drama of motion. . . .[13]

His words suggest that the terms *abstract* and *literal* are not opposites. While he talks about transcending the literal he speaks of the "literal figure," and he does not want his pieces to be without meaning. Quite the contrary, he uses the seemingly contradicting words "abstract metaphoric language." The word *language* reappears throughout his writing, indicating a strong conviction that motion is communication. This is neither new nor bound to any specific non-narrative dance form, because perceiving movement beyond any verbal language as a means of communication was one of the founding ideals of modern dance, which tried to emancipate itself from the theater arts and the spoken word. Sensitizing dancers and audience to kinetic communication and stimulating empathy when watching dance has been a central goal in the American as well as European modern-dance tradition.[14] When modern dance was not yet established, audiences had problems perceiving the emotional impact of Martha Graham's works, because they seemed stylized and abstract.[15] The dance critic John Martin found it necessary in the 1930s to explain to the audiences that "emotional experience can express itself through movement directly" and that "metakinesis," and "muscular sympathy" can evoke direct emotional contact, which functions outside the realm of language and simple mimetic movements.[16] Indirectly, Nikolais draws on that tradition. However, he uses motion to communicate a different content, which is no longer organized around a clear semantic understanding. Instead of replacing the literal with something that is entirely abstract, the physical means of communication becomes the center of attention. Accordingly, a "drama of motion" can be enacted that functions on the classical modern-dance notion that movement can evoke emotions directly. In the way these emotions are interpreted, it becomes clear that Nikolais' dances remain in the sphere of emotion as well as content.

Furthermore, the insistence on abstractness needs to be interpreted in its post-war historical frame. Problematizing the notion of the anti-emotional touches on the understanding of abstraction. If abstractness is seen as a result of missing emotion, it is hardly precise and needs to be re-evaluated. Even my initial reaction to Nikolais' works was one of feeling slightly estranged, because the dances did not seem "abstract" in the way that I had understood the concept from Nikolais' words and in scholarly writings. Rather, Nikolais' dances showed a simple concreteness, figures and masks that were symbolically charged, a flatness of colors and costumes in an abundantly materialistic assemblage, as well as an adherence to a sort of formalism close to that of modern ballet. As such, I think the continuous insistence on abstractness is due to the specific art-historic discourse that values abstraction.

Nikolais' abstractness shares traits with both Abstract Expressionism and the Pop Art movement. His work shows similarity to the work of contemporaries like Mark Rothko (especially through the colorful slides that are projected onto stage and dancer), and with the dynamism of Jackson Pollock. More, Nikolais' work is on the verge of Pop Art in his reliance on objects, and his focus away from the pondering individual and the Jungian myth of struggle that still fed some of the alienation that drove the Abstract Expressionists. With the Pop Art protagonists Nikolais shared a concern for abstractness that was weakened to some extent by using very concrete and realistic elements. What Robert Rosenblum or Suzi Gablik define as some of the main characteristics of Pop Art could describe the work of Nikolais. They identify the use of simple, regularized forms and flat, unmodulated colors; the presentation of emblematic imagery; and the adoption of impersonal machine-like surfaces as key elements of this art form. I see dancers in costumes with patches of colors, carrying objects and moving like puppets. Objects are hardly abstract; they are recognizable as disks, tents, pillars, etc., and they demand a movement that is very task driven. This similarity reaches beyond the visual appearance; the mode of presentation also invites this comparison. "Deadpan delivery, irony, paradox, and humor," which Sidra Stich sees as the characteristic elements of Pop Art, are all part of Nikolais' performance style.[17] Nikolais' repeated insistence that he wanted to create abstract art that denies a narrative structure places him within the post-war American art debate about form and abstraction. Being abstract was artistically more worthy, more self-reflexive than the figurative in Pop Art, with its references to daily objects and photos.[18] Nikolais was aware of this, and he might have referred to it when writing that the "dancer can use his literal figure to enact a drama of motion." While there are no classical characters embodied and no attitude of representation in Nikolais' early work, there are nonetheless very clearly formalized figures. The dancing figure is not yet a casual body, as it will appear to be a few years later in the context of the dance avant-garde at Judson Church.

But with stylization it is difficult to render the body totally abstract. It always reappears through its concreteness, even more so when it is treated like a thing, when mask and props transform it into puppets. Despite all the talk about abstractness, Nikolais' figures reverberate with a social and cultural significance. A certain form of stiffness might even enhance the notion of a symbolic meaning as it does, for instance, in *Imago*. The initial appearance of stiff, puppetlike beings is created by movements provoked by long tubular costumes that prevent wide steps, bends, or the lifting of legs. The feeling of length and the vertical is enhanced by the stripes reaching from the top to the bottom of the costumes. The limitations as well as the appearance might be associated with a form of prison suit. At the beginning, the movements of the body are very linear and never rounded. But there are tiny edging outs— the coherence of the group is slightly disturbed by a staggered execution of movements that renders the organization arbitrary and thus appears out of order with the strict stiffness of the costumes and the focus on the vertical line. A series of sideward jumps and contractions that seem neither synchronized nor appropriate for the costumes, appear like a failure. They are movements that could be executed without the costumes, and have a humorous and liberating aspect because they are measured against the stiff execution of movements that shape the entire setting. Only in that contrast does the symbolic meaning appear. It seems to be that peculiar battle that generates empathy with these figures. We cannot help but associate characteristic types with certain forms of movement, as the sociologist Talcott Parsons[19] has shown and as a critic demonstrates when describing a section from *Allegory* (1959):

> Here the maddest fantasy takes command as a collection of old moss-stained tops of columns have somehow managed to stagger one atop the other. Now they totter about, performing some strange and ponderous gavotte, snapping their middle sections futilely at the empty air as they maintain a precarious balance.
>
> The largest of them (presumably Murray Louis) acts as a kind of dowager chaperone, wonderously condescending and pompous. It is Louis' secret as to how a costume so completely insane and all-obliterating can still convey so strong a personality. Come to think of it, this must be the first time that column tops have ever been considered to have personalities. . . . [20]

With this ambivalent perception in which the critic is aware that she is provoked into seeing something that is not mimetically embodied, we have everything that Nikolais might have described as figures that enact "the drama of motion." As such, I think that the center of this discussion on abstraction is not the denial of emotion or the literal, but a specific body concept that challenges notions of the "natural" body that was paramount to the early modern dance.

2. *"Finials," a section of* Allegory *(1959). Photograph David S. Berlin, courtesy of the Nikolais/Louis Foundation.*

The Technical Body, Forms of Contact, and Power

While we can interpret Nikolais' dances as human and emotional, his conceptualization of the body is different from that of early modern- dance. Nikolais' work does not hide the techniques by which it forms the body and by which the choreography is constructed. He does not adhere to the belief of the "natural" body or the body as the carrier of emotional depth that can be elucidated by true listening to the inner self or by training. Accordingly, he can be read against a modern-dance practice that has successfully managed to hide its strict training and rather exemplifies "the contrived distortions of movement that modern society incurs, (while) the ideal body inheres in a primal experience of integration within one's self and within society."[21] Laban still believed in a body that should move organically, by which he meant as an integral thing. This does not hold true for Nikolais, however.

Nikolais makes the dancers oscillate between subject and object positions. In this process, the body cannot be imagined as an integral source of identity and movement. The dancer is not an independent individual striving to express his/her own sentiments. Nikolais describes this as follows:

> I think much of my choreography reflects this point of view, the dancer is sometime man on stage and he is sometimes thing. He is sometimes related to objects and he is sometimes related to environments and situations, but rarely does he dominate them; he rather lives with them, he becomes part of them. . . . In some of my works perhaps there are subtle satirical comments—his silly behavior in having the urge to move . . . but he does not have a clear-cut focus. . . . [22]

The thinglike status is often enhanced by light effects or in combination with technically generated sound collage. In this field of technological tricks the figures sometimes appear like animated automatons. Critics often saw these as "dehumanizing" tendencies and pointed to similarities in theater concepts reaching back to Heinrich von Kleist's "Marionettentheater," Gordon Craig's "Übermarionette," and Oskar Schlemmer's dance experiments at the Bauhaus. Nikolais was familiar with this history and with puppet theater. He also saw no negative connotation in technical means or media that enlarge the body.[23] As such, Nikolais' work not only resembles esthetically the dance experiments of Oskar Schlemmer, especially "The Triadic Ballet," but also resembles them conceptually, because Nikolais and Bauhaus protagonists share similar beliefs in the opportunities of technical advances. While they were critical of the exhaustion of the body in industry, they thought that technology could make life more fulfilling and easy and that new design would help create a new world. They saw themselves as craftsmen who should integrate different artistic means, sharing a belief in a communal working atmosphere that was inspired by the old school of cathedral building, where all crafts were assembled in one workshop.[24] This ideal was linked to a political position; the manifest of the Bauhaus states that it could help overcome class differences and the separation between artist and craftsman. This is a political vision that probably was not shared by Nikolais. However, his emphasis on the larger context in which humans move echoes some of that idealism.

This unbroken belief in progress is very much in line with the general public belief in America in the 1950s. However, what is different from the 1920s is that the technical advances and scientific discoveries that are the foundation of this belief in progress could no longer be grasped completely. There was a general notion that the world is too complex and the individual no longer the center of things. Nikolais' art works within a seemingly neutral

3. *Nikolais perfected the technology of slide projection to place individual images on the bodies of dancers, as here in* Scenario *(1971). Photograph P. Berthelot, courtesy of the Nikolais/Louis Foundation.*

stance. At the same time, it is highly affirmative, believes in the process of creation, and uses the possibilities of technical advancements for the creations of scenic illusions. However, Nikolais' choreographies can also be seen as exposing the mechanization of the body so obviously that it can be read as both something to detest or admire.

Despite a focus on relationality, Nikolais' body concept generates a very different movement vocabulary and physical appearance and has different political implications and readings from both classical modern and contemporary dance. This can be exemplified by comparing Nikolais' work to contact improvisation, which today may be the epitome of a relational dance form and has significantly influenced the contemporary dance scene as, for instance, in Sasha Waltz' pieces. The focus on relationality and the close contact between objects and dancers, as well as dancers, and dancers in Nikolais' early works prefigure astonishingly a movement vocabulary that can be associated with a dance technique that developed in the 1970s.

Sensitivity to the movement of others, flow and relaxation, use of leaning into space, putting oneself out of balance as a point initiation, taking the impulse of one movement to another as the starting point in Nikolais' dances, come very close to what has become the esthetic of much contemporary dance. Another part of *Imago* makes that apparent. There is a funny section, which totally denies any straightness and firmness. Colorful costumes having the unappealing shape of potato sacks reaching from the neck down to the knees, hang around the dancers so that their bodies seem to be without any joints or organs. Even while steps are smallish and fast as dancers stumble out into space, the bags seem to have an independent life that enhances the illusion. The whole thing seems to flow, to have the consistency of jelly, and when the characters "accidentally" bump into each other they generate a wave through the others bodies—producing a slapstick effect. A comic image arises from the ostensible loss of control.

It is this slapstick quality next to the thinglike appearance that somehow reduces physical sensitivity by generating comic encounters, which produces the contrast with contact improvisation. Clearly this is linked to the historical context in the post-war era. Nikolais started working when the encounters between bodies were still regularized by a strictly sexual reading of full-body contact. The physical transgression that is linked to sensing of others via skin and feeling was not yet possible. However, contact improvisers resist the notion of a body that can be considered a thing. Today contact improvisation and the relationality between dancers is imbued with a sense of the antitechnical and with democratic notions of being together and sensing each other. It suggests an alternative, nonhierarchical way of being with each other in a world that is increasingly violent towards bodies. In this way Sasha Waltz would describe the importance of her focus on the awareness of space and her debordering physical activity.

While Nikolais was not explicitly political, he nonetheless does not stay outside the realm of politics, because crossing borders and challenging stability is always linked to aspects of power. Power lies in the ability to divide, clarify, and separate as well as in the capacity to motivate and mobilize bodies toward desired ends. How transcendence or dissolving of borders is used may alter, but it links dance and its theory to the realm of politics. Means of transcending esthetic, physical, and ideological borders remain key issues in dance, and thus Nikolais' work has proved to be a starting point for reflection on these fields. Improvisation, limitation and freedom, formalism and dissolving conventional movements stand right next to each other in Nikolais work, showing how these cannot be captured as dichotomies. Nikolais provides an education in how borders could be complicated and surmounted. What is at issue then is that dance can not only resist certain boundaries and dichotomies, but also undermine them in our analytical perceptions.

NOTES

1. *Körper* (*Body*) and *S* were the other two parts of this trilogy.

2. Vgl. Erika Fischer-Lichte, *Ästhetik des Performativen* (Frankfurt am Main, 2004).

3. See Alwin Nikolais, "Day at Night," transcribed interview with James Day, 29 November 1973. The New York Public Library for the Performing Arts, Jerome Robbins Dance Division, 7.

4. Rudolf von Laban, *Choreographie* (Jena, 1926), 2.

5. Laban, *Choreographie*, 2f.

6. See Laban, *Die Welt des Tänzers* (Stuttgart, 1920). ʼ

7. For an extensive discussion of the political dimensions of community culture, movement choirs see Yvonne Hardt, *Politische Körper. Ausdruckstanz, Choreographien des Protest und die Arbeiterkulturbewegung.* (Münster, 2004) and Hardt, "Relational Movement Patterns: The Social Significance of Movement Choirs in the Weimar Republic," *Proceedings of the Society of Dance History Scholars* (Limerick, Ireland, 2003).

8. My description of three sections of the 1963 full-evening-length *Imago* are based on a 1993 reconstruction recorded for the five-volume video series *The World of Alwin Nikolais* (New York: Nikolais-Louis Foundation for Dance, 1996). The excerpts are in program five.

9. See Deborah Jowitt, "Man, the Marvelous Mechanism," *The Village Voice* (19 October 1982), reprinted in Jowitt, *The Dance in Mind* (Boston: Godine, 1985), 199. See also P. W. Manchester, "The Playhouse Dance Company in Masks—Props—Mobiles, 27 December 1955, Henry Street Playhouse," *Dance Magazine* (February 1956), 54f.

10. A good performance of *Tensile Involvement* can be seen on *Kennedy Center Honors* (US: CBS-TV, 1978–1991). *Tensile Involvement* was performed during the 1987 ceremony honoring Nikolais and is recorded on cassette two.

11. Jowitt, *The Dance in Mind*, 200.

12. Doris Hering, "Runic Canto and Premiere of New Dances by Alwin Nikolais, Henry Street Playhouse, 27–29 December, 1957," *Dance Magazine* (February 1958), 59–60.

13. Alwin Nikolais, "Growth of a Theme," *Dance Magazine* (February 1961), 30–34.

14. The German word *Mitschwingen* signifies both to radiate and to swing and was used to describe this form of communication. See Fritz Böhme, *Tanzkunst* (Dessau, 1922). For a discussion of this concept see Inge Baxmann, *Mythos: Gemeinschaft. Körper- und Tanzkulturen in der Moderne* (Munich, 2000), 219.

15. Mark Franko points out in his discussion of the modernism of modern

dance that the early works of Martha Graham were often perceived as lacking in emotional meaning because they were so highly stylized in their poses. See Franko, "Emotivist Movement and Histories of Modernism: the Case of Martha Graham," *Discourse* (1990–91), 111–128.

16. John Martin, *The Modern Dance* (New York: A.S. Barnes & Co., 1933; reprint edition, Princeton, N.J.: Princeton Book Company, 1965), 18.

17. Sidra Stich, *Made in USA: An Americanization in Modern Art, The 50's and 60's* (Los Angeles: University of California Press, 1987), 3f.

18. Stich, 10.

19. When people are asked to describe a triangle, a small triangle, and a ball moving together, they give them human characteristics, the bigger one who move fast is seen as aggressive, etc.

20. P. W. Manchester, "Allegory, by Alwin Nikolais, at Henry Street Playhouse, N.Y. Jan 30, 31 and Feb. 1," *Dance News* (March 1959), 7.

21. Susan Leigh Foster, "Dancing Bodies," in *Incorporations,* edited by Jonathan Crary and Sanford Kwinter (New York: Zone Books, 1992), 487.

22. Nikolais quoted in Winston Grant Gary, *The Dance Theatre of Alwin Nikolais* (Ph.D. dissertation, University of Utah, 1967), 38.

23. See Claudia Gitelman, "The Puppet Theater of Alwin Nikolais," *Ballet Review* (Spring 2001), 84–91.

24. See *Dokumente zum Bauhaus,* Bauhaus Archiv Museum für Gestaltung, *www .bauhaus.de/bauhaus1919/manifest1919.htm.*

CHAPTER 6

Being Motion

. . . .

ALWIN NIKOLAIS' QUEER OBJECTIVITY

REBEKAH KOWAL

In a 1960 review of choreographer Alwin Nikolais' *Totem*, Doris Hering, a critic for *Dance Magazine*, compared the work to a childhood memory in which she watched couples dance at a Chinese restaurant. She remembered: "Every so often the lights would dim; a most marvelous mirrored orb would revolve above the dance floor; and a battery of colored lights would be focused upon it so that as the couples two-stepped sedately, they were bathed in swirling pellets of colored light."

"What made this especially exciting," she recalled, "is that right before the dancing and right after, these were ordinary people. But while they were on the dance floor, they were magically transformed."

Hering used this analogy both to praise and find fault with Nikolais' choreography, which on the one hand "created an enchanting world of the senses," and on the other hand, so distanced the dancers from everyday experience that it seemed to dehumanize them. As she put it, "Because he gives [the work] no points of reference with reality, one feels that his dancers are in some way betrayed. We are forced to forget they are people. And in so doing, we are forced to forget that art in its fullest definition implies emotional involvement."[1]

Hering's conundrum is emblematic of a general critical ambivalence toward Nikolais' work at mid-century. Some, like John Martin and Walter Terry, believed that Nikolais had revived tired and anachronistic modern dance with his improvisational approach to choreography and his use of costumes, props, special effects, and other production elements to add dimension to the moving body.[2] As Martin put it in 1956, "Mr. Nikolais, indeed, has tracked [modern dance] down to its essence, knows what it is and how it operates, and is engaged in developing and extending his knowledge into the *objective* terms of performance with results that may be far reaching" (italics mine).[3] Martin saw merit in Nikolais' investigation of performance on its own terms, as an object with components (of which the body was one) that could just as readily operate independently from one another as they could in conjunction. However, others like Lois Balcom, a reviewer for *Dance Observer*, thought just the opposite, that Nikolais' concentration on what she called "surface elements" "depersonalized" his work. She wrote of *Totem* in 1960:

> Perhaps it is by sheer multiplication of surface elements that the large group numbers . . . are on the whole the most impressive. Yet the real high spot of the evening . . . was a duet called *Rite IV,* beautifully performed by Gladys Bailin and Murray Louis. Here we saw a man and women dancing . . . *It was the only glimpse of humanity in a whole evening of depersonalized arms, legs and torsos—sticks, scarves and stools—light rays, tones and flashing colors*[4] [italics mine].

George Beiswanger best summarized the terms of the debate in 1957 when imagining dichotomous possibility of seeing "the props dance and the dancers prop." He continued: "Now one may take this in two ways, as dehumanizing the dancer or as animizing the thing."[5]

How might we account for this heated debate about the value and implications of Nikolais' post-war work? Had Nikolais' nonconformist artistic practices revived a tired and anachronistic dance idiom? Or did his egalitarian approach to the elements of the choreographic medium, which did not elevate the status of the moving body within the overall scheme of any performance event, degrade modern dance's humanistic aims? Finally, had his conception of the dancer as object inaugurated a new approach to the embodiment of a danced subjectivity or simply reduce the dancer to a sentient machine? Focusing on Nikolais' thought and work between 1945 and 1960, this essay investigates the cultural meanings of his aesthetic strategy of objectivity, which, when deployed, produced choreography that looked and operated differently than the norm in post-war modern dance. My contention is that objectivity disrupted normalization on the registers of the aesthetic and the social. It cleared a conceptual space outside of the prescriptive expressive economy of the artistic establishment in which to explore both the possibilities of physical movement and the mechanics of the performance event. Nikolais interrogated aesthetic and social constructions of normativity by presenting dancers whose appearances did not conform to cultural expectations. In this space of objectivity, perhaps ironically, he embodied another kind of subjectivity, queer not only because it interrogated, exceeded, and even violated conventional aesthetic and cultural conventions, but also because it arose as a result of dancers pursuing their own movement impulses within the context of his overall choreographic vision.

"Freedom from the Domination of the Concrete": Nikolais' Novel Conception of Danced Subjectivity

As it had the lives of many men, World War II interrupted Nikolais' early career as a dancer and choreographer. At the time of his conscription to the army's Signal Corps in 1942, Nikolais, a latecomer to modern dance, had recently opened a dance school in Hartford, Connecticut, and begun an artistic collaboration with Truda Kaschmann,[6] a former student of German expressionist choreographer Mary Wigman. According to Murray Louis, Nikolais' life-partner and a principle dancer in his company, "Nikolais felt his career had been launched. A year of recitals in the New England area and a growing school all made his arrival at a North Carolina army base the following year a ruthless and severing end to an era and the beginning of a new time."[7] On his return to civilian life Nikolais resumed his life in dance. Between 1946 and 1947 he served as Hanya Holm's assistant and, beginning in 1947, as a teacher in her New York school. In 1948, Grace Spofford, director of the Henry Street Settlement House, offered him the chance to establish a school at the Henry Street Playhouse, which, with its stage and two small rehearsal studios, could also serve as a residence for a dance company. Nikolais embraced the opportunity, especially since the institutional support of the Settlement House gave him a sense of creative security. As Louis observed, "With his own school and theater, Nikolais withdrew from the pressures and coercions that the dance field can so devastatingly heap upon its own."[8]

At Henry Street Nikolais began developing a theory of dance and experimenting with ways of conveying it in theatrical terms. Moving away from the expressionism of the traditionalists, who believed that dance movement externalized inner feeling, and which he associated with a preoccupation with sexual matters, Nikolais sought to express his ideas abstractly—as he put it, seeking "freedom from the domination of the concrete."[9] He associated concreteness with the literal, which meant anything biographical or psychological, including sexual preferences or love interests, precisely because these aspects of life were subjective and eventually led back to the personal life of the artist. He preferred instead to think in larger terms. As he expressed it, "Since sexuality is an invitation to self, when you move away from that as your impetus for life, you have to go into environment—the relation of man to nature, the relation of man to things other than fellow man, the need to make peace with things other than fellow man."[10] This was a novel way of conceiving subjectivity in modern dance, as something primarily relational and therefore not rooted exclusively in the realm of personal experience. According to John Martin, it placed Nikolais "oddly out of line with the 'expressiveness' of modern dance."[11]

In these efforts to reform modern dance, Nikolais was in esteemed company. At mid-century, he, along with other choreographers like Merce Cunningham, Paul Taylor, and James Waring, sought ways of invigorating modern dance practice, avoiding what they saw as the pitfalls of narrative-driven compositions, which, they thought, predetermined the result of a choreographic process. Specifically they rejected the post-war penchant for adapting canonical works of literature for choreographic uses (e.g., Martha Graham's *Night Journey*, 1947, and José Limón's *The Moor's Pavane*, 1949, to name two), eschewed structural devices that necessitated that dancers play characters or enact dramatic situations, and looked for other reasons to move besides expressing emotion.

Alternatively, they used choreographic structures to motivate action around imposed contingencies, making movement itself what any dance was about. Cunningham, for instance, subjected his choreographic choices to chance, making decisions about step sequence, phrasing, body position, spatial pathway (in general, choreographic content and structure) based on the random outcome of "chance operations."[12] Taylor focused on body posture, translating what he observed people doing on the street into gestures and phrases that could be performed on stage.[13] Likewise, Waring concentrated on action. According to Jack Anderson, "The important thing, for him, is the movement itself, not its purpose or literal meaning. His list of 'things I don't like in dancing' includes 'drama, psychology, myth, symbol, literature, logic.' He prefers each of his dances to be its own world, subject to its own laws."[14] Of Cunningham, Mark Franko contends, "Cunningham's work did not originally dismiss expressivity as much as it sought to redefine it. As long as Cunningham was actively putting expressivity into question, he manipulated the expressive model in new ways."[15] Franko's observation applies not only to Cunningham but also to Taylor and Waring, both of whom, in Cunningham-fashion, "pried physical sensation loose from the emotional impression that purportedly created it."[16]

While Nikolais shared similar aims—expanding the "expressive model" for modern dance—he, more than any of the others, however, pursued neutrality, even objectivity, looking to science for a model of artistic inquiry that "could bring man into symbolic communication with the unknowable."[17] Distinguishing his work from that of the traditionalists, whose work he associated with acting, Nikolais sought to work "motionally" as opposed to "emotionally."[18] As he explained, "Emotion is the result of motion or the lack of it," giving the example, "If you have the desire to do something and you cannot do this thing because of certain tensions or restrictions, then you have the resulting emotions of gladness, sadness, madness, or whatever obvious ones that we know of." He thought that moving caused a dancer to feel "sensations" rather than emotions—"reaction to the fact that you're in movement." Emotion was a "reaction to sensation," and therefore a secondary result of movement. It was not therefore, as the traditionalists contended, the impetus for it.[19]

Taking great pains to move away from what was personal, Nikolais devised an aesthetic philosophy that, above all, stressed objectivity. Applied to the creative process, his stance demanded an almost scientific empiricism that was coupled with, oddly, a brand of mysticism. Thus, in a composition, Nikolais strove to embody what he called "an object in mind," an "idea" that emerged for him as a result of a conversation he had with the "universe"; he called it "the history of a conclusion emerging from the impress of the universe upon the artist and his perception of it." Once conceived, the idea supplied him with the "motivations for the form of the composition—the themes, phrases, reiterations, developments, climaxes, etc," which he called "the vehicle." The vehicle was the conveyer of the idea, a highway for "its intended traffic," or, in other language, aspects of choreographic design like movement vocabulary, phrasing, spatial patterning, and production elements. Finally, the body's role was that of an "instrument," making visible the elements of the idea and its vehicle, the composition, in the illustration of "time, space, and dynamics."[20]

As removed from the choreographic process as this sounds, Nikolais did exercise judgment in determining the form of the composition, deciding where and how to "place emphasis to give weight to certain aspects of the idea."[21] Subjugated to the priority of objectivity, these choices came almost as an afterthought, as acts of aesthetic discrimination rather than as the impetus for a given composition. Unlike his esteemed peers, Graham, Limon, and Humphrey, whose inspiration for choreography was, in part, rooted in the artist's psychic or emotional life, Nikolais' approach was more rational, grounded in concepts akin to the scientists and logicians of his age who devised systems for understanding the world that coordinated mental and physical objects. In fact Nikolais' move away from compositional constructs that would suggest human relationships was meant to neutralize, or at least to downplay, the significance of his dancers' personal identities.

Nikolais coached dancers to think in these neutral terms as well. When choreographing, for example, he asked them to think of themselves as abstract qualities, not as characters or even as people with lives outside of the theater but as "instruments" whose efforts to solve movement problems led to danced action. According to Mazo, they "are persons in an environment, and they are dancers, but they are not specific individuals with carefully defined histories or relationships."[22] In these explorations, he directed them to avoid movement that signified a literal meaning—like handshakes or embraces—or even kinds of eye contact or touching that would telegraph any subtext. Instead the dancers physicalized "primary" or "pre-psychological" gestures, movement for its own sake that had no emotional (and sexual, for that matter) valence or intent.[23] These methods did not altogether block the expression of feeling, but they situated it secondary to the generation of movement for its own sake. Action resulted from dancers' responses to constraints placed on them by any given compositional rubric: "the environment, the rules of the game, is what links the incidents in most Nikolais dances; there is no immediate cause-and-effect relationship between the action of one performer and the movement of another."[24] Additionally, costumes, props, and other visual effects minimized distinguishing features of the dancers' bodies, thus disrupting the viewer's ability to discern the dancers' gender, age, or race. The result was a concept-driven formalism. Nikolais' motivation was physical (anatomical, spatial, temporal), his aim to elaborate the body's potential for action—action not as a reaction to a psychological or dramatic conflict but in response to the exigencies and limitations of physical reality (e.g., a dancer's physical range, gravity, time and space).

Nikolais' shift of emphasis away from the dancer-as-individual and toward the dancer-as-body is significant. In contrast to choreographic precedents that saw the body as an expressive conduit for emotion, Nikolais saw the body as a materialization of motion. His approach altered the balance of emphasis in traditional modern-dance compositions that tended to revolve around a protagonist or group of related characters. No longer at the "dance hero" of the composition, the Nikolais dancer played a complementary role in the overall theatrical spectacle, what the choreographer called a "polygamy of motion, shape, color and sound."[25] As an element in the environment of the composition (nothing more, nothing less), the dancer's body expressed the "sentient values" of a physical "media" via the elements of motion, shape, time, and space.[26] In this departure, he opened a space for movement and artistic invention, making explicit that while a dancer's movement was governed by contingencies like time and space, it also produced them.

Also significant is the way Nikolais "decentralized" the spectator. Whereas the modern-dance traditionalists strove to open channels of communication between audiences and their work through a process of interpretation—in which viewers would attempt to make sense of what they were watching by organizing a series of visual and aural cues—Nikolais deliberately left out such cues. "I like to give images that allow the public to make their own associative reaction," he commented, continuing, "I think this is probably one of the things that I'm master of and have been for years. The image by itself is not so important as its being the catalyst into the onlookers for their own reverberations. . . . If it's spelled out too strongly on the stage, then you're robbed of that privilege."[27] Repositioning viewers to the periphery of the theatrical spectacle, as both witnesses and participants in the total environment, Nikolais hoped to make them aware of their presence within and outside of the world he created onstage. A microcosm of the work of scientists, he altered a viewer's frame of reference, situating him simultaneously in relation to the small spectacle, and that small spectacle in relation to entities infinitely larger.

Nikolais' early approach to choreography has theoretical overtones. It suggests that dance, a form of human action, arises in response to limits, be they physical, or even cultural. And it illustrates that in solving problems posed by such limits dancers find possibilities for action not previously imagined, avenues that did not present themselves at the outset. The phenomenologist Sondra Horton Fraleigh argues that dance is a metaphor for embodiment, a way in which we "celebrate our living, concrete reality."[28] Nikolais' work, in and of itself, makes a similar assertion. He not only produced dances that had merit for their own aesthetic sake, but the dances themselves also offered models of human action that, in offering new options for moving, embodied alternative ways of being and living, thus laying a foundation for an alternative reality. His work had social implications; it embodied ways in which choreography can, at the same time, reinforce conventional modes of action *and* interrogate them, meeting even as it exceeds cultural expectations in its embodiment of possibility. In Nikolais' assertions—that the meaning of movement be assessed purely on its own terms and that the bodies of his dancers could signify outside of conventional terms (that they could be, in effect, genderless, raceless, ageless, etc.)—was a distinctly contrived conceit that Nikolais imposed on his spectators. It demanded that in order to ascertain the meaning of his dances on his terms viewers would have to change their own frame of reference, donning social blinders, so to speak, so as not to see (or to pretend not to see) any information that would contradict Nikolais' illusion of objectivity.

Objectivity as a Form of Silence

Nikolais' objectivity was not unlike the approaches of other gay male artists within and outside the dance world, whose investigation of the impersonal took many guises from the pedestrian, to the found, to the aleatoric; whatever their path to composition, they all found delight in compositional opacity and relished the defiance of critical interpretation.[29] Scholarship on artists working in this vein has largely focused on a milieu of gay men whose work challenged the dominance of expressionism, embodied in large part by the Abstract Expressionist movement. This group includes composer John Cage and visual artists Jasper Johns and Robert Rauschenberg, as well as Merce Cunningham.

There are parallels, for example, between Nikolais objectivity and Cage's fascination with "silence," not only because objectivity defied the dominant aesthetic mode in dance (i.e. expressionism), but also because it minimized the role of the choreographer (and his subjective impressions) in the creative process. In "Finishing School: John Cage and the Abstract Expressionist Ego," Caroline Jones recalls a lecture that Cage gave at the Artists Club in 1949 entitled "Lecture on Nothing." Among those who listened were "the dominant abstract expressionists" who "may have recognized themselves as the bull's-eye in Cage's target." According to Jones: "To that audience, obsessed with subjects, Cage offered subjectlessness; to men captivated like Narcissus with their own bodies' parts, a bodiless philosophy; to the protectively arrogant leaders of the New York school, an exercise in Zen discipline and discipleship."[30] Similarly, Nikolais' objectivity arose in direct response to the choreographic mainstream in modern dance at the time, choreographers who didn't hesitate to use their emotional lives as reference points as they choreographed their dances. Furthermore, as Nikolais contended, objectivity shifted the emphasis from the choreographer to the surrounding world. Again he thought like Cage, who posed silence "against . . . epic egoism . . . reminding his listeners that the subjects being obsessed about were not trapped within the subconscious, in need of extrication, or figured in the body of the artist; rather they were all around, to be discovered in simple, silent wonder at the world."[31]

As Jones and Jonathan Katz have observed, Cage's aesthetic of silence had numerous social and cultural implications, not only as an antidote to the hyper-masculine self-indulgence of the abstract expressionists and the milieu they cultivated in New York City, but also in the context of post-war debates about the affiliation between modern art and communism. One of the most colorful examples of this cultural predilection for aesthetic transparence comes from the world of post-war visual art. In the wake of post-war anti-Communist fears, it reared its head in a public uproar over a traveling art exhibition. Called "Advancing American Art," it was organized by the U.S. State

Department's Office of International Information and Cultural Affairs and curated by J. LeRoy Davidson, former curator of the Walker Art Center in Minneapolis, known for his progressive (and Europhilic) taste. Davidson supervised the purchase by the U.S. government of seventy-nine oil paintings and thirty-eight watercolors with the intention of exhibiting them abroad over at least five years. He favored abstract works, aligned with the reigning interwar Europeanist aesthetic rather than American regional and more prosaic painting.[32] To accommodate the State Department's wishes, and with the hope of international exposure, artists and dealers had sold the paintings at prices far below market value.

The exhibition's troubles began with criticism by the disgruntled in the art world, academics whose works had not been selected and critics who did not share Davidson's taste.[33] According to a 1949 article in *Newsweek*, "The principle attack centered . . . on the fact that the show emphasized modern art." It continued, "That the examples chosen did not reflect the a-tree-is-a-tree school aroused yowls of rage and sarcasm." Taking the lead from the disapproval of the American art community, members of the press continued an assault against the exhibit. Hearst publications, owned by the conservative mogul William Randolph Hearst, followed by *Look* magazine and others, featured sarcastic comments about the exhibition, often including mockingly derogatory captions underneath illustrations. For example, Hearst's *New York Journal American* reproduced O. Louis Guglielmi's painting *Tenements* accompanied by the caption: "If you contemplate adding to the suicide rate, we recommend this picture for the guest room."[34]

The salvos continued, even after the show's opening at the Metropolitan Museum of Art in New York City, as planned paintings from the exhibit represented the United States at the opening of the first general UNESCO conference in Paris.[35] Perhaps President Harry Truman's remarks aroused the most attention. When asked by a reporter at a press conference to comment on Kuniyoshi's *Circus Girl Resting*, an exaggerated portrait of a circus performer wearing a revealing dress and half-stockings, he offered that it showed "a fat, semi-nude circus girl," and added that "the artist must have stood off from the canvas and thrown paint at it. . . . if that's art, I'm a Hottentot."[36] Ripples from this debate extended into the late 1940s and early 1950s, the public interest fueled by McCarthyist anticommunism. Senator George Dondero of Michigan led the charge equating modernism with communism in several speeches on the Senate floor.[37]

Such attacks on modernism, and on artistic freedom, attracted a host of defenders from artists to museum curators, art critics to newspaper editorial boards. Nonartists mounted a direct and verbal assault on their adversaries through letter campaigns, editorials, and speeches. Republican Congressman Jacob Javits from New York, for example, issued the following response to Dondero in a speech on the Senate floor: "I would fight to the last breath to preserve to my colleague the right to make his case against any particular artist or his work, but I feel it is my duty to protect just as vigorously any effort to smear all modern art and contemporary art with one brush as communistic."[38] Others like editorialists Emily Genauer of *Harper's Magazine* and Howard Devree of the *New York Times* pointed to the hypocrisy of the equation of modern art and communism citing the wartime purge of modern artists from Germany by the Nazis. In Devree's words:

> That speakers and writers in the country should employ the same methods of attack and use almost identical terms with those made infamous by the Nazis and by the suppressive forces in the Soviet Union can only arouse wonder. For it is the sturdy individualism, the refusal of modernism to become propaganda or to cater to the anecdotal and the illustrative that have led to its suppression under totalitarian governments. Must that be pointed out over and over again?[39]

Like Devree, others such as Thomas J. Colt, director of the Portland Art Museum, made the point that modernism embodied a central tenet of democracy—that citizens be allowed to think and act freely. "Modern art is a product of our democratic society, which grants each man the right and freedom to search his own soul, discover his own values, and to express his feelings," he contended.[40] In whatever way they found to undercut Dondero's accusations, these advocates of modernism supported the idiom on grounds exactly contrary to his logic; each argued that modernism embodied U.S. cultural dominance as a symbol of the individualism engendered by democracy, and therefore that it was a form of moral suasion against communism.

Compared to the nonartist defenders of modernism, artists adopted a more indirect approach. Rather than address pointedly the claims of their accusers or be explicit in their advocacy of artistic freedom, they tended to prove the virtue of modernism through demonstration, not verbal argument. Visual artists, for example, took the offensive in an attempt to shape the public's perception of their work. They presented their work on their own terms, speaking with art audiences in public forums and curating exhibits. In New York City, abstract painters William Baziotes, Robert Motherwell, and Mark Rothko, who were later joined by Barnett Newman, organized a series of artists' lectures in Greenwich Village during the academic year 1948–1949. Part of the academic program of a cooperative school that the artists had started, the discussions, which were open to the public, had been intended to introduce students to other accomplished artists who had been invited to speak.[41]

The next year, teachers from the New York University School of Art Education took over the responsibility for the lecture series. They culminated its final year, 1950, with a closed session moderated by Alfred H. Barr Jr., curator at the Museum of Modern Art and a foremost scholar of modernism; Richard Lippold, a sculptor; and Motherwell. In the spirit of self-representation in the midst of a politicized environment, the artists engaged in a discussion that revolved largely around aesthetic issues, not political ones. They addressed the following questions: What is abstract art? How does one know when an abstract work is finished? What is the function of the title of an art work? What binds abstract artists together? To what extent is American modern art derivative of European precedents? What is more important to the contemporary artists, reason or intuition? Is art a form of self-analysis? Finally, what is the subject of abstract art? The session took place during three days in April 1950 and is documented as a conversation entitled "Artists' Session at Studio 35 (1950). Seeking to define themselves on their own terms, not those of demagogues like Dondero, curators Motherwell, Ad Reinhardt, and Barnard Karpel assembled an exhibition as part of the lecture series. According to their mission statement, they intended to highlight the "sustained achievement" of post-war American art in spite of the "recent great attention paid to Abstract Art [that had been] characterized by an erratic concern, full of prejudice and confused by misunderstanding." In their words, "This biennial . . . promises to come to grips with that central situation. Through works and documents of its own making the scope and nature of the struggle will be self-revealed."[42]

When diverging from the status quo implied abnormalcy at best, and political subversion at worst, those whose views and life practices were considered outside the mainstream or that did not conform to dominant expectation, like visual and performing artists as well as those in the film industry, were held suspect, their works coming under fire, their lives under scrutiny.[43] Understandably, these comments about the ability of art to justify its merits on its own terms—through "self-revelation," if you will—are opaque compared to the sharp line of attack employed by other public figures like Javits, Genauer, Devree, and Colt. Yet, even so, they exemplify the points made by Katz and Jones about the artists of the abstract expressionist school; many defended their art against charges that it was communistic on the basis that it embodied each the artist's subjectivity.[44] Peter Grippe said as much during the closed conversation during the biennial when responding to the question "How do you know when a work is finished?" He explained: "A work of art is never really 'finished.' There is a feeling of trying to express the labyrinth of one's mind—its feelings and emotions, and to fulfill one's personality. Each work is trying to complete the expression of that personality."[45]

By contrast, artists like Cage and Nikolais did not have such lines of defense at their ready because their artistic practices deliberately distanced the artist from his work. In Cage's case, scholars have observed that, at a time when some equated homosexuality and communist subversion, his refusal to say anything about the meaning of his work, his silence, so to speak, functioned as an excuse for not exposing anything about his personal or interior life, a "dissimulation, camouflage, hiding" that cloaked his idiosyncrasies, his difference.[46] His silence, then, acted as a closet for his sexual identity. Yet both Katz and Jones intriguingly assert that the performance of not saying anything suggested the contrary—rather than diverting attention away from Cage, it drew attention to his efforts to cover up. Thus, even though silence did not offer any concrete information about his thoughts or his life, it highlighted his difference from artistic peers who saw their work as a means of formalizing (in the sense of giving form to) their emotional lives.[47] Jones takes this further, arguing that Cage's silence was also resistive. She argues that in operating "alongside" speech, it marks the spaces of communication that exist within dominant discourse and yet whose contents are not determined by it.[48] Thus, it "constitutes a kind of critique": "secrets and silence may be enforced by the oppressor, but they can also hide the oppressed (or the liberator, or beauty, or love) from the controlling, panoptical view; . . . silence is both shield and protest."[49] I believe that Nikolais' aesthetic of objectivity functioned in a similar way. It protected him in that it frustrated the viewer's attempt to make a connection between the choreographer's life and his work. But it also licensed and prompted his odd portrayal of the world, which embodied not only his refusal to abide by the prescriptions of the modern-dance standard bearers but also his assertion of new ways of thinking and being.

Choreographic Objectivity and Visible Difference

In this comparison we see, ironically, the extent to which analogies between Cage's silence and Nikolais' objectivity go only so far in explaining the aesthetic and social impact of the latter's artistic practices. While silence is, in some ways, comparable to objectivity in that it allows the artist to absent himself (i.e., his subjective judgment) from the creative process and repositions the spectator in relation to the work of art, the two modes are different when it comes to the matter of the body. Nikolais' choreography necessarily involved the human body, its representations and constructions, whereas Cage's compositions did not. As Katz explains in a perceptive essay on Jasper Johns' plaster cast paintings, the body "possesses an authoritative significance that is able to transcend delimiting context and conditions,"[50] thus guaranteeing the body's presence in ways profoundly unlike the absence of sound.

What does a consideration of the significance of the moving body, as figured in Nikolais' choreography, add to the cultural picture established by precedent scholarship on Cage's silence? What were the aesthetic and social ramifications of Nikolais' aesthetic practices, specifically to what extent did Nikolais' aesthetic of objectivity allow his dancers to operate in ways not restricted or directed by their gender identities, thus interrogating conventional constructions of gender? And, in what ways did those same practices affirm and possibly reify convention? An examination of several of Nikolais' mid-century works will begin to address these questions.

Consider Nikolais' use of props to disguise dancers or modify the images of their bodies for instance. In *Noumenom Mobilis* (1953), for example, dancers' bodies were fully encased in stretchy fabric that made them look like giant amoebae. Their costumes disguised performers to such an extent as to erase all signs of their identity. At first, the shapes appear to be resting on barrel-like pedestals. As they shift subtly, rocking back and forth in unison, they heighten the viewer's sense of horizontality—we perceive elongated and malleable forms, not prone dancers. Sometimes the forms pose on single points of contact, presumably the dancers' feet, and look like a series of rectangular planes, each balanced on one corner and extending out into space. The taut casements, framed by the points of the dancers' outstretched limbs, erase all evidence of the skeletons inside them, distorting the viewer's perception. As planar shapes, not dancers, the forms look looming and larger than life. What is more, since we cannot see the dancers' faces or make out their anatomical features, we lose a sense of their spatial orientation. Are they facing front or back? On which body part are they balancing? Which body part is creating which bulge? Our curiosity is addressed in the last image of the dance, when the performers gather their casements around their necks revealing what appear to be their human heads. Nikolais' exploration of the impact of costuming on an overall theatrical spectacle was in line with the experiments of early twentieth century European modernists such as German expressionist Mary Wigman, Dadaist performer Hugo Ball, movement theorist Rudolph Laban, and Bauhaus artist Oskar Schlemmer. Like them, he imagined that a costume could function like a puppet and the dancer's body like a puppeteer.[51]

Nikolais' experimentation in this realm is also analogous to the work of Loie Fuller, a modern dancer who, at the turn of the twentieth century, revolutionized the dancing image in her investigation of motion. Expanding the contours of her body in swirls of diaphanous fabric, manipulated by her hands and even long prosthetic arms, Fuller envisioned her dancing body as a "site of metamorphosis."[52] Julie Townsend argues that such "object-based dances removed the thing (serpent, butterfly, or flower) from any recognizable scenario or story line," thus relieving Fuller of the expectation that she needed to play a woman.[53] Fuller demonstrated the potential of portraying the body as object because unlike a human being an object could exist outside of normative structures for making meaning.

We see this not only in Nikolais' *Noumenom Mobilis*, but also in dances of the same period, like *Kaleidoscope* (1956), which explored ways the body's structure could be extended, or its contours distorted, to create unusual visual effects within a multimedia, theatrical environment. A suite of dances, it made theater out of dancers' manipulation of various props, including discs, a long pole, skirts, enormous capes, paddles, and straps. In the section called "Discs," for example, Nikolais investigated the movement possibilities and aural effects caused by wooden circular discs strapped to the dancers' right feet. The dance begins simply, as seven dancers, standing evenly spaced, mechanically extend and retract their legs in unison. Each time they replace their feet they clap their discs on the floor. Both the regular motion of the dancers' legs and the clap of the discs evoke a feeling of industry. In time, their movements become more complicated: the dancers swing their right legs like pendulums, use the discs as pivots for twists and full turns, or seem to glide on the discs in arabesque. In one sequence, the dancers lie on their backs with the bottoms of their feet facing the audience. Then, each person gestures his or her right leg to trace an arc with the circular disc. The disc attachments enhance our sense of the dimensionality of the leg gestures; thus, rather than just seeing a group of legs move, we perceive the patterns the discs make in space.

The premise of "Pole," which included two dancers and a prop, was similar. The pole functioned like the discs in that it focused the viewer's attention to the dancers' interaction with the prop and with space—as much as on their relationship to each other. Although one of the performers is male and the other female, in their costumes they look nearly identical. They wear close-fitting body suits, which display Mondrian-like geometric designs, and pointed

1. Murray Louis and Gladys Bailin in "Pole" from Kaleidoscope *(1956).*
Photograph David S. Berlin, courtesy of the Nikolais/Louis Foundation.

hats. When we first see them, they are standing on their left legs, facing stage left, and balancing a long pole on their flexed right ankles. Exercises in coordination and concentration, their movements are incremental and in strict unison—the object is not to drop the pole. We are aware of the performers' intense concentration, an aspect of their presence that highlights their teamwork rather than their feelings toward each other. They resemble Thai court dancers, whose poise and intricate handwork and footwork convey stateliness. The mood shifts momentarily, as the dancers become more playful. Now they look like circus performers in a high-wire act, using the pole for balance as they walk a fine line. For a moment, the man takes the pole so that his partner can enjoy a whimsical solo of turns and jumps. Then she takes hold of the object, giving her partner his freedom. When he finishes dancing, they sit down together, the woman on the man's lap; however, nothing is made of this gesture; it is accomplished with matter-of-fact neutrality. They rise to perform a last antic; while the woman stands on the pole, the man raises it to his shoulder, making a ramp on which she slides down.

The other dances in the suite proceeded in a similar fashion. In "Straps," the dancers contended with stretchy bands that are attached off stage. On one hand, the straps limit the dancers' mobility, but on the other, they make it possible for them to do things that would otherwise be impossible. Balances are a good example; supported by the strap, the body can extend out into space way beyond where it ordinarily could without falling. Both "Capes" and "Skirts" investigated how partially or fully obscured bodies can create extra-ordinary shapes in space. Male and female performers wear the same costumes and execute the same movement phrases. The various ways they manipulate their garments make moving zones of color; our vision is directed to the kaleidoscopic effects the dancers create rather than to their relations with one another. In examining these early works, one is struck by a redolent dichotomy. On one hand Nikolais' objectivity created a space for alternative modes of action and appearance. On the other hand it was prescriptive in not allowing certain kinds of physical interaction that implied intimacy among the dancers or was suggestive of narrative content.

Nikolais' ambivalence was a product of his time; it resonated not only with the efforts by members of the modern-dance establishment to normalize the aesthetic practice of modern dance, but also with a broader cultural anxiety surrounding gender and sexuality that marked the Cold War era. This anxiety was the byproduct of fear and uncertainty about social change on gender roles and family life in spite of widespread efforts to mitigate its effects through a preoccupation with traditional values.[54] Political and social rhetoric during the Cold War era cast the nuclear family as a key player in the nation's pursuit of security.[55] In this cultural atmosphere, gender roles hardened around traditional ideals that acted as thresholds of normalcy used to determine what was and was not normal.[56] Michel Foucault calls this differentiation process "normalization," a measurement of the "'nature' of individuals" that "traces the limit that will define difference in relation to all other differences, the external frontier of the abnormal. . . ."[57] In other words, normalization establishes the bases for individual conformity, or norms, by defining the extremes.

One way that normalization played out during the early Cold War years was through a cultural debate about what social scientists called "gender convergence." Sociologists like David Riesman, William H. Whyte Jr., John Seely, R. Alexander Sim, E. W. Loosley, Jules Henry, and Talcott Parsons used this term as a code for nontraditional gender practices in an attempt to explain the popular perception that gender roles were becoming less and less distinct.[58] But the discussion about gender convergence did not stop in the academy. Popular magazines of the time discussed the subject in terms of stereotypical figures such as the so-called she-man and he-woman.[59] She-men were men who displayed "feminine" characteristics—they were typically stammering, hen-pecked husbands, like the father in *Rebel With-out a Cause*, whose lack of initiative and deference to their wives were interpreted as marks of weakness. He-women were their female counterparts—the relentlessly demanding and aggressive wife or the shrewd career woman.

Alternatively, in order to be deemed normal, one needed to conform to an ideal type. A prescriptive discourse supported these types by articulating a set of standards by which a person's outward appearance and behavior could be judged by a viewing public. The point was to determine the extent to which a person's demeanor conformed to conventional expectations of that person's gender. Within this visual economy, women were assumed to exhibit the qualities of docility, dependence, sexual availability, and emotionalism, while men were supposed to show strength, aggression, remoteness, and rationality. With so much riding an individual's presentation of self, or what Erving Goffman called "the arts of impression management,"[60] the coherence of a person's self-presentation was key to a favorable audience reception. If a person's appearance conformed to social expectations, he or she would be deemed normal, if not, judged aberrant.

In what ways did Nikolais' objectivity situate his work outside of this system of normalization and in which ways within it? Consider the implications of Nikolais' focus on motion. His idea, to prompt movement invention by asking dancers to solve movement problems, expanded the movement vocabulary in modern dance. His work outside of narrative constructions enabled dancers to dance without assuming character roles, introducing the option for dancers to express their presence simply, in terms of physical action. These innovations took away the psychological angle of interpretation, thereby shifting the viewer's frame of reference outside the binary discourse of normalcy and aberrance. On a phenomenological level, these changes embodied new and nonconventional ways of acting and being in the world, ways that were different in both choreographic and social arenas. Nikolais distortion of dancers' appearances on the one hand, and his equalization of men and women in costume and movement on the other, made some trenchant, if inadvertent, comments about gender construction. Implying that identities were mutable, these interventions suggested that gender was founded on contrivance, not nature, that it could be put on and taken off at will. Additionally, his choreography downplayed dancers' athletic physiques in its alteration of their bodies. Thus, even though the dancers' well-trained bodies affirmed gender convention in the ways in which their appearance met contemporary ideals, they challenged it in their performance of oddity. In sum, in a society in which gender differences de-

2. Tent *(1968) in a 1993 reconstruction. Photograph © Johan Elbers 2007.*

terminate, these ambiguous portrayals envisioned alternative, even queer, constructions.

Nevertheless, for all of these modifications, which disrupted normalization, there are other ways in which heteronormativity still operated in Nikolais' work, mitigating its expression of nonconformity. Take his "object-ification" of the body, for example. Even though this approach ushered in new options for movement and ways that dancers could interact, its Cartesianism, its almost defensive separation of mind and body, substantiated normalization as well. His perception of the dancer's body as an "instrument" implied that the body was a physical object. As sentient as it was, therefore, the body was also capable of doing things irrespective of the emotional results of its actions, either for the person doing the action (the dancer) or for those involved (others in the company)—a morally ambiguous position at best. Furthermore, while his approach capitalized on the body's capacity for movement invention, it privileged certain kinds of movement while denying others. While he

3. Christine Lamb and Raul Trujillo in Graph *(1984). Photograph Peter Koletzke, courtesy of the Nikolais/Louis Foundation.*

placed a premium on the sentient capacities of human living, these could not include the erotic, sensual, or sexual, and emotionalism was certainly downplayed. Thus, while Nikolais mined the body's potential for movement, he also limited it based on his aesthetic and philosophical predilections. This goes the same for partnering conventions, which Nikolais modified in allowing same-sex partnering. Unlike mainstream modern dance, which predicated such partnering on character conflict or scenario, Nikolais' gave license to it on its own merits (without a dramatic excuse, so to speak). Yet these instances in which men danced with men and women with women maintained the conceit of chastity.[61] That is, they deliberately did not use dance movement to express homosexual desire.

Conclusion

Michel Foucault asserts that it is often the case that embodied responses to power relations are themselves indicative of the characteristics of the very formations to which they are responding.[62] How did objectivity operate in Nikolais' work and what were its cultural meanings? Objectivity was a term Nikolais adopted as a way of describing his aesthetic strategy. It characterized an approach to the presentation of the moving body that situated the body as an object, one element in the total performance event. It was also the idea behind Nikolais' efforts to disrupt the visual economy of spectatorship. In this case, objectivity was a tactic of disillusionment "decentering" viewers from the privileged perspectival position at which all vantage points converged and giving them the same status as any of the other components of the performance experience. Finally, objectivity made doing and viewing movement the foundation of choreographic production. In other words, the component parts of choreographic production could be investigated in and of themselves and independently of one another; and, while they could express an emotional tone or feeling idea, they were not subordinate to them.

Peggy Phelan has observed the potential of performance to interrupt "the reciprocity of visual exchange"; works that confuse the categories of hierarchical binaries, in effect, "disrupt the neat substitutions of the psychic economy of seeing."[63] Performance makes visible different ways of being and doing and therefore has the capability of unsettling social and cultural convention. In this case, charges like Balcom's and Hering's, that Nikolais' work dehumanized the dancer or depersonalized the dance, must be interpreted on several registers at once. On the one hand, they reveal the intensity of belief of some in the modern-dance establishment that there was a compulsory way of doing things. Leveling such charges, therefore, was tantamount to accusing Nikolais of denigrating the humanism of modern dance and of negating the operating assumption that dance was the externalization of human emotion. Yet there was more to it than that. As I think Balcom's comment—that a duet between Bailin and Louis was the only "glimpse of humanity" that evening—makes clear, such charges were code for heteronormativity. What bothered viewers like Balcom was not only that Nikolais made his dancers look different, but also that their oddity destabilized normative assumptions that governed both the aesthetic and cultural realm. Put another way, objectivity made manifest a visible difference that countered the aesthetic and social pressures of normalization. Yet it did more than this. Ironically, Nikolais' objectivity led to the embodiment of a new kind of subjectivity, which was queer not only because it destabilized aesthetic and cultural convention but also because of what it allowed dancers to do: follow their own movement impulses, exercise their own judgment on a moment to moment basis, and pursue the realization of self in movement terms.

NOTES

1. Doris Hering, revision of *Totem, Dance Magazine,* March 1960: 69–70.

2. See for example: Walter Terry, revision of *Kaleidoscope, New York Herald Tribune,* 19 August 1956: 32; John Martin, revision of Prism, New York Times, 6 January 1956. Both reviews are in the collection of the New York Public Library for the Performing Arts, Dance Division. For an extended discussion of expression in modern dance see Mark Franko, *Dancing Modernism: Performing Politics,* (Bloomington: Indiana University Press, 1995). Franko, however, does not consider the work of Nikolais in his book.

3. John Martin, "The Dance: New Life," *New York Times,* 19 February 1956. See also by Martin: "Experiments in Grand Street," *New York Times,* 6 January 1956; "The Dance: Bright and Augury," *New York Times,* 26 February 1956.

4. Lois Balcom, "Alwin Nikolais' 'Totem,'" *Dance Observer,* March 1960: 40.

5. Beiswanger is quoted in Jack Anderson, "Alwin Nikolais, Versatile Pioneer of Modern Dance, Is Dead at 82," *New York Times,* 10 May 1993. The parameters of the debate represented here were consistent in Dance Panel deliberations about sending Nikolais and his company abroad under the aegis of the U.S. Department of State and President Eisenhower's Emergency Fund. See Naima Prevots, *Dance For Export: Cultural Diplomacy and the Cold War* (Middletown, CT: Wesleyan University Press, 1998); 58–60.

6. Kaschmann and Nikolais collaborated on *Eight-Column Line,* an evening-length piece set to a contemporary score by Ernst Krenek.

7. Murray Louis, "The Contemporary Dance Theater of Alwin Nikolais," *Dance Observer* January 1960: 6.

8. Louis, 6.

9. Nikolais, "The New Dimension of Dance," *Impulse*, 1959: 43.

10. Nikolais quoted in Joseph H. Mazo, *Prime Movers: The Makers of Modern Dance in America* (New York: Morrow, 1977), 232.

11. John Martin, "The Dance: New Life."

12. David Vaughan, *Merce Cunningham: Fifty Years* (New York: Aperture, 1997), 58. Vaughan documents that Cunningham and John Cage began using what they called "chance operations" in 1951 in their collaboration on *Sixteen Dances for Soloist and Company of Three.*

13. Paul Taylor, *Private Domain* (New York: Alfred A. Knopf, 1987), 75–81. Taylor writes about his first experimentation with posture with respect to *7 New Dances.* As he recalls: ". . . I decide to start over from scratch. Some kind of building blocks were needed, some clearly defined ABCs that could be ordered into a structure that would be antipersonality, unpsychological (no Greek goddesses), would achieve a specific effect (no Merce dice decisions), and would be style free from the cobwebs of time (no ballet). So it is easy enough to know what not to do, and since it seems unlikely to find a solution in other people's work, I go out and look around in the streets" (76).

14. Jack Anderson, "The Paradoxes of James Waring," *Dance Magazine*, November 1968: 64–67, 90–91. See also: Lisa Wroble, "James Waring," *International Dictionary of Modern Dance*, Taryn Benbow Pfalzgraf, ed. (New York: St. James Press, 1998), 809–811.

15. Franko, 75.

16. Franko, 77.

17. Nikolais, "The New Dimension of Dance," 43.

18. Nikolais makes this distinction in Elinor Rogosin, *The Dance Makers: Conversations with American Choreographers* (New York: Walker and Company, 1980), 82. Here he explains, "The character [in dance] should be created from the motional point of view; that's the dancer's job. . . . You will lose a lot of the sensitivity of your movement behaviorism if you take it from the actress's point of view."

19. Rogosin, 82.

20. All quotes from Martha Coleman, "On the Teaching of Choreography: Interview with Alwin Nikolais," *Dance Observer*, December 1950: 148.

21. Coleman, 148.

22. Mazo, 238.

23. Coleman, 148.

24. Mazo, 238.

25. Nikolais quoted by Jack Anderson, "Alwin Nikolais, Versatile Pioneer of

Modern Dance, Is Dead at 82," *New York Times*, 10 May 1993. For more on the Niko-lais' philosophy of dance see Selma Jeanne Cohen, Alwin Nikolais: No Man From Mars," *The Modern Dance: Seven Statements of Belief,* (Middletown, CT: Wesleyan University Press, 1965), 63–76; Mazo, *Prime Movers;* Marcia B. Siegel, ed. "Nik: A Documentary," *Dance Perspectives* 48, Winter 1971; Kathy Duncan, "Nikolais . . . ," *Village Voice,* 28 February 1977: 60; Deborah Jowitt, "Man, the Marvelous Mecha-nism, *Village Voice,* 19 October 1982: 83; Anna Kisselgoff, "In a Nikolais Work, There's Always Depth With the Dazzle," *New York Times,* 24 January 1993: 22.

26. Nikolais spoke about the art of choreography in scientific terms in "New Di-mensions of Dance," 43.

27. Rogosin, 85.

28. Sondra Horton Fraleigh, *Dance and the Lived Body: A Descriptive Aesthetics* (Pittsburgh: University of Pittsburgh Press, 1987), xvii.

29. Susan Sontag celebrates this move in her essay "Against Interpretation," in *Against Interpretation and Other Essays* (New York: Farrar, Straus & Giroux, 1966).

30. Caroline Jones, "Finishing School: John Cage and the Abstract Expression-ist Ego," *Critical Inquiry,* Summer 1993: 643.

31. Jones, 644.

32. Virgina Mecklenburg, "Advancing American Art: A Question of Style," *Ad-vancing American Art: Politics and Aesthetics in the State Department Exhibition, 1946–48* (Montgomery, AL: Museum of Fine Arts, 1984), 41. According to Mecklenburg, Davidson had "tacitly rejected a nativist philosophical slant that would probably ensured the project's success."

33. Many of the artists whose works were not selected for the show were mem-bers of the American Artists Professional League, an association of academic painters and illustrators. In 1947 this group filed a formal complaint to the secre-tary of state, George C. Marshall. For more see Margaret Lynn Ausfeld, "Circus Girl Arrested: A History of the Advancing American Art Collection, 1946–48," *Ad-vancing American Art,* 17.

34. "Debunking State Department Art," *New York Journal American,* 19 Novem-ber 1946.

35. Ausfeld, 11.

36. Ausfeld, 20.

37. See, for example, George Dondero, "Communist Art in Government Hospi-tals," *The Congressional Record,* Volume 95, Parts 2–3, February 21–April 9, 1949: 2317; "Modern Art Shackled to Communism," Ibid., August 31, 1949: 11584; "Communists Maneuver to Control Art in the United States," Ibid., March 25, 1949: 3233–3235, and "Communism in the Heart of American Art—What to Do About It, Ibid., Vol-ume 95, Parts 4–5, April 11–May 31, 1949: 6372–6375.

38. Jacob Javits, "Modern Art—A Response to a Colleague," *The Congressional*

Record, Volume 95, Parts 8–9, July 21–August 31, 1949: 12099. Also under this heading are a number of letters written in defense of modern art that Javits submitted for inclusion in The Congressional Record.

39. Howard Devree, "Modernism Under Fire," *New York Times*, 11 September 1949: 1.

40. Thomas C. Colt, letter written to Senator Wayne Morse, included in The Congressional Record, Volume 95, Parts 8–9, July 21–August 31, 1949: 12100.

41. Robert Motherwell and Ad Reinhardt, eds., Modern Artists in America (New York: Wittenborn Schultz, Inc., 1950), 9.

42. Motherwell and Reinhardt, 7.

43. Victor Navasky, *Naming Names* (New York: Viking Press, 1980).

44. Eva Cockcroft, "Abstract Expressionism: Weapon of the Cold War," *Artforum* June 1974: 39–41; William Hauptman, "The Suppression of Art in the McCarthy Decade," *Artforum* October 1973, 48–52; Jane de Hart Mathews, "Art and Politics in Cold War America," *American Historical Review*, October 1977, 762–787; Serge Guilbaut, "The New Adventures of the Avant-Garde in America," *October*, Winter 1980, 61–78; Max Kozloff, "American Painting During the Cold War," *Artforum*, May 1973, 43–54; David and Cecile Shapiro, "Abstract Expressionism: the Politics of Apolitical Painting." *Pollock and After: The Critical Debate*, Francis Frascina, ed. (New York: Harper and Row, 1985).

45. Motherwell and Reinhardt, 12.

46. Jonathan D. Katz, "John Cage's Queer Silence: Or, How to Avoid Making Matters Worse," *GLQ* 1999: 231–252.

47. Katz, 238. Jones, 628–665.

48. Jones quoting Michel Foucault, *History of Sexuality: An Introduction*, Robert Hurley, trans. (New York: 1978), 27.

49. Jones, 646.

50. Jonathan Katz, "Dismembership," in Amelia Jones and Andrew Stephenson, eds., *Performing the Body/ Performing the Text* (New York: Routledge, 1999), 177.

51. Susan Manning compares the full-body mask to the puppet and puppeteer in *Ecstasy and the Demon: Feminism and Nationalism in the Dances of Mary Wigman* (Berkeley: University of California Press, 1993), 71.

52. Julie Townsend, "Alchemic Visions and Technological Advances: Sexual Morphology in Loie Fuller's Dance," in Jane Desmond, ed., *Dancing Desires: Choreographing Sexualities On and Off the Stage* (Madison: University of Wisconsin Press, 2001), 77.

53. Townsend, 76.

54. Elaine Tyler May, *Homeward Bound: American Families in the Cold War Era* (New York: Basic Books, 1988); Lynn Spigel, *Make Room for TV: Television and the Family Ideal in Postwar America* (Chicago and London: University of Chicago Press, 1992).

55. Elaine Tyler May, *Homeward Bound*.

56. Michel Foucault, *Discipline and Punish: The Birth of the Prison*, Alan Sheridan, trans., (New York: Vintage Books, 1979) 182–183.

57. Foucault, 182–183.

58. Wini Breines, "The Other Fifties: Beats, Bad Girls, and Rock and Roll," *Young, White, and Miserable: Growing Up Female in the Fifties* (Boston: Beacon Press, 1992), 30.

59. Elizabeth Dunn, "What Is a Man?" *Newsweek*, June 1948: 64–65; George Lawton, "Proof that She Is the Stronger Sex," *New York Times Magazine*, 12 December 1948: 7+; Russell Lynes, "Is There a Lady in the House?" *Look*, 28 July 1958: 19+; Marybeth Weinstein, "Woman's Case for Women's Superiority," *New York Times Magazine*, 17 April 1955: 26–27; "Men are Weaker Sex," *Science Digest*, March 1950: 34; "Mind Your Wife and Live Longer," *Better Homes and Gardens*, November 1951: 122+; and "I'd Hate to Be a Man," *Coronet*, January 1955: 130–140.

60. Erving Goffman, *The Presentation of Self in Everyday Life* (New York: Anchor Books, 1959), 51.

61. Susan L. Foster, "Closet's Full of Dances: Modern Dance's Performance of Masculinity and Sexuality," *Dancing Desires*, 147–207.

62. Michel Foucault, *The History of Sexuality: An Introduction*, Vol. 1, Robert Hurley, trans. (New York: Random House, 1990), 48–49.

63. Peggy Phelan, *Unmarked: The Politics of Performance* (New York and London: Routledge, 1993), 26.

CHAPTER 7

Flights of Angels, Scattered Seeds

. . . .

HERBERT BLAU

I am not an Orthodox Jew, nor even very much reformed, since there was never any clear reverence to fall away from. If not by doctrine, then by some instinct of divided mind I recall—as I think about where the theatre will be fifteen, or fifty, years from now—Walter Benjamin's remark that "the Jews were prohibited from investigating the future." They are, however, instructed in *remembrance*, which strips the future of its magic. Perhaps the future has been prematurely given a bad name, stripped too caustically of its magic by certain prophetic Jews—if not the chiliastic Marx, the discontented Freud— although it is in the tradition of the prophets to understand that a look into the future is a remembrance of things to come, in the belabored nightmare from which we are trying to awaken, a salvaging of the spilled seeds of time, putting the best complexion on the forbidden.

What I want to do here, more or less at random (and maybe in the sere), is to pick up some of the seeds, as a reflex of speculation—not unlike the theatrework I've tried to do over the last dozen years, which so far as I can see, still remains to be done. In the *thought* of such a theatre the subject *is* the future, but with a particular consciousness about the *remainder,* in the doing *as* it's done, doing it over and over. It is a theatre of *reflexions* with the actor in the space between predication and the prediction, without resolving the difference between them, but entrusting it to the moment, as if the subject were the self. We've become accustomed in our time to structures of momentary thought, associative or additive, going over the same ground, serially, but aside from the (un)grounding, no promises that anything will add up. How? By what measure? And *who* would know? For isn't that the sticking point, the summary other (*what* audience?) of the recurring subject? In which thought becomes a *process* with no other evidence but itself—the Geiger counter in the Lacanian mirror? It is a silverless mirror with indeterminate frames

Herbert Blau's "Flights of Angels. Scattered Seeds" was originally published in *Blooded Thought: Occasions of Theatre* (Performing Arts Journal Publications, 1982). This is a revised version of the essay, used by permission of the author.

whose outside danger is solipsism. With the solipsist, as in outer space, time warps into the future, catching us from behind, disturbing the circadian rhythms, and the problem is where we came from, assuming we know where we are.

These are all questions *in* the future of the theatre, which may be read in the scattered seeds, and *represented* in the theatre of the future. The imminence of another orthodoxy is already in the scattering, and it's hard to imagine theatre activity of any importance that does not accept it as something like second nature, to which, naturally, there may develop an internal resistance, as there is in what I say. In the habit of the modern, the emphasis is on the process, but refusing to take for granted the perpetual present moment in which the future is *only* the subject, self-perceived, almost wholly specular fiction; which is to say, *theatre,* the sum of moments to be watched, which has been almost wantonly appropriated by not only the other arts but also the most seductive critical theory, as it tried to assume the character of a performance.

It should already be apparent that this is very circuitous thought, divided about the subject, but to the extent we are talking about theatre we are talking about *division*—here and now, now and then, body and thought, in the engendering of the subject, sex and substance, self and other (which in the mirror in infinitely divided), the future and its object—which, by narrowing the distance between art and life, may be a better theatre, but is always life and death. If the theatre has any future, it is in wanting to do away with it, the futures, theatre, and division, for that has always been *its* subject, the millennial desire, the "future in the instant," the undivided subject, in an incessancy of becoming act and being One, with the moment as its medium taking us where it will. We used to think of theatre as Faustian, but it's really the same subject even if laid back, chewing upon the seeds.

We can also pretend, of course, that the seeds are no longer there, only the scattering, like a memory trace on the mystic writing pad, which Freud used to explain the perceptual apparatus of the mind and the discontinuity in the currents of innervation from the unconscious, which may be "at the bottom of the origin of the concept of time." But as I think about the possibility, seeding the possibility, I do so with equivocal feelings about affiliated tendencies, in thought and performance: the addiction to process itself, the aleatory, the evasive habitudes of chance, disjuncture, and condensation, and the encyclicals of seriality that would otherwise, in the performance of thought, authorize a more elliptical procedure.

I

Say, rather, we are following in the wake (I wanted to say *dialectically*, but let it pass) of Benjamin's angel of history, drawn from Klee's *Angelus Novus*, moving away from something that, in the picture, he is "fixedly contemplating." As Benjamin reads the image his/its "face is turned to the past." Fifteen years? Fifty years? Assuming we endure them, these years are likely to make no essential difference whatever the apparencies of change, because of the sovereignty of the chance refusing the essential, as if the ancient forms of theatre in their incarnating myths have accurately recorded history in advance. Their angel is no fuzzy archetype from the *illud tempus* or occult fancy from the *Anima Mundi*. The angel is moving *in* history. Or *with* history. Yet the more we study the gaze the less sure we are in what direction he is moving, or whether it is he who is or we who are, the geography of the temporal being confounded: "Where we perceive a chain of events, he sees one single catastrophe which keeps piling wreckage upon wreckage and hurls it in front of his feet. The angel would like to stay, awaken the dead, and make whole what has been smashed. But a storm is blowing from Paradise; it has got caught in his wings with such violence that the angel can no longer close them. This storm irresistibly propels him into the future to which his back is turned, while the pile of debris before him grows skyward. This storm is what we call progress."[1]

II

In a period that seems to be advancing scandalously to its ruin, progress also has a bad name. So long already, it smells to high heaven. But now (as I write) as Madison Square Garden where, during the Democratic convention, the word is being used so liberally and with such unexpected sincerity—by Ted Kennedy or by Muriel Humphrey before the testimonial film about Hubert—that it is almost touching, like a lapse of history. Or the effect of photography itself, and film, with its power to elicit sentiments that are moving, memorial and—even when not merely documentary, in the most admirable state of the art—maybe meretricious, because of its insidious manipulations of time. The threat of the photograph was absorbed into the theatre in the foreground of *The Wild Duck*, as if to keep it away from time. But as with other perplexities of our age, we are now dealing with *quantity*, the exponential powers of swifter production, the inestimable forces of distribution, and the rabid critical publicity about the quality of photographic art.

III

The qualities of photography that are saturating the image-system—
annotating history with a nonexistent code—are not to be discounted in the
future of the theatre, another reproductive system, saturated with time, whose
credibility has been so undermined by the analogical plentitude of the other
that is has sometimes tried to behave, in recent years, as if it *weren't* theatre.
Or, in order to be more convincing, it has had to insist that more *work*—that
is, productive labor—go into the *making* of its images, the construction exposed, whereas in older realistic acting we didn't want the work to show, as
in the cinema, where what is exposed is not the construction, but, as they say,
the visible presence of the invisible. No wonder we've seen a generation of actors, who, in their psychophysical exercises, have learned to sweat. There is
also a sweat that comes with the invisible, as when you see a ghost, and the
body may be drenched with both, but with no way to work it off. It was a new
labor force that was uncertain about the future from the beginning, nurtured
through catastrophe in a cloud of unknowing, the wreckage in its memory
like a strip of film, no longer sure what images are supportable—nor where,
with any scale, they might be performed if they were made. That's what we
saw at the end of the sixties—after, at Chicago, they chanted, "The whole world
is watching!" and maybe it was, for the moment—in the breakdown of body
language, and the sweat became a strain without the amplitude of history.

IV

The alternative seems to be a public solitude (Stanislavski) without a public. Still, vigilant as we may be about what the course of history represents—
about the history of representation itself, with its illusions, one of which is
progress—it's hard to think about the future at all without the illusion of
progress sneaking in, if only as an isotope of relief over survival, as if the mere
fact that we've made it so far is an improvement. Or as if the different things
that happen are the things that really should, the capacity for distinction
blurring in the sheer abundance, as with photography—or solo and private
performances (an alternative to unemployment as well as repression)—so
that we don't know whether we're getting on with it or disappearing into the
profusion. I remember feeling something like this when, quite a few years
ago, I went over to the Henry Street Settlement and first encountered the
dance-theater of Alwin Nikolais, its unexpected bounty and magical gift of
abstraction, the puppetry and projections of that swiveling conceptual ex-

1. *From left, Murray Louis, Dorothy Vislocky, Beverly Schmidt, and Phyllis Lamhut in* Web *(1955). Chimera photograph courtesy of the Nikolais/Louis Foundation.*

cess, as if the tactile abundance were invested *avant la lettre* in what Jean Baudrillard was about to call "the superfetation of thought." In a period of minimalism that was also a period of conceptualism, but sometimes, as with Nikolais, in paradoxical profusion, it might have been authorized on theoretical grounds, as with the always surprising, structurally rich, effervescent provocations of *Tensile Involvement*, a swirling cat's cradle of spatial thought, to be perceived—with elastic strips joining the dancers ("involvement" hardly the word), as if they were one performer—by the impromptu stretch fabric of a susceptible mind. If there is an idea of progress there, it is sustained by lights, sounds, motion, noise (all of it subtly eccentric), the ecstatic and ekphrastic impasse of parabolic bodies, on which, as Nikolais once said, "non-literal dances are hung," in an articulated incessancy, knowingly indeterminate, of—to use a Beckettian phrase—"nowhere on." And so it was, too, in the swift liquidity of a piece I remember as *Lythic,* its unison not quite mythic, with steps you could hardly measure, the dancers on their toes, and if they were getting on with it, nowhere so, with a preinstinctual energy receding into the psyche— or (as if Freud were merely fantasy) whatever was there before it.

V

On the wincing anvil of a premonition: There is a pulsation of something like this—a progressive vanishing? or a vanishing progress?—in the "*fixed gaze*" of Beckett's Clov (who wants to be a solo performer, outside of history), resembling the *Angelus Novus,* something taking its course that he can't quite keep out, the long trail of repeatable catastrophe, two thousand years of western history like a propagating stalemate in his voice. "Finished it's finished, nearly finished, it must be nearly finished. (*Pause.*) Grain upon grain, one by one, and one day, there's a heap, a little heap." We might very well have been discouraged, but the heap is fabulous. I am not exaggerating, I am being very discrete. There is an anti-entropic nominalist signal (*Watt:* "No symbol where none intended") in the permutating stasis, with its simulacra of motion exquisitely denying change, or rather change denying motion. The heap is not quite the Smithsonian sublimity of the *Spiral Jetty* or *Amarillo Ramp,* but it is moving subliminally in a similar whorled and oxymoronic direction.

VI

The difference between the outburst of Beckett's Hamm—who wants to be a *whole* actor, playing all the roles—and most "conceptual" performances is that the latter have lost the high humanistic velocity of the seemingly static desire traveling over vast spaces of thought, which invented the *idea* of a future that, relinquished too much to the *moment,* we're now struggling to preserve by discontinuous structures that draw it out. The next fifteen years are likely to be, not always with Wilson's brilliance, a disjunct holding action.

VII

Once they called it Destiny and now we call it Structure. I don't mean they are the Same. For the kind of experience we have at any time depends upon the degree and quality of *resistance* to the moment, even when you think you're letting it be, and a sense of its *duration*, which determines the features we attribute to time, a river, a rosebud, a sediment, or a dream, a sparrow through the meadhall or a falling star, a figure with a wallet at its back or a blank check for a linguistic event, the kneejerk interval of a conception or a limitless metonymic space where, as a dance or a play of light or other impulses of behavior by human bodies or other objects, the A-series is reducible to the B-series since A-determinations can be performed in terms of B-relations between events, or vice versa . . .

VIII

Today we live, it seems, in a dispensation of moments or infinite profusion of instants that the weakening human presence of theatre can barely endure, yet with an avidity for the instants that we want to see imaged, out of some obsessional hunger for figuration that nobody understands. The demand is insatiate, as if we were suffering in a colloidal suspension of images from sensory deprivation. We call for a Theater of Images to keep up with the proliferations that not even the flashing and clicking ubiquity of photography can appease. The moments, the instants, the images, now and then in performance, as in the muscular eruptions or isolations of Nikolais' dancers, a digit, a leg, a torso, even if you can't quite see it, like the blink of an eye, it's nevertheless there like a heartbeat, which you have to take on faith, the instant's abstraction human, and maybe unforgettable, or remotely there in the mind. But when we pick up the camera again, and the click turns negative, there is something about its still-enshrouded photochemical processes piling up memories for the future like a loss of memory, which is the wrong kind of remembrance—the anecdotal accumulations of an information system storing up alms for oblivion, as if in dread of being forgotten. All those images, unregenerately *out of touch*. A double dream of *nature morte*, like the achievement of duration without desire.

IX

That is not the duration of theatre. But if all the world's becoming the stage, which was once a metaphor of the world, most of it is now on film, while the metaphor clings to the theatre, with its bodily mortgage of time. What we once saw in the forms on stage (like John Ashbery in Parmigianino in his own convex mirror) was a certain measure of ideality, there because we saw it, dreaming *what* we saw—until an emptiness is tangibly there whose meaning we cannot see, though we can't deny it *is* there—not by the meaning but the tangibility. Whatever it is we see is nourished by the dream of seeing, which is the reversed image of a desire to *be seen*, which—in the gluttony of our scopic drive—is almost being exhausted on film.

X

Louis Lumiere, whose claw-drive for the filmstrip gave the projective impetus to cinema, said about his own invention, "The cinematograph is an invention without a future." Historians of the cinema have condescended to the remark, which seems so naively far from the dominant reality of the cinematic apparatus, but it remains to be seen who has the last laugh. For it may be that the cinematograph has indeed come full circle, like most mechanical inventions, to the end of its progress—unless it once again comes to terms with theatre. We can already see that occurring in film theory, which scorned the theatre after Bazin. We can also see it in the performative clues of the most abstract films (without open evidence of dramatic narrative or actors). The enigmatic traces give the invisibility away by leaving, say, sprocket marks or a lock of hair upon the film, like that left by the filial stranger upon Agamemnon's tomb. After years of insistence upon the autonomy of the film. the antioedipal discourse of cinema seems not to be able to rid itself of theatre, whose death appears now as its most demonic illusion, or something like an interminable disease.

XI

I am speaking of the theatre in which (the oedipal) *filiation* is still the issue, and the enigma, the disease or villainy of which the drama has said much and I shall want to say more. The theatre of the future will certainly be affected by the labyrinthine outreach of the cinematic apparatus, as it has been in the no-win competition for audiences. It will also respond to whatever technology surrounds it, which may even change our ideas as to what constitutes an audience. The point is that we must conceive of technology now as something other than machines. The stress in social thought is on systems of communication, with mechanisms of production and distribution in the unconscious, a technology that is mirroring "epistemic codes" or the performance of "desiring-machines."

1.

For captions see "A Guide to Color Plates," page ix.

2.

3.

4.

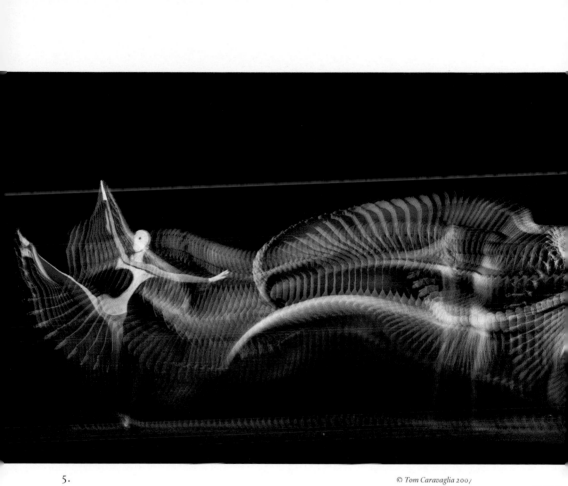

5.

6.

7.

8.

9.

10.

11.

12.

13.

14.

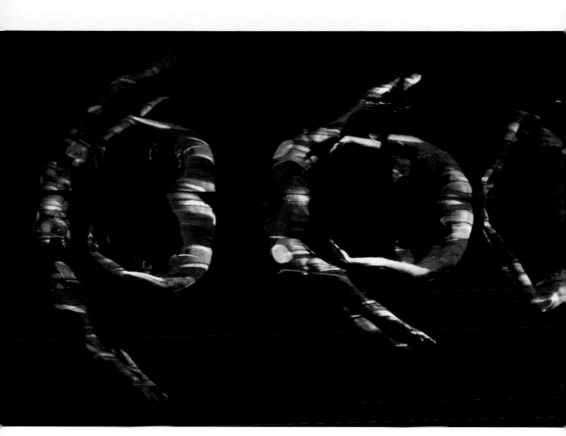

15.

16.

XII

In these processes, the industrialization of imagery by the movies, and by video, may be the controlling force, since there is a technological obsession with *recurrency*, the looping concatenation of fragments (splicing, cutting superimpositions), a new allegorical neurosis of recycling, feedback, bio-degradability ("loop gains" and "returnratios" mimicking, efferently, the proprioceptive signals of the body and the central regulatory programs of the species), a whole new repertoire of replicative strategies that will have to be reassessed (and is being reassessed) by social theorists, because they are, ironically, strategies of *accumulation*, like a shadow play of the old disreputable system—the computer terminals disconnected before they are installed in every home, because the metaphor of an uninterrupted series, the dream of repetitive sequences of ceaseless differences and timeless moments, the systematic disjunctures of a spatiotemporal experience with no apparent organic limit of magnitude has turned out to be (like the "geometric grammaticality" of Sol LeWitt's cities of cubes and the ontological hysteria of Richard Foreman) a systematic variant of uninterrupted illusion, like the society of overabundance and no scarcity that preceded it and encountered, in the syntagmatic chain of events, a broken-down economy, stagflation, and the paratactically rising expectations of OPEC, whose member countries not only have the oil but an organic corner, to end this period, on the tradition of the arabesque.

XIII

We used to believe that theater reflects society. If it remains to any extent a public form, holding the (split) mirror up to nature, then we will expect experimentation in the theatre to keep pace somehow, in whatever subterranean ways, with the more activist projections of a post-industrial world. Theory and fantasy conspire in a promise of recombinant wonders through the displacement of labor into information, instantly transmitted by satellite, the terminals at every elbow, in a cybernetic transfer of the dematerialized body of thought. As for the body itself, there is the incalculable cracking of the genetic code and a new genesis by implantation. We are asked, as with abortion, to think through the right to life as we haven't really done since the reported death of tragedy. These will also be space laboratories that can achieve in surgery, at zero gravity, another fusion of fragments impossible on earth, medical miracles of levitation, a transcendent healing of the dismembered body, as if there we'll finally have the shamanism at which the theatre has been pretending, with the dull substance of its flesh, shoes left at the door, its unfortunate feet on the ground. (Mircea Eliade, by the way, disturbed by the percussive presumptions, called it "family shamanism.")

XIV

When we imagine theatre on other planets, we are not really imagining a future (no less with extraterrestrial intelligence) but indemnifying the past, whose "secret heliotropism" is always at work—as Benjamin says in a Blakean image—like the flower turning itself to the sun, in the unenvying present, which doesn't want a future, only itself.

XV

Thus, coming back to earth, like Gravity's Rainbow . . .

XVI

The actuality is, for the time being, not what the future planners are predicting. Not yet, not probably for the fifty-year limit of our ruminations. What we are more likely to see is another holding actions, the revitalization of heavy industry that, through a long period of overweening consumption and improvident underinvestment, left us holding the bag from which, in the energy crisis, the seeds were running out. The theatre had been predicting that crisis with almost hysterical energy through the history of modernism, as Woyzeck's running razor, like Occam's gone berserk, widened into Wedekind's Jack the Ripper, and the tower that Solness built had, in the hallucinations of Strindberg, a crack in the chimney before the oneiric remembrance of the petrifying fall—and what else are we talking about in the amortizing paralytics of Beckett, the bag in the mud of Comment c'est?, which is why I have been returning to him as the locus classicus of the problematic of the future.

XVII

With a more direct experience of the scattering on impact, after the Blitz and the Bomb, Germany and Japan had the almost ontological advantage of beginning over again, building fuel-efficient factories along with higher-mileage cars, and now, with a cultural gift for miniaturization, Japan apparently has better superconductors for the cybernetic universe when it finally establishes its dominion. Over the overseeable future, and despite the necessity for going solar or nuclear or both, we are still likely to be digging for coal—and in a world of images, that image is still germane to the future of the theatre, with the rumor of its long ascent from the underground and, like Freud, like Kafka, its history of excavations. *Comment c'est?* Whether beginning or ending (and picking up the pun), it seems to be in language or, as they say semiotically, in the language systems. In the post mortems of the anti-verbal sixties (which are being recycled in critical theory), we have had some strip mining—as in the language games of minimalism and conceptual art—but insufficient explorations of the geological strata of our fossiliferous words.

XVIII

Whether or not the words acquire the luster they once had, the strategies of theatre over the next fifteen years will be conceived after the spacious model of *language*. Whatever the linchpin with the body, the body cannot think of the future, as only language does. Only language has the amplitude we long for, and the indeterminacy, in its precisions. If there is also an accrual of the fabulous around the nominalism, a mythicizing of the model, that may be because whatever there was in the beginning, with or without the Word, there is still the theoretical suspicion that there would be no theatre without it, no future, and no theory. The etymological linchpin between theatre and theory is in the place and act of watching, that is, *speculation*, even before the words were sounded, as with the basilisk in the garden reading the situation, that smooth talker, *hypocrite lecteur*—the first actor?

XIX

If the quickest eye is in the mind, and words as swift as thought, the quick objects of the mind are not, in the gross actual world, as moveable as thought. So with the more superconducting cybernetic illusions. Post-industrialization, with its pure brain theory realized in silicon chips, will probably have to wait on reindustrialization (hopefully not as dull as the Democrats, with their long commitment to the unions, make it sound), blue-collar workers with old-fashioned muscle-power. And nothing is better suited to reflect that than the theatre, with its long tradition of manual labor and new vocabulary of ideographic sweat. There were always those who felt something like that: Craig, who wanted his puppets, and Duse, who wanted to kill all the actors and start

2a (above) *Murray Louis in* Prism *(1957). 2b* (right) *Herbert Blau in* Prism *(1957).*
Photographs David S. Berlin, courtesy of Nikolais/Louis Foundation.

over, and even later in dance, the critique of Nikolais, where the dancer's egos were coeval with projections upon their bodies and the sovereign art of motion might be part of an ensemble, not merely with other dancers, but with dripping water, jackhammers, mirrors, automobile parts, puppets too, of course, as well as tape recorders and Oriental instruments, then with film and the Moog synthesizer, the dancer's body one of the elements in the orchestration of multimedia. As for Brecht—wanting only to restrain the actors, not intending to minimize the human presence—he nevertheless gave us, in our time, the cue for more distrust, warning us about the emotion, which implied a future that is *overdetermined,* and therefore, in its fated cadence, unsusceptible to change.

Flights of Angels, Scattered Seeds : 119

XX

The sculptor Richard Serra has given us, however, a suggestive image of post-modern reconversion of heavy industry—long past the early modern romance of the machine or the facile new deconstructing parodies—in his film of a railroad turnbridge, where the graceful architectural swivel of the track is no mere exercise in perception like, for instance, his own earlier film *Frame* (1969). (The development is taken farther in the documentary about the forging of his seventy-ton cube in a German steel mill, which included interviews with the workers whose relationship to the oppressiveness of their work is not changed by the presence of sculpture, through they are quite able to perceive that it's "a work of art to bend a shaft, to forge it nicely.") Whatever the film does for the dialogue of art history out of which so much art, and performance, is being made, it also reminds us, like Serra's precariously leaning lead plates, of what in the predictable future we are most likely to be living with, without the relief of an easy condescension to replace the lapsed nostalgia.

XXI

It's been a while since theatre has been in such a business—at least in this country, and not in the grandiose ascetic spirit of Artaud's "No More Masterpieces." If Artaud wasn't thinking of monuments, he was certainly thinking of ruins. It was never a question of scale. One of our theatre's problems, that of scale, is that nobody is going to underwrite anything like those lead plates of Serra, no less a seventy-ton steel cube. It wasn't quite the same when in the cultural explosion of the fifties, the fringe benefits of a permanent war economy put up a number of buildings for regional theatres whose stability is still either too uncertain or too incurably mediocre to even think of such a problem. When we think of scale in American theatre today, we might remember that Lee Breuer has taken over a football field or that Robert Wilson has received financing for the magnitude of his projects, once at Persepolis, once at the Met; but if his gift is idiosyncratic, it is also remarkably entrepreneurial, and the subsidy is now mostly from Germany, where magnitude has been the mode and the problem is scaling down—the most experimental directors worrying along revived Marcusean lines about preemptive tolerance in the large state theatres that support their work. Here—with funds dwindling and the touring circuit narrowing with the budgets—some of our more experimental directors are probably quite ready, like Morris with Kennecott Bingham, to go into business, if not with Broadway, then with the regional theatres, covering up the vacancies, if they can ever really afford it. I don't think much of this will really be happening, not on anything like the German scale, in the next fifteen years. Earthworks, like performance art, which came out of the desire to outflank the gallery system, were reappropriated by that system, whose possibilities of lucrative patronage are not yet available even for the best practitioners in the experimental theatre. Nor can the disappearing continuity of companies be mapped and photographed, like Christo's running fences, for sale, when it is no longer there.

XXII

But leaving the almost unreclaimable landscape to the longer dimensions of time—when it may be, according to some future thinkers, impossible to distinguish between technological and biological forms—let us return to the large-scale felicities of Serra's film. For us in the theatre, it is interesting because it allows itself what Serra does not allow in his sculpture, whose massive minimalism still refuses representation (which doesn't mean it can be successfully refused). While the sculpture is allied to theatre by its physicality in space, the film is closer to theatre through the play of analogy, its trafficking with appearance; the duplicitous substance of theatre, still, however, keeps it at a distance, because it is focused on the outside world, the bridge, a social artifact whose designation as such is never formally obscured in the site specificity of its perceptual transformations. As a reflection on technology, theatre shares the circular momentum, from the turn of the bridge to outer space, of Wilson's *Einstein on the Beach*, but is without the autistic surrealist patina. Nor does it have, in the social impulse that led (somewhat accidentally) to *Steelmill*, anything like the cultish politicism of Joseph Beuys, with its invented aura of a personal myth of origins. It is nominalist, with scale, not asocial, neither anachronizing nor derogating its materials—and I should like to see more of it in the theatre.

XXIII

With the caveats about a technology registered in the computer but waiting their turn, we should also remember that there is a sense in which there is no such thing as *innovation* in the theatre (after the second actor, and the third) except at the level of *external* technology, starting with the mask and costume, musical instruments (as both sound and scenic utensils), some other

semblance of scenery, periaktoi, or eccyclema, properties, the startling ob-
trusion of a curtain (possibly the major innovation in theatre history), and
then the mechanisms for changing the stage or moving the platforms or super-
imposing light or, now, electronically turning the tables or mixing the media.
But it's apparent that none of these things are *in themselves* of the essence or,
if so, as historical moments that may be—as by withdrawing the curtain and
letting it drop again, or cutting it in half—recapitulated. And whenever we
find ourselves redefining the theatre or projecting its future, if the mechanisms get in the way we will get rid of the mechanisms, in favor of the naked
stage or the poor theatre with the naked actor, which are now—like shifting
the theatre back to the landscape—also historical moments.

XXIV

Recapitulating: To the degree that we began to suspect that the drama, like
the dematerialized technology, was a mechanism of power, a duplicitous structure of appearances, we tried to get rid of the drama, about whose true nature
we have been arguing since Aristotle—though the argument about the theatre went back to the immaterial presences in Plato's cave.

XXV

Actually, the theatre can only sustain itself so long in either direction, with
too much drama (melodrama) or without it (plot exposed, banished, or scattered), *as spectacle,* whether with the mechanical technology or the naked
actor, depending on the speculation in the spectacle, and the quality of its
voyeurism, the power of its specular obsessions—as if Aristotle, who seems
far afield from the indeterminacy in the eye of the beholder and the contemporary breakdown of the conceptual categories, had anticipated it all, including film, when he wrote in *De Anima* that "the activity of the sensible object
and that of the percipient sense is one and the same activity."

XXVI

To the degree that the theatre's future is bound up with developments in
technology, it will not have evacuated itself of the idea of progress, which has
been its subject matter through the history of the avant-garde. The belief in
radical change on a progressive axis is always contradicted, however, by the
equally radical regressions of the avant-garde, essentially reactionary, but it is

doubly so in the theatre, because of the inherently skeptical nature of the form. Why skeptical? What else can it be, fastened as it is to a dying animal, the mystery of whose self-consciously absurd persistence never leaves the stage, even if the stage is scattered like, today, the belief in a continuous self, and the animal is no longer there? If the mystery is not there, whatever else it may be, it will not be theatre. Yet we live in a period of demystifications, severely distrustful of theatre—source of the self's illusions and the illusory self—and given to *theatricality* as a means of disarticulating the mystery (the "that" within "that passeth show"), whose origins are dubious, ghostly, and whose end is never in sight, though you can feel it coming, thereby obscuring the moment by arousing false desire.

XXVII

Which is always desiring desire, the memory of (an illusory?) gratification that can never be appeased, the future always denying the instant. In recent years, we have had performance events that have tried to preserve the integrity of the instant by minimizing or cooling down desire, which is presumably tricked into being by ideology, which is what the mystery is really about. The egocentric actor doing his part didn't always know it, and thus became its corrupted and corrupting agent. (I suppose that's why they were cautious about introducing more than one actor: one ego was enough.)

XXVIII

In trying to *construct* a future with no ontological mystification, we have sometimes tried to forget that in some time-warped corner of remembrance there may still be something interminably waiting (*in* the technology but *not* the technology) to trammel up the consequence. The kind of theatre we may do in the future depends upon just how illusory we think that is. Or how afraid of it we are, assenting or denying, so that we develop our own mechanisms in self-defense, which also resemble theatre structures (Acconci, Anderson) or theater structures resembling happenings that, in "the aesthetic semantics of the event itself" (Nikolais), are forms of musicality, seemingly impersonal, but not without anxiety for all their magical panorama. For want of certain knowledge about the remembrance, the emphasis has been in the theatre and other performance events upon the clarifying task or structure, with more or less psychic content, sometimes expressionist and autobiographical, more or less desperate (Gray, Montano), in more or less "real-time"—but

3. Images projected onto the dancers' bodies in Scenario *(1971). Photograph. P. Berthelot, courtesy of the Nikolais/Louis Foundation.*

equivocating between *presentness* (as in the presentness of the past) and, whether cooled down or heated up, a desire for *presence* with no illusions. And we want it right *now*, undisguised, though it always seems to be putting us off.

XXIX

"Who, if I cried," said Rilke in the first elegy, "would hear me among the angelic orders?" If we remember correctly (and the classical anthropologists, through all rationalistic error, touched some nerve end of origins), the theatre was born of such a cry taking its chances. Over the last fifteen years, along with the toning down of desire in some of our art, there was a compulsion of *innateness*, evangelized by Artaud and methodized by Grotowski, to experiment with the birthright and raise the cry again. If there is one tendency of the post-modern to thwart disguise by keeping it all on the surface, there is another wanting to scourge it by having it all out, confessionally, palpably, to the point of exhaustion, ripping through the vocal chords to the source of the Utterance, if only in theory now, the gristled and muzzling "*writing aloud*" (Barthes) of the carnal actor of Artaud, the stereophony of an avenging angel, bereft, outscreaming the paradisal wind.

XXX

That was not the case with the primal scream. It was quickly exhausted. So were the hieratic incantations, which all sounded so much alike, like the answers that come before the question. The cry has since diminished in its intensity, subsiding from Persepolis into the murmurs of history, paratheatrical solemnities in the forest, the network of underground or solo performances, and the infatuations of theatricality in everyday life that seem to make theatre redundant, and it may not be getting through the noise. And the angels may be tired of listening, and the orders no longer there, and the metatheatrical tendency of the post modern is to ignore it (with inflections of pain, sometimes exorbitant, or with "minimalist reduction"—which doesn't mean it doesn't hurt—in body art), playing with the arbitrariness of the signifiers in the insufferable debris.

XXXI

Blown about the wreckage, we return to the *bricolage*. In the systems of estrangement, we strain to read the signs. In the prophetic soul of the wide world dreaming on things to come, it is important to remember that whatever experiment is currently going on in the theatre is still playing out the consequences of an intimidating history—all the more so because of an increasing *theoretical* emphasis in the arts and other disciplines on radical discontinuity, epistemologically taking for granted "the universe of discourse," what the scientists are cosmologically debating about the universe of quasars and charmed quarks. It is a debate that hasn't come to any conclusion since Einstein remarked about Heisenberg's principle of indeterminacy, that God doesn't play dice with the cosmos. For want of any conclusiveness in the cosmos, the ethos of discontinuity, which is a refusal of the inseminating Word, is a perhaps necessary counterfiction to the falsifying cadence of an illusory coherence. But it is something other that what Wallace Stevens meant by the Necessary Angel—an imagination pressing back against the pressure of the real, mastery of the words in a world made (so far as we know) out of words, which have returned to the theatre, but with nothing like the stature they had, and surrounded by critical subversions of the Authorizing Text. If we listen to the theory, the Text is rubble of the wreckage, a catastrophe in itself.

XXXII

Nor is it the first vision we've had of the death of theatre in the terminal revolution, or the birth of theatre in the ecstasy of carnage. And of course there's a difference between saying it and doing it, and in any case, "*Ophelia remains on stage, motionless in her white wrappings,*" and through Müller is male and East German and fighting personal battles through the maimed figure of the woman, *using* her again for his own political purposes, as she was used in the Old Plot. The actor-who-plays-Hamlet destroys the portraits of Marx, Lenin, and Mao with the poleax of the Father, after being instructed with all the Author's self-contempt to tear up the photograph of the Author, who is trying to find *his* way honorably into the future behind the hideous Wall, by surrendering his identity, and his text, to a process on the other side of history; which is to say, in the unconscious, the staging place of the permanent revolution, which does not represent time, identity, or death. As long as we're on that other stage, however, on the other side of the Wall . . .

XXXIII

The trouble with the theatre is that, if the actor is *there* (and we are seeing theatre without actors), too much artfulness is required—as concealment or unconcealment—to mediate the problem with Electra, who is speaking for the victims of illusion that cry out for no more theatre. The theatre has taken the cry to heart, but what can it do but theatre? Whether theatre is a phantom of ideology (Marx) or ideology a phantom of theatre (Bacon), the theatre is in an ideological double bind—which may be what it is to *be* theatre, and I suspect we'll see more of that. I mean more thinking about it in the theatre over the next fifteen years. Even when the theatre is being candid about its theatricality, it always seems fake. That's the problem—we saw it in Brecht, the actor is always pretending, even when he's pretending he's not. The purer appearances of film seem realer, because the actor isn't there, only his image, whereas in the theatre the actor is there *with* his image, like the "unperfect actor on the stage," in the other sonnet, "Who with his fear is *put besides* his part. . . . " The emphasis is mine, and it is a very strange ontological problem. Even Shakespeare didn't understand it, though he knew enough to make it the center of his theatre, which is why he remains even now, despite Brecht's critique and subsequent deconstructions, close to our best intuitions of what the theatre *is*.

XXXIV

If the actor isn't there in the theatre, we seem to be evading the problem, and the theatre seems a little anemic. The more arduous theatre of the future—I mean a theatre equal to our love of the truth we can no longer believe in or adequately embody in any gender that we yet know, that is, *the truth of the actor*—will come, I think, out of the other end of this theoretical dilemma. I wish I could be confident that it will only take fifty years. Nietzsche thought, starting about twice fifty years ago, that "this is the great spectacle in a hundred acts reserved for the next two centuries in Europe—the most terrible, the most questionable, and perhaps also the most helpful of all spectacles." We used to do things faster in America, so perhaps we're nearing a solution, though I doubt it (or fear it), but here's how he puts the theatrical issue, not sure that he has an audience: "What meaning would *our* whole being possess if it were not this, that in us the will to truth becomes conscious of itself as a *problem?*"

XXXV

After more than half a century of intensely self-conscious theatre, theatre about theatre, its discourse and modes of production, the whole illusory apparatus of deception, it would seem we've played through all the phallocratic horns of the dilemma. But there is still the double bind (propounded by Pirandello and doubled over by Genet), and my impression is that we have only played around with it in recent years, as conundrum, parody, concept, more or less polysemous, in successive etiolations of the play-within-the play, forgetting that the play is not only *within*, innate, but within *the play*—with the inevitable trivialization, in the autonomy of play, of the *idea* of play itself.

XXXVI

As a result, the actor—at precisely the time he has been liberated from the realistic constraints that are more endemic to the cinema, and from servitude to the Director, the Playwright, and the authoritarian Text—finds himself, with a more limber body and a new ideographic expressiveness, not really knowing what there is to say, as in the vapidity of the recent *Rearrangements*, where charter members of the Open Theater seemed to be rehearsing pallid and spastic versions of themselves up to their old games, with a sort of bittersweet schmaltziness they would have once derided in the Actor's Studio, as if in disavowing the self-indulgent Method, the method of physical actions were playing the superobjective backwards. Even with more time on stage, in self-determining structures, there is now a peculiar sensation that our actors have a somewhat diminished function, less to do than it first seemed when they were released from the old script—not unlike what instrumental musicians experienced (actors never had their training) with the emergence of atonal music, a sense of virtuosity wasted (when they did get some training) in an excess of what was required.

XXXVII

There are nowadays new performers, like Stuart Sherman and John Zorn, who have created personal scores independent of the old notion of a text. And this has been a period of performance art—in theatre and the galleries and other sites—where along with the emphasis on highly trained *performers* (the word has been preferred to *actor*) we have also cultivated the amateur and developed events for participants without professional skills. Over the next fifteen years we will continue to see performance pieces with nonactors, or without actors, in a staging of (unpejoratively intended) bloodless objects seeking a subject, as the characters once sought the Author. He was actually still very much there at the time, on the periphery, before he was drummed out of the theatre by the dissidence of the sixties, which thought it was distributing power, and dismembered ever since by the sparagmos of theory, which is subliminally running the show, or holding it in escrow until "the closure of representation" (Derrida on Artaud).

XXXVIII

And so, all over the world, whatever the forms of desire, the figure in the carpet is worn. As the current story goes, it has faded like origins into the sometimes barely perceptible, undiachronic but not unsystematic inflexions of indeterminacy in everyday life, where the self has been dissociating itself as theatre. Or, with various degrees of anxiety and mastery, resisting the pressures of the real, into the suspensions, conspiracies, or final solutions of silence. But while there has been a lot of high-powered propaganda about the disappearance of the ego-centered self, along with the humanistic image of man, the figure in the carpet is obdurate, if not decipherable, and at least surreptitiously there. The issues of authorship and the authority of the Text are caught up in the threads, like Agamemnon in the polymorphous net. Almost all controversy over what the theatre should be has to do—from the cavity of Plato's iridescent thought to any conceivable future without mimesis—with the propriety of its lingering presence. Of the most consequential theatre that will be, at conscious and subliminal levels, the unavoidable subject—as if corresponding to the reemergence of the Middle East, where the carpet was first woven and the theatre seems to have been born.

XXXIX

Meanwhile, we permutate the hybrids. In an age of systematic hybridization, that's mostly what we'll continue to do through the next generation and into the next century, whether in the spectacular, or somnambulant, dimensions of opera, or the slapstick disjunctures of movielike collage, doubly missing the media, or in underground or solo performances by troupes of communitarian anarchists or actors like stand-up comedians with nothing but themselves on stage, or with talismanic personal objects hermetically arrayed in lofts, living rooms, factories, sidewalks (the quality of the politics in the streets depending on the stage of industrialization of the political setting), or in feminist collectives, or with suggestions of terrorism, or in summoning up defunct myths in abandoned gas stations, with masks and puppets, like a palimpsest of all these, oneirically at the edge of the sea.

XL

The subject of the theatre, as I have written elsewhere, is not only the illusion of a future but also the future of illusion, which is still blowing through history in the paradisal gaze. Outside the normal precincts of theatre, in the minimalist proclivities of performance art, the objective was to put the questions of illusion up front, settling it once and for all, on the *surface*—which even without actors, turned out to be a very porous mass. With actors, or in body art, the surface bleeds into itself as in Kafka's penal colony, skin scraped by metaphysics, or retreats into the unconscious, where all the wreckage has settled, a Möbius-strip topography of ruinations that refuses to be leveled out. As for the ecstatic extremities of Artuad's vision—the actor like an angel signaling through the flames—they have largely tapered off in practice, while being, as I've suggested, hypostatized in theory. The sonorous body of his own forked thought is inscribed upon our brains, however, and the prospect of a theatre as a ruthless physiology of signs matches Marx's ruthless critique of everything existing, with the illusion of its being nakedly attainable, like the memory of a second Creation. The legacy of the alchemical vision, with its unremitting desire to pulverize all the mediating signs, still seems to be impelling Grotowski, but, after his visit to America, as if by way of Esalen into a kind of Gothic Gestalt. His paratheatrical activity since *Holiday* is sure to be emulated in this country in the ever-recurring novelty of a congenital primitivism, which would dematerialize the last remaining distances between art and life.

XLI

What we will see, I think, in the next half century, is an intricate distancing of that desire, a playing out of the refusal in the contradiction and the contradiction of the refusal, arrested at each end by our new awareness of the possible forms of play, which is never gratuitous: mimetic and methetic, frank artifice and utter naturalism, inner and outer, announced play and disguised pretense, surface and depth, alienation and empathy, the secret *and* its exposure, not merely as oscillations as by *infiltrations*. What we are coming to realize—with resistances that are human and ideological, and no doubt unable to be eliminated—is that *all of these are appearances of the other*, erasures, allusions, perturbations, corrections, misprisions, overlays, reversals, and provisional end stops. All of them will lead, when pressed to the utmost logic of the most illusory desire, around the not-quite-synchronous edges of the metamorphic circle—the actor looking at himself or being looked at, looking at herself looking, in a new consciousness, labile and feminine but not unpatriarchal, of the available spectrum of acting (if not action), playing off the incremental concepts of person-self role/subject/character/persona/mask, with no impediment between the improvisational and the analytical, between doing it and thinking it. We have learned after years of understated method that to act less is sometimes to act more, more or less, depending on where you are in history, the future in the seed.

XLII

The acting will appear self-reflective or presentational, decentered or umbilical, at a hallucinatory distance or clinically close up, as a subjective drama of presence, or an objectifying narrative in the second or third person that is absorbed before you know it in the hallucinatory stream. Or there will be purported event irrespective of person, through concrete tasks or hypothetical objectives, with the promissory insistence that there are no strings attached. But there will be the recension of a lot of writing between the lines that will, probably, be spoken more and more, in the exposures of ideology, *as images,* denying the exposure, each playing off the other in a calculus of perceptions, shadows, double projections, intimations of prospective behavior, playing with identity or identifying the prospect of play, since the one thing that can no longer be the same is the pretense that there is only the one way—though if we'd followed the angel of history through the backward movement of time, studying the theatre's changes, we would have known it was only a pretense and that, in order to liberate the theatre in the future, we may have to arbitrarily pretend again.

XLIII

Today we are pretending, some of us, that we can do away with illusion, and thus with the substance of theatre, even while we are pretending that performance is the means. It is a remarkable proposition in its most strenuous theoretical form. I think it is the most interesting proposition about theatre. There is, however, a self-evident logic that the assault on representation would undermine, that says the theatre's future is in *remaining theatre,* and making the most of that illusion. But to know what it is to want the remainder, you have to approach the illusory edge where it hardly seems to matter, the most duplicitous moment of all. When the theatre looks to the future, it always comes back to that. There may be more desirable states of being than that obscured by the duplicity, but in imitating nature—as the theatre irreparably does—the theatre is the illusion of what appears to be left of life.

NOTE
Walter Benjamin, "Theses on the Philosophy of History," *Illuminations* (New York: Schocken, 1969), 257–258.

CHAPTER 8

The Music of Alwin Nikolais

. . . .

A PROVISIONAL STUDY

BOB GILMORE

By the time of his death in 1993 Alwin Nikolais was an internationally re-
nowned choreographer of considerable distinction. His impact on modern
dance was pervasive, the magnitude of his accomplishment incontestable.
Lauded and honored in the United States and Europe, his place in dance history was a matter of record. Amid all the critical commentary, one peculiar-
ity of Nikolais' work rarely failed to attract comment: that Nikolais was much
more than simply a choreographer. The *Encyclopedia Britannica* describes him
as an "American choreographer, composer, and designer," whereas his long-
time associate and collaborator Murray Louis has characterized Nikolais, with
perhaps a little affectionate exaggeration, as "the father of mixed media."[1]
Nikolais' early training was in scenic design, acting, puppetry, and music
(performance and composition); far from abandoning these pursuits once
dance became the center of his activities, he continually sought ways to en-
fold them into his practice.

Of all his parallel lives, the one to which Nikolais devoted most time and
effort—besides choreography—was music. Beginning with *Masks, Props, and
Mobiles,* premiered at the Henry Street Playhouse in New York in January
1953, Nikolais played the leading role in composing, selecting, and editing
the "sound scores" of the majority of the eighty or so choreographic works he
created in the remainder of his lifetime. Purely in terms of the time he spent
composing, listening to, and selecting from other people's music, improvising (on piano, percussion, and, later, synthesizers), coaching musicians (including the Playhouse's own percussion group and the tape engineers and
studio technicians who worked on many of his productions in the 1950s and
beyond), and preparing the finished master tapes for his performances, the
degree and intensity of Nikolais' absorption in music could hardly be clearer.

And yet to date, music has received short shrift in the writings on Nikolais. There remains no substantial article devoted to this aspect of his work, a
situation that seems in need of correction given the importance this endeavor
clearly held for the choreographer. There are a few useful sources: an article
by Nikolais himself published in the magazine *Dance Perspectives* in 1963; the

worthwhile, if brief, liner notes by Murray Louis for the CD of Nikolais' music released by CRI in New York in 1993; and a valuable e-mail discussion string triggered largely by reminiscences from Nikolais' associate Ruth Grauert, posted on the Internet in 2002. For the most part, however, discussion of Nikolais' music has been largely confined to reviews, press releases, and the published recollections of those who worked with him. If the music itself was insubstantial or lacking in interest, then the absence of commentary could easily be explained away. On the contrary, Nikolais' music, while hardly meriting the same sort of posterity as his choreographic achievement, is of much more than passing interest. For one thing, his choreographic work would have taken very different forms without it.

For the musicologist, Nikolais' sound scores pose some fascinating challenges: they are preserved today as recordings (Nikolais notated very little of his music) and therefore require more imaginative approaches than the conventional methods of musical analysis; his collaborative practice in working with other musicians raises fascinating, if complex, issues of authorship and of individual versus collective creation; the need to shape his music to the dictates of dancers (and his own choreographic imagination) raises questions about the primacy of one imaginative faculty (choreographic) over another (musical). Then there is the knotty issue of Nikolais' use—or some would say, appropriation—of other people's music and related questions of attribution and fair use, given that this fugitive material was then integrated into a sound score that often had only one name attached to it: Nikolais' own.

The present article is subtitled "a provisional study" because a good deal of further work needs to be done on Nikolais' oeuvre before all the questions about his creative practice can be adequately answered. Because of the way Nikolais created dance as well as music, there are probably some things that will never be known, or known in detail, about his working methods. Although I have tried to be scrupulous about the research data presented here and my various extrapolations from it, this first extended study of Nikolais' music is necessarily provisional to some extent. Nonetheless I have tried to present an overview of what we presently know about an under-documented subject: Alwin Nikolais the musician.

Nikolais learned the piano as a child at the insistence of his German mother, who herself had no particular musical aptitude but believed in the importance of such an education for her children. He became a competent pianist and organist. Among the first uses he found for these abilities was as a pianist in silent movie houses in Westport, Connecticut, and other locations. This particular practice—selecting and improvising music as accompaniment to moving images—is, of course, uncannily prophetic of the use to which Nikolais would put his musical talents in the work for which he is now remembered. His interest in dance was stimulated initially by attending, in his early thirties, a performance by the German dance artist Mary Wigman. He was impressed both by the qualities of the dance and by the fact that the performance made use of percussion music, a new sonority in early 1930s America, and one that caught the youthful Nikolais' ear: it is very unlikely he had heard anything like this before. The use of percussion that characterizes so many later Nikolais works has its origins in this early encounter with Wigman.[2]

After his dance studies, Nikolais' first substantial collaboration on a new choreographic work came in the spring of 1939 with *Eight Column Line*, with music by the Viennese émigré Ernst Krenek. (The choreography was created in collaboration with Truda Kaschmann.) Krenek, recently arrived in the States after his expulsion from Austria the previous year, following the Anschluss, was in his late thirties and was a figure of a certain notoriety, partly thanks to the blacklisting of his opera *Karl V* by the Nazis, and partly because of the uncompromising modernity of his musical language. The newly composed sixty-minute score for *Eight Column Line* used a chamber ensemble of nine players. Although it is all but forgotten today, the work's Hartford premiere enjoyed a successful critical reception and helped to launch Nikolais' career. It is notable that the work that marked Nikolais' emergence into the public arena should align him with the European-American avant-garde rather than with the more audience-friendly forms of Americana then becoming prevalent in the dance world, such as Aaron Copland's scores for Eugene Loring's *Billy the Kid* (1938), Agnes DeMille's *Rodeo* (1942), or Martha Graham's *Appalachian Spring* (1944). Nikolais' involvement with the cutting edge of American musical modernism (and later, with the American experimental tradition) was thus in evidence right from the outset.

However, the works Nikolais created as part of the Federal Theater Project series in Hartford in the years up to 1948 (interrupted by his years of service in the army during World War II) give little indication of what was to come. He worked on eighteenth- and nineteenth-century operas such as Flotow's *Martha,* Paisiello's *The Barber of Seville,* and Gounod's *Romeo and Juliet,* and choreographed recent music by Prokofiev, Gershwin, and others, in other contexts. The first of his substantial collaborations with a musician, that with Freda Miller, also began in Hartford (with a work for children, *Fable of the Donkey*) and continued after Nikolais relocated to New York in 1948 to become director of the Dance Division at the Henry Street Playhouse. Several other works for young people followed until the breakthrough year of 1953, which heralded a new chapter in Nikolais' career.

The first work that placed Nikolais' name among the leaders of modern dance was *Masks, Props, and Mobiles*, premiered at the Henry Street Playhouse on January 26, 1953. Right from the outset, critical opinion about this new work was divided. Many critics refused to accept it as dance at all. One section, "Tensile Involvement," was a virtuoso piece in which the dancers became entangled in a weblike structure of their own making. Nikolais' use of stretchable bags to conceal and transform the dancers' bodies in "Noumenom Mobilis," although intended as an exploration of "the dancer in relation to external substances," was branded in some quarters as "dehumanizing." Nikolais was concerned with circumventing what he regarded as modern dance's preoccupation with the self, using props to extend the body, and he looked to nonrepresentational art to nourish his interest in shape, color, and texture. Equally noteworthy—and, for some, fuel for the accusation that Nikolais was dehumanizing dance—was the highly unconventional music he used.

To get a fuller sense of the kind of music used in Nikolais' earliest characteristic productions at the Henry Street Playhouse, let us examine five representative works of the mid-1950s in greater detail. These works are:

- *Village of Whispers*, premiered February 13, 1955
- *Masks—Props—Mobiles*, the new version, premiered December 10, 1955
- *Kaleidoscope*, premiered August 17, 1956
- *Prism*, premiered December 27, 1956
- *Cantos*, premiered December 27, 1957

By the time of *Village of Whispers*, the general pattern of Nikolais' sound scores of this period had been set. For the most part the individual dances were accompanied either by percussion music performed by the Playhouse Percussion Group, or by passages of prerecorded music by various composers taken from LPs. Nikolais himself made all the decisions about the choice of music and the sequencing and duration of the individual pieces, although in the surviving printed programs of this time (the mid-1950s) he does not credit himself as composer. The names of composers used are given in the programs, although only in the most direct way and with no further information, such as the name of the composition, the performers, the catalogue number of the LP, etc.[3] (One representative example, the program for *Kaleidoscope*, is reproduced as Fig.1.) The percussion group's music was evidently arrived at by an amalgam of ideas from Nikolais, general improvisation, and a spirit of group endeavor, while always under the shaping hand of the choreographer. If any of this music was scored out in musical notation, no manuscripts of it would seem to have survived. (The personnel of the percussion group changed over the years; in one of the few programs of these years that mentions the musicians by name—that for *Forest of Three* in 1953—five musicians are listed: Phoebe Abelow, Leonora Birnberg, Natalie Jaffe, Sonia Savig, and Marilyn Wood.)

The pre-existing music in *Village of Whispers* consisted of extracts (Nikolais rarely used whole pieces or even whole movements) from compositions by Carlos Chávez, Henri Dutilleux, Béla Bartók, John Cage, Harold Farberman, and Julián Carrillo. With the exception of Bartók, none of these names would have been well known to New York audiences in 1955. Cage, then in his early forties, was still generally considered a maverick and not to be taken seriously, whereas the twenty-five-year-old Farberman had only recently graduated from Julliard, was working as a percussionist with the Boston Symphony, and had just produced his first compositions. No less unconventional a choice was the *Preludio a Colón* by the Mexican Julián Carrillo (1875–1965), composed in 1924 and one of the earliest examples of microtonal music, music using intervals smaller than the equal-tempered semitone. Nikolais must have got his hands on the original Columbia recording of the piece and been captivated by the haunting, otherworldly sounds: a soprano singing in very fine shades of pitch, and a small ensemble—Carrillo's mysteriously named "13th Sound Ensemble" of Havana—that included a newly built harp-zither tuned in sixteenth tones and an *octavina*, a sort of contrabass guitar. Appropriately, the Carrillo music is used for the penultimate section of *Village of Whispers*, "Styx." But it seems that the most lingering impression in the minds of those who attended the performance in the mid-fifties was made not so much by the pre-composed extracts but by the new music. Ruth Grauert, Nikolais' stage manager at that time, recalls that in *Village of Whispers* "he relied on the sounds—voice and percussion—made both by him and the dancers in the wings and on stage."[4] These passages, to judge from the surviving recording, must have made a powerful impact—a piercing woman's scream, followed by loud crashes on metallic percussion, laced into a texture of recorded spoken words, fragments of dialogues that are intense but incomprehensible. This music is perhaps crude but certainly effective, suggesting a paranoid, post-McCarthy world in which interpersonal communication is problematized and violent outbursts are unavoidable.

Masks—Props—Mobiles, "an experimental program in which the dancers are depersonalized or in which their motions are extended into external materials," was staged in December 1955 (program notes). Again, three percus-

Presents

First Event of the 1956 - 1957 Season

ALWIN NIKOLAIS'
HENRY STREET PLAYHOUSE DANCE COMPANY
IN
KALEIDOSCOPE

Choreography and direction by	Color design by
Alwin Nikolais	George Constant
assisted by Ruth Grauert	Sound Technician, David Berlin

DANCERS

Gladys Bailin - Murray Louis - Beverly Schmidt - Phyllis Lamhut
Dorothy Vislocky - Coral Martindale - William Frank

1. DISCS (Percussion) .... Company
2. POLE (Ethnic) .... Gladys Bailin, Murray Louis
3. PADDLES (Edgar Varèse and Percussion) .... Murray Louis, William Frank
4. SKIRTS (John Cage) .... Company

15 Minute Intermission

5. BIRD (Percussion) .... Gladys Bailin, Phyllis Lamhut, Murray Louis
6. HOOP (Carlos Chavez) .... Beverly Schmidt with William Frank,
Coral Martindale, Dorothy Vislocky
7. STRAPS (Percussion) .... Gladys Bailin, Murray Louis, Coral Martindale
8. CAPES (Carlos Chavez) .... Company

Percussion scores composed and played by the Playhouse Percussion Group

Electronic tape recordings by David Berlin

Incidental Music by George Antheil, Edgar Varèse, Alan Hovhaness,
Heitor Villa-Lobos, Henry Brandt and from Ethnic Sources

Stage Manager for Mr. Nikolais .... Ruth Grauert

Technical Assistants .... Joseph Cooper, William Smith

Lighting Crew: Clive Driver '57, Terrell Fredericks '59, Thomas
Keena '58, James Olsen '58, Donald Ramsey '57,
Stanley Simon '58, Robert Thirkield '58, Alan
Thompson '57, David Wing '57.

Immediately after the performance, members of the audience are invited to meet
Mr. Nikolais and the members of the Company at the Davison Art Center.

NOVEMBER 3, 1956

1. *Courtesy of the Nikolais/Louis Foundation for Dance.*

sion sections were interspersed among pre-composed music. This time the composers featured were Jean Sibelius (then still alive, at the age of ninety, in Finland), the Mexican Carlos Chávez (whose music had been used in *Village of Whispers*), and two relatively unknown Americans, both around Nikolais' own age and both defiant nonconformists: Henry Brant and Alan Hovhaness. The Montreal-born Brant had been based in New York for many years and earned his living there as a commercial orchestrator. As a composer, he possessed a fresh and exciting ear for novel sounds; moreover, only a few years earlier he had composed the first of his works that call for spatial separation of the musicians as an essential part of the compositional design, an approach he developed in the years ahead. (Brant is today recognized as the pioneer and principal exponent of what has become known as "spatial music"; hearing his music on records, Nikolais would have got only the flavor, not the full sonic reality of this spatial aspect of Brant's work.) Not only the "Noumenom Mobilis" section of *Masks—Props—Mobiles* but also the following year's *Kaleidoscope* and *Prism* use extracts from Brant recordings, specifically the newly released Columbia LP of *Galaxy 2* and *Signs and Alarms*, two of his earliest spatial scores, and the much earlier *Angels and Devils* (1932), a concerto for flute and flute orchestra.[5] Alan Hovhaness had first made a mark on the New York concert scene the previous decade, with works that were tonal (or, more often, modal), reflecting his Armenian heritage. His music turned its back on most of the hallmarks of musical modernism: dissonance was ousted in favor of consonance, often harmonically static or drone-based, the fragmentation of phrase and irregularity of rhythm characteristic of musical modernism was nowhere in evidence, and metrical rhythm, florid passagework, and quasi-Oriental ornamentation embellished the melodic lines. In 1955 MGM Records had begun issuing records of Hovhaness' music (largely prompted by Leopold Stokowski's successful premiere of the second symphony, *Mysterious Mountain*). Like Brant, but for an even longer period, Hovhaness would remain a favorite of Nikolais.[6]

Kaleidoscope, from August 1956, continues the basic pattern established by its immediate predecessors, but departs from it in small but significant ways. Besides the percussion music and the fragments of pieces by contemporary composers (in this case Edgard Varèse, John Cage, Carlos Chávez, George Antheil, Heitor Villa-Lobos, Henry Brant, and Alan Hovhaness), Nikolais for the first time introduces fragments of recorded music "from ethnic sources"— primarily Japanese—in this case, koto music most prominently. It is clear that he had begun listening to non-Western music more closely than before. Occasional non-Western instruments even turn up in the instrumentarium of his percussion ensemble from this point onwards (an African mbira, for example, is used in the percussion sections of *Kaleidoscope*). In this respect Nikolais was reflecting a tendency that several American composers displayed in their music at that time (Hovhaness, for example, also Henry Cowell, Lou Harrison, and Harry Partch), an interest in the forms, textures, and instrumental sonorities of non-Western music, and the attempt to learn from such sources in contemporary composition. A second innovation in the sound score of *Kaleidoscope* is that Nikolais superimposes recorded material upon his percussion music. "Paddles," the third of the work's eight main sections, begins with a recording of the opening of Varèse's *Density 21.5* (1936) for solo flute. After some ninety seconds of the Varèse, percussive sounds (from the Playhouse Percussion Group) begin to fade in, and the two sources, more or less equal in volume, continue together for a further minute until the flute stops and only drum sounds remain. The percussive music continues for two minutes; when it stops, the Varèse (in its original, "unaccompanied" form) resumes and ends the section. This is a modest, although prophetic, departure on Nikolais' part. Rather than simply using other people's music—as any choreographer does—he has begun to recompose the borrowed material, placing it in new aural contexts. (One wonders what Varèse's attitude to this would have been!)

Prism, first performed on December 27, 1956, and revived at the Henry Street Playhouse in January 1958, is yet another significant step forward. The printed program, as given to the audience, gives less of a detailed listing of the music accompanying each dance than previously, and simply notes: "The music and sounds accompanying PRISM are original recordings and arrangements of ethnic music with the exception of [the seventh section] "Paratint" (Hovhaness) and [the last section] "Glaasch" (Antheil)." Not only was Nikolais becoming less scrupulous in crediting other composers' music, but also his whole way of describing the sound score becomes more vague, possibly intentionally so. What, for example, is meant by "original recordings"? And what exactly does "arrangements of ethnic music" mean? Listening to the surviving tape of *Prism* is more revealing (although it cannot be taken as wholly definitive, as Nikolais would often make changes in subsequent performances of a work, omitting or adding material). The main difference from the immediately preceding scores is that *Prism* feels much less like a succession of set pieces and more like an aural collage. Most of the music used is presented in fragments, some as short as forty seconds and with only one extended passage (of music for prepared piano, lasting over five minutes). There are snatches of gongs (from an LP, Asian, but otherwise difficult to identify precisely); several passages of didgeridoo music; some African drumming;

whistling and vocal sounds; a brief snatch of Brant's *Angels and Devils;* improvisations on piano and percussion; and, notably, some electronic sounds that are created by Nikolais manipulating tape, using some simple techniques of *musique concrète* (splicing, playing the tape backwards, fiddling with volume levels and playback speed, etc.). Hearing this recording today is a curious experience. On the one hand, it is perhaps the most "creative" sound score Nikolais had produced to that time; on the other, the tape does sound very dated because of the crudeness of the techniques employed, such as the extremely unsubtle use of splicing and the too-quick fade outs and fade ins. What it still retains, however, is the choreographer's evident excitement at his discovery of a new creative tool: the reel-to-reel tape recorder.

The program for the performances of *Runic Canto* and *New Dances* at the Playhouse in late December 1957 (a work that would subsequently be known as *Cantos*) states, once again rather unhelpfully: "Sounds by Playhouse Percussion Group unless otherwise noted." Quite a few exceptions are noted: composers whose music is used include two great pioneers of French *musique concrète*, Pierre Henry and Pierre Schaeffer, as well as Daniel Pinkham, Henry Brant, and Alan Hovhaness. As a general observation, it is worth noting that Nikolais' programs of the mid- to late-1950s (such as those for the works discussed above), despite their lack of information, do not seem consciously designed to conceal or misrepresent, or to withhold credit from the composers and performing musicians who appear on the recordings used in the performances. Rather, they seem typical products of more innocent, pre–litigation-conscious times, when the need for permission and correct attribution was simply less of a pressing concern. By our standards today they may be sloppy, but it seems to me that it is going too far to accuse Nikolais of willful dishonesty.

By the end of 1959 there has been a sea change. In a program for a performance presented at the Department of Theatre at Smith College on December 8, consisting of excerpts from *Allegory* and preview extracts from *Rituals*, the sound score is listed as being by Nikolais himself without further qualification.[7] The program also notes: "These sound scores are included on a new recording now published by Hanover Signature Record Company, entitled *"Choreosonics," Music of the New Dance Theatre of Alwin Nikolais."* Released in 1959, this LP shows how seriously Nikolais was now taking the sonic aspect of his work. It seems that by the end of the 1950s, Nikolais' long trajectory toward assuming total authorship of his artistic creations had reached its final stage.[8]

It is worth exploring Nikolais' working methods of these years in more detail, as a description of how he worked gives much insight into the music he created. Whereas his earliest works were often piano based—the music Freda Miller composed for the works for children in the late 1940s and early 1950s, for example, was played live in the performances by Miller and Nikolais on the piano—as the 1950s wore on he increasingly came to rely on electronic devices. When he used recorded music, as in most of the works of the 1950s, the records would be played on a turntable, not an easy process given that one had to find the exact spot on the vinyl where the desired extract began. Perhaps for this reason, most of the extracts Nikolais used are from the beginnings of pieces, which could be more easily identified thanks to the bands that separated tracks on the LPs. But for Nikolais, the real liberation was the reel-to-reel tape recorder, which offered many more possibilities of a creative nature. Ruth Grauert, Nikolais' associate, describes how he worked with the machine:

> With the introduction of the tape recorder Nik's pallet of sounds was greatly enhanced. He directed [and recorded] his company members as they made all kinds of concrete sounds with cooking pots, pipes, cardboard tubes, glasses of water, and Nik's favorite—an old gas tank from a Model-T Ford. Nik would improvise on the piano, which he might intersperse with recorded music, and which the sound engineer (David Berlin) might alter electronically.

Characteristically, much of Nikolais' composition was done on the spot, in the studio with the dancers around him. Grauert continues:

> The sound would be played as the dancers danced and frequently part or parts needed to be rerecorded, sounds altered, tempos revised, tonalities changed. But it was Nik's musical ear that always said aye or nay. . . . The motion came first. As the company members improvised on themes that he proposed, Nik would accompany with percussion. When a substantial phrase or phrases of motion were set, he would time them with a stopwatch, note rhythms, and aesthetic intent. He would go back to his music room in his apartment and compose. The following rehearsal he would play the tape as the dancers moved. The first attempt was usually not totally satisfactory, so notes on changes were made. Often he would make cuts and resplice and replay during rehearsal.[9]

Nikolais himself describes the process in an article published in 1963:

> It was the unique communicative values of sound and the fascination of its interrelation with motion that originally brought me to dance. It was the

invention of electronic tape that brought me the means to relate these two areas within the scope of my own manipulation. None of this was a deliberately planned experiment. It "grew like Topsy." I had always used percussion accompaniment, but then the tape recorder came along. At first I used straight recordings but soon became intrigued with the results one could achieve by manipulating this tape into another abstractional sound area. Unwittingly I moved into the realm of *musique concrète*. Thus by slowing, speeding, filtering, rearranging, overlaying, dissecting, etc., I had the values of a whole instrumental combine at my one-man-manipulatable disposal. Further, by such manipulations, it was possible to achieve a new area of sound values, which emphasized even more the unique abstract qualities of sound.[10]

These working methods placed Nikolais firmly in the domain of the avant-garde. In fact, Nikolais' description of his evident delight at the "one-man-manipulatable" resource of the tape recorder echoes John Cage's sentiments, some two decades earlier, at his invention of the prepared piano as a medium for accompanying dance, replacing his previous use of a percussion ensemble; the prepared piano was a sort of percussion ensemble under the control of two hands.[11] Not only were Nikolais' composing means up to the minute, but also the sounds that resulted were, to say the least, challenging to much of his audience. There is not much melody or harmony in these scores, though sometimes patches of recognizable, danceable, metric rhythm emerge. Indeed, listening today to the tapes of the sound scores of the late 1950s we can almost understand the charge of dehumanization leveled at Nikolais; the tapes are filled with passages of music that seem to be snatched from their organic context and placed into a modern container, always tailing off crudely and abruptly into silence. The sounds may be engaging, fascinating, or compelling, but they are rarely warm or charming. (It might be noted, however, that the dance audience, then as now, often approaches such new sounds with ears that are more open and less prejudiced than those of the contemporary music audience.)

In the 1960s there were further developments along lines initiated the previous decade that expanded Nikolais' sonic vocabulary still further. The first was the opportunity to work with James Seawright (husband of Playhouse Company member Mimi Garrard), who worked at the newly established Columbia-Princeton Electronic Music Center, the first fully functioning institutional electronic music studio in the United States. This connection gave Nikolais access to equipment that far surpassed the sonic capabilities of his reel-to-reel tape recorder, notably the recently installed RCA Mark II music synthesizer, a huge device that occupied much of the available wall space in the studio in which it was housed. Although he did not work directly with the machine, Nikolais immediately saw its potential: as distinct from the tape recorder, which could manipulate pre-recorded sounds, the synthesizer actually created new sounds. The RCA Mark II synthesizer had a frequency/tone generator, with oscillators and white noise; a pitch glide and vibrato generator; a volume and envelope controller; a timbre (tone color) controller; and amplifiers and mixers.[12] Its complex set of controls, which enabled the user to shape the various parameters of sound, promised unlimited resources for the experimentally minded musician. The music for Nikolais' *Imago*, which was premiered in February 1963, was produced though this collaboration with Seawright and using the resources of the Columbia-Princeton Electronic Music Center.

If *Imago* was a tantalizing glimpse of a new world of sounds, it would not be long before Nikolais was able to embrace synthesizer technology directly. In September 1964 he attended an Audio Engineering Society (AES) convention in New York and came across one exhibit in particular that attracted his attention: a display of several handmade synthesizer modules by the American engineer Robert Moog, still a largely unknown inventor, but who would soon become a legendary figure in the electronic music world as the first person successfully to market the voltage-controlled synthesizer as a commercial product. On seeing what were essentially prototypes at the AES convention, Nikolais immediately ordered one from Moog; he was in fact arguably the first owner of the now-classic Moog synthesizer.[13] When it arrived in his studio in 1965 the new machine became a staple of Nikolais' sound work, and almost all the scores of his dance works of the next ten years incorporated—or were made solely using—the Moog.

As might be expected, the use of the synthesizer opened up many new musical possibilities for Nikolais and transformed his sound world. Listening to the earliest scores in which he used it, one thing is immediately clear: that quite apart from the new sounds, the one parameter of Nikolais' music that had been transformed the most is rhythm. His music for Murray Louis's *Chimera* (1966), for example, bubbles along in a light-footed way that seems far removed from the sometimes ponderous improvisations in his scores of the mid-1950s. The style of the music is not, perhaps, vastly original—it is not so different in its genial polyrhythmic feel from Cage's prepared piano music of the 1940s (which Nikolais had used a decade earlier)—but there is the unmistakable feeling of a new departure, a refreshing of his musical language.

The later sixties and seventies were for Nikolais a time of international acclaim and consolidation, especially overseas. Following the Playhouse company's highly successful 1968 Paris season at the Théâtre Des Champs-Elysées, Nikolais' work began to make a considerable impact on the French dance world: he began a long artistic relationship with the Théâtre de la Ville in 1971, and in 1978 received an invitation from the French National Ministry of Culture to form the Centre Nationale de la Danse Contemporaine in Angers. Meanwhile his innovations, both in dance and in music, showed no sign of slowing down. His later music, from the 1970s and 1980s, retains its dependence on synthesizers but keeps up with the times. In general the music is lighter in tone; it shows the influence of the use of the synthesizer in pop music; and it is tuned in to the world of the dance music of the time, even to certain features of disco (but, thankfully, without the backbeat). It sometimes displays a sense of humor—for example, the music for *Blank on Blank* of 1987— that the earlier scores generally lacked. Nikolais' incorporation of fragments of spoken text (in the later 1980s these fragments became referred to as "samples") can be genuinely delightful and sometimes very funny, as in the music for Louis's *Pierrot* of 1986. (An earlier effective use of spoken text is the "Overture" to *Gallery*, premiered in 1978.)[14]

Some of these innovations are due to two new keyboards that Nikolais had acquired. The Moog synthesizer was joined first by the Synclavier, the first commercially available portable digital synthesizer. (It is not clear when exactly he started working with this keyboard; the earliest models were sold around 1976.)[15] Then in the early 1980s he acquired an Emulator, which, as Murray Louis has observed, henceforth became "the major instrument in the Nikolais sound room."[16] The Emulator was a digital sampling keyboard, the first synthesizer of its kind in general circulation. Its sample time, only two seconds, is very short by today's standards, but Nikolais made effective use of these short samples ("Dance 3" from *Pierrot* is a good example). The machine offered eight-voice polyphony (in other words, it could sustain up to eight different sounds at once) and a real-time looping feature. Looping, in which a short musical pattern is repeated many times over (analogously to the use of tape loops on reel-to-reel tape recorders some two decades earlier), is an almost irresistible technique for anyone encountering it for the first time, and Nikolais was no exception. "Dance 4" from *Mechanical Organ,* created in collaboration with David Darling, offers a simple example of looping, and "Dance 1" from his music for Murray Louis's *Ten Legs* (1989) a more sophisticated one.

Nikolais' involvement with the newest technology did not mean he had

2. *Nikolais working at a keyboard synthesizer in mid-1980s.*
Photograph © Tom Caravaglia 2007.

abandoned his earlier ways of working. Marc Lawton, who worked with him in France in the late 1970s, recalls Nikolais' continuing use of tape:

> In 1978, for our first lecture-demonstration, Nik had some French jazz musicians improvise with us for two weeks at the *coupole* (top floor) of Théâtre de la Ville and then edited the stuff to fit our one-hour performance. We were all very impressed watching him cut and splice meters of tape on the Revox recorder right next to the stage where we were rehearsing (and quite close to the premiere!).[17]

Jon Scoville, who collaborated with Nikolais near the end of the choreographer's life, recalls:

> He very rarely used a piano while accompanying a class, mostly utilizing a small collection of percussion instruments—floor toms, cymbals and the like. I heard him play on a number of occasions and was always struck by how delicate and understated his touch was. I presume he felt that the real motivation for movement should come from within the dancers rather than being imposed externally by forceful and dynamic (read loud) accompaniment.[18]

Nikolais' work in abstract dance theatre and his sense of the dancer as part of a total environment, already a concern in his earliest breakthrough works of the 1950s, had expanded into a vision of "total dance theatre" in which he increasingly shaped all aspects of the performance as part of the creative process.[19] And whereas it is generally true that the broad picture of his career shows a tendency toward ever-greater control over all the aspects of his productions, some important musical collaborations of the last two decades of his life should be discussed to give a more complete picture of his later work. Such collaborations became more common after the mid-1970s, and it is not unreasonable to wonder why this should be the case. In fact the reasons may be quite simple. "Nik was really used to composing his own scores," remarks one of his collaborators, David Gregory, "but as he got older this became much more of a chore for him and Murray [Louis] convinced him it might be easier for him if he left it to someone else."[20] His last collaborator, Jon Scoville, who worked with him in 1992, comments: "Nik was nearing the end of his life at the time and probably felt he lacked the energy to produce both the music and the choreography. Also—and this is speculative—both the Emulator and the Synclavier, which had replaced his old friend the original Moog, were much less user-friendly and thus perhaps took more time to program and generate the kinds of sounds in which Nik was interested."[21]

The list below gives the main musical collaborators Nikolais worked with in his later years. (Where possible, the wording of the acknowledgement of their contribution is quoted from the printed programs that accompanied the original performances.)

Styx (1976): "Gamelan improvisations by members of the Music Department, Wesleyan University. Andrew Rudin assisted in creating and integrating some of the electronic sounds and the editing of the score."

Triad (1976): "Some sections for the sound score were improvised by Robert Benford and members of the Paul Winter Consort. Other sections incorporate sounds created and edited by Andrew Rudin."

Guignol (1977): "Music improvised by the Paul Winter Consort with the exception of the electronic sounds."

Aviary (1978): music by Daniel Harris and Les Thimmig; later rejected by Nikolais and new music composed by him.

Mechanical Organ (1980): "The score is improvised by the David Darling Ensemble under the direction of David Darling and Alwin Nikolais. Tapes compiled and edited by Alwin Nikolais."

Schema and *Five Masks* (1980–81): "The score is improvised by the David Darling Ensemble under the direction of David Darling and Alwin Nikolais. Tapes compiled and edited by Alwin Nikolais."

Talisman (1981): "The score is improvised by the David Darling Ensemble under the direction of David Darling and Alwin Nikolais. Tapes compiled and edited by Alwin Nikolais."

Lenny and the Heartbreakers (1983): music by Scott Killian.

Persons and Structures (1984): music by David Gregory. (At the premiere performance February 16, Edgard Varèse's *Poème Electronique* was used.)

Video Game (1984): music by David Gregory.

Graph (1984): music by David Gregory.

Aurora (1992): music by Jon Scoville.

These collaborations were not always a straightforward matter. The original score for *Aviary,* as used at its premiere in Madison, Wisconsin, in 1978, was a collaboration between Daniel Harris and Les Thimmig. "Even though it was done very much under Nik's direction," recalls dancer Dudley Brooks, "he was never happy with it (nor were they happy with the way he created one particular sound by lifting up their synthesizer a couple of inches and banging it down on the table). . . . It frequently appeared to me that their music was doing just what he had requested, but when he finally was (somewhat) satisfied with the results it seemed to contradict the original instructions he had given them." This original score was only used in the Madison perform-ance. "Nik completely re-did the score himself when we returned to NYC," Brooks adds, "and there are no other credits."[22] Nikolais would occasionally reject scores offered to him by potential collaborators—he rejected David Gregory's first attempt at a score for *Graph* (1984) on the grounds that the music didn't fit his choreographic ideas, but then went on to create a new dance for the existing music (which became *Video Game*). And he could be touchy about the admiration some of his musical collaborators received: "I once committed a terrible faux pas," recalls Dudley Brooks, "by telling him that I liked [the music for *Triad*] the best of all his music, to which he replied, rather frostily, that he didn't write it."[23]

The collaboration on his last work, *Aurora,* premiered in New York in Janu-ary 1992, was a much happier experience. Nikolais commissioned the music from Jon Scoville, who had composed a score for Murray Louis the previous year, and Louis, pleased with the results, had suggested Scoville's name to Nikolais. (Scoville's wife, Tandy Beal, had studied with Nikolais in the mid-1960s and had danced in his company for two years.) Scoville describes the working process on *Aurora:*

> Initially I was told that the piece was going to be a dialog between city and rural landscapes and psychic states. I was asked to come up with 35 min-utes of music (and to be completed in a month). . . . I sent Nik a number of sketches and completed episodes. He picked out the ones he liked, asked me to make several changes on some of them—in fact, in at least two instances he took the music and made splices and cuts in the tape and sent them back—and asked me to insert a few surprises. I then had another two weeks to complete it and well remember with great relief and subsidence of adrenaline when I sent the finished tape by express mail, just meeting the deadline.[24]

How, then, should we regard Alwin Nikolais' musical achievement overall? In a sense this question has no real answer, as Nikolais' musical activities did not have the goal of creating a body of work that would have an existence in-dependent of dance. "For Nik, the sound did not come out of any sense of melody or harmony or any other conventional musical structure," comments David Gregory. "Sound for Nik was an abstraction of either shape, space, time, or motion. . . . If you listen to his compositions without watching a performance then you are missing half the experience. You wouldn't watch a movie without the sound. Nik did not compose music for people just to listen to. If you want to do that as an academic exercise, since I can't imagine it would be that aesthetically pleasing, then try to decide if he is defining shape, space, time or motion with the sound, because that will be what it is all about."[25] This does not mean that Nikolais' music cannot or should not be listened to on its own, merely that it is unfair to judge it in that isolated context. The problem may be that in the context of Western music we still tend to define the word "composer" very narrowly, as though anyone who creates music necessarily aspires to the condition of Beethoven. There are many other applications of compositional activity, and it is in these other domains that Nikolais' work resides. "The music was there primarily to provide motor and atmosphere rather than structure," observes Jon Scoville. "To say that he was unstructured and not involved with composerly choices, while accurate from a traditional point of view, might be trying to compare apples and onions."[26]

In one sense, Nikolais' combination of activities—as a composer, an improviser, and what might be termed a curator of other people's music, with the boundaries between them being not infrequently blurred—marks him out as a very modern figure. His musical work is in some ways prophetic of the activities of many young musicians at the beginning of the twenty-first century, to whom the distinctiveness of these various roles seems ever less relevant in an age of high-speed connectivity. Nikolais' way of making other composers' music (almost) his own problematizes the question of single authorship and the authorial voice, issues that are highly relevant to a discussion of the contemporary arts today. His practice of compiling libraries of sounds on tape is an analog-era equivalent of present-day libraries of digital samples. His gathering of obscure or exotic LPs and the incorporation of them into his work can be seen as having much in common with today's mania for downloading music from the Internet and the creative practice of many DJs. Equally forward looking are his collaborations, from the mid-1970s onwards, with musicians equally at home in "serious," "popular," or "crossover" domains, such as the saxophonist Paul Winter or the cellist David Darling; the contemporary dance world has continued its fascination with this type of musician.

There is, of course, another view of Nikolais, one that directly contradicts the above description. It could be argued that he looked not forwards but backwards, to a nineteenth-century model, that of the selfish, manipulative, ungrateful, ego-driven "author-God" (to use Roland Barthes's phrase), enfolding and absorbing everything that came his way into his own autocratic vision of art. In that sense Nikolais seems like a latter-day Wagner creating his own *Gesamtkunstwerk,* one in which dance, rather than music, stands at the pinnacle of all the arts. It is true that not all of his musical collaborators felt they received due credit for the work they had done for him, and some composers remained unaware that Nikolais had used their music at all.[27] This lack of full accreditation persists in aspects of Nikolais' legacy even today, as can be seen in the column about music in the "Chronology Of Choreographic Works By Alwin Nikolais" on the official Web site of the Nikolais-Louis Foundation for Dance.[28] But, as I have argued above, it feels wrong to accuse Nikolais of consciously trying to deceive.

It is surely the case that an accurate view of Nikolais' musical achievement lies somewhere between these two extremes. All great artists look both backwards and forwards, Nikolais as much as anyone. In his unswerving pursuit of innovatory artistic practice, Nikolais used anything and everything that appealed to his creative imagination. "We need only be wary of rules," he wrote. "I have no specific method. I do whatever I feel may produce the desired result."[29] Nikolais' music—whether original, collaborative, or borrowed—is an integral part of a body of work that has enriched the creative arts and that continues to stimulate new adventures in the correlation of music and dance.

ACKNOWLEDGMENTS

I am grateful to Claudia Gitelman for the suggestion that I write this article, and for her help with access to archival materials. I am grateful also for help from Judith Connick, Special Collections librarian and archivist of the Alwin Nikolais and Murray Louis Papers at the Robert E. and Jean R. Mahn Center for Archives and Special Collections, Ohio University, Athens, Ohio. Murray Louis kindly supplied music from original performances in the 1940s and 1950s for purposes of my research. Sound recordings of Nikolais' works are preserved and archived at Ohio University.

NOTES

1. Murray Louis, liner notes to *Alwin Nikolais: Electronic Dance Music,* CRI CD 651, 1993. This CD, which includes extracts from Nikolais' music for *Revels, Ten Legs, Mechanical Organ, Frail Demons, Tribe, Pierrot, Blank on Blank, Aviary, Graph, Chimera, Styx, Gallery, Contact,* and *Crucible,* is the best introduction to his later music. The earliest music included (*Chimera*) dates from 1966, whereas all the other scores are from the years 1975 to 1989.

2. Much of the biographical material on Nikolais in this and the following two

paragraphs is summarized from Alwin Nikolais and Murray Louis, *The Nikolais/Louis Dance Technique: a Philosophy and Method of Modern Dance* (New York: Routledge, 2005), ix–xii. (Although most biographical accounts give 1934 as the date of Nikolais' encounter with Wigman's work, the German dance artist was not in the United States that year. Her three U.S. tours were in the winters of 1930–1931, 1931–1932, and 1932–1933.)

3. Programs in the New York Public Library, Jerome Robbins Dance Division, and in Alwin Nikolais and Murray Louis Papers at Ohio University.

4. Ruth Grauert, e-mail November 6, 2002, to "The Chatterbox," an e-mail discussion list, available online at http://bearnstowjournal.org/chatterbox2.htm

5. The LP of Brant's *Galaxy 2* and *Signs and Alarms* was on Columbia ML-4956. Despite at least one reissue by the company, it has long been unavailable and can be found only in libraries or on the shelves of a few discerning music lovers; so far the recordings, in common with most of Columbia's more interesting recordings of contemporary music, have not been released on CD. *Angels and Devils* has been recorded several times after the release of the recording Nikolais possessed, but at the time of this writing no commercial recording of the piece is available.

6. Nikolais' *L'enfant de la Lune* of 1961 features music by Hovhaness.

7. An erratum to the program of *Allegory*, however, notes—admits?—that the final extract from *Allegory* uses music by Varèse and Chávez.

8. A further contributing factor in this change may have been Nikolais' fraught and unhappy collaboration with the composer Harry Partch in the winter of 1956–1957. Nikolais had been asked by composer Ben Johnston of the University of Illinois at Urbana-Champaign to undertake the choreography for the production of Partch's *The Bewitched* to be given at the university in March 1957. The disaster that ensued was a confirmation, if confirmation were needed, that simply choreographing another composer's music was not the way Nikolais wanted to work. I have written about this episode in detail, including extensive quotations from Nikolais' correspondence, in my book on Partch (Bob Gilmore, *Harry Partch: a Biography* [New Haven and London: Yale University Press, 1998], 243–252), which incorporates material first published as an article: "'A Soul Tormented': Alwin Nikolais and Harry Partch's *The Bewitched*," in *The Musical Quarterly* 79 no.1 [Spring 1995], 80–107). According to his associate Murray Louis, Nikolais' collaboration with Partch convinced him that he would thereafter work with "sound, not music" (Murray Louis, personal communication).

9. Ruth Grauert, e-mail November 6, 2002, to "The Chatterbox," an e-mail discussion list, available online at http://bearnstowjournal.org/chatterbox2.htm.

10. Alwin Nikolais, "Composer/Choreographer," in *Dance Perspectives* 16 (1963), 35. Writing in the same journal a few years later, Nikolais gives a more cynical view of the matter: "I had a not altogether enviable music background which led to a

theater background, which led to a dance background, which led to an early tape machine (to save musician money), which led to *music concrète* (by virtue of broken tape, sloppy splicing, and punching the wrong speed control), which led to electronic sound. . . . "; cf. *Dance Perspectives* 48 (1971).

11. Cf. "How the Piano Came to be Prepared," in John Cage, *Empty Words: Writings '73 to '78* (Wesleyan University Press, 1979).

12. The Columbia-Princeton studios are described in detail in Thom Holmes, *Electronic and Experimental Music,* second edition (New York and London: Routledge, 2002), 105–122. Holmes briefly mentions Nikolais' involvement with the studio on p. 112, and his commissioning Robert Moog on p. 165, acknowledging that Nikolais bought Moog's "first production model."

13. Nikolais' Moog synthesizer, purchased with the help of a Guggenheim Fellowship, is today at the Museum of Musical Instruments at the University of Michigan, Ann Arbor.

14. All the music mentioned in this and the following paragraph is included on *Alwin Nikolais: Electronic Dance Music,* CRI CD 651, 1993.

15. After Nikolais' death, his Synclavier was given to Jon Scoville, who describes it thus: "A Synclavier 1 with a behemoth for a CPU [central processing unit]. In an enormous Anvil case weighing around a hundred pounds and sporting a massive 512 kilobytes of memory. What an elephant! Elegant and very very slow." Jon Scoville, e-mail to the author, July 31, 2005.

16. Murray Louis, liner notes to *Alwin Nikolais: Electronic Dance Music.* In his notes, Louis misremembers the date slightly: the Emulator appeared on the market not in "the mid 1970s" but in 1981, and it is very unlikely that Nikolais could have owned one prior to that date.

17. Marc Lawton, e-mail November 8, 2002, to "The Chatterbox," an e-mail discussion list, available online at http://bearnstowjournal.org/chatterbox2.htm.

18. Jon Scoville, e-mail to the author, July 17, 2005.

19. Phrases such as "abstract dance theatre," the dancer "as part of a total environment," and "total dance theatre" are usages of the Nikolais-Louis Foundation for Dance, Inc.; cf. http://www.nikolaislouis.org/NikolaisBiography.html.

20. David Gregory, e-mail to the author, July 18, 2005.

21. Jon Scoville, e-mail to the author, July 17, 2005.

22. Dudley Brooks, e-mail to Claudia Gitelman, May 15, 2005: quoted by permission.

23. Dudley Brooks, e-mail November 7, 2002 to "The Chatterbox," an e-mail discussion list, available online at http://bearnstowjournal.org/chatterbox2.htm.

24. Jon Scoville, e-mail to the author, July 17, 2005.

25. David Gregory, e-mail to the author, July 18, 2005.

26. Jon Scoville, e-mail to the author, July 17, 2005.

27. The composer Henry Brant, for example, when asked about his work with Nikolais for purposes of this article, replied: "Concerning Alwin Nikolais, I've never met him nor had any communication or collaboration with him." Henry Brant, e-mail to the author, May 17, 2005.

28. See http://www.nikolaislouis.org.

29. Alwin Nikolais, "Composer/Choreographer," *Dance Perspectives* 16 (1963), 36.

CHAPTER 9

Motional Abstraction

. . . .

ALWIN NIKOLAIS' FORMALISM

PHILIP AUSLANDER

Whereas other contributors to this volume discuss Alwin Nikolais in relation to the aesthetics of European dance, I wish to situate him in a distinctly American context: the aesthetic debates taking place within the New York School of visual artists, which developed contemporaneously with Nikolais' dance aesthetic. The period from 1948 to 1953, from the time Nikolais became director of the Dance Division at the Henry Street Settlement and founded the Playhouse Dance Company to the creation of *Noumenom Mobilis*, the first work to reflect his mature choreographic style, was a significant phase in the development of the New York School of painters and sculptors as well. This configuration, which had it roots in relationships begun during the Depression-era Works Progress Administration's art projects, was by 1947–48 a well-established bohemian scene; a year later, an illustrated feature in *Life* magazine would make the painter Jackson Pollock a household name.

Dore Ashton argues in her intellectual and cultural history of the New York School that Martha Graham was the choreographer whose work most paralleled the painters' aesthetic concerns: "The emphasis on original gesture, harsh and without charm, divested of pretty stories, was at that moment considered to be highly desirable in painting" (145). Described in this way, Graham's work might be said to parallel the expressionist aspect of Abstract Expressionism. But New York School aesthetics did not emphasize expressionism exclusively. In fact, the art critic Clement Greenberg, perhaps the school's single most important theorist, explicitly emphasized abstraction and formalism over expressionism and built a sophisticated theoretical edifice upon that foundation.[1] It is primarily with Greenberg's ideas that I wish to compare Nikolais' aesthetic, to show strong parallels between the way Nikolais thought about his own work in dance and ideas being debated at the same time in New York School circles.

What follows is primarily a close (though admittedly selective) reading of the philosophical writings by Nikolais included in *The Nikolais/Louis Dance Technique*. If I discuss Greenberg first and Nikolais in comparison, it is because Greenberg is famous for having codified a distinctive version of modernist formalism and Nikolais is not usually discussed in those terms, not to imply that Nikolais' ideas were in any way derivative or that he necessarily looked to Greenberg or others for inspiration. Neither do I wish to imply that Nikolais' aesthetic was more connected to the visual arts than the world of dance. It is clear that his ideas paralleled those of some dance theorists, that his artistic practice was in "the major choreographic tradition" initiated by Loïe Fuller (Copeland and Cohen 104), and that he shared an orientation toward formalism and dance for dance's sake with other choreographers of his generation (Selma Jeanne Cohen 11–12).[2] Nevertheless, I think it is productive to consider Nikolais in relation to ideas that emerged from the creative and intellectual ferment that was taking place on his doorstep. I see Greenberg and Nikolais as parallel figures simultaneously exploring the same aesthetic problematics in relation to different art forms and arriving at very similar ideas in proximate, but different, artistic milieux.[3]

Beginning in the late 1930s, Greenberg developed a controversial formalist and historicist account of modern art in which he defines the modernist impulse as the progressive purification of each art form through reduction to its most essential characteristics. This entailed a rejection of representation in favor of "art for art's sake": "In turning his attention away from subject-matter or common experience, the poet or artist turns it in upon the medium of his own craft." Taking its own procedures as its subject, art thus becomes "the imitation of imitat*ing*" rather than the representation of anything outside of itself ("Avant-Garde" 23).

Greenberg argues that a crucial step in the development of modernism was the choice of music as a model for the other arts, because

> the effects of music are the effects, essentially, of pure form; those of painting and poetry are too often incidental to the formal natures of these arts. Only by accepting the example of music and defining each of the other arts solely in the terms of the sense or faculty which perceived its effects and by excluding from each art whatever is intelligible in terms of any other sense or faculty would the non-musical arts attain the "purity" and self-sufficiency which they desired. . . ("Towards" 41).

The material of music is sound, which appeals to the ear directly rather than through mimesis. Greenberg saw the development of modern painting, the art form with which he was most concerned, as moving in a parallel direction toward a practice of painting that would appeal to the eye through pure visuality rather than representation.

Greenberg's idea of formal and perceptual purity as the goal of modernism obliged him to identify the essential characteristics that had progressively become the subject matter as well as the means of each art form. In the case of painting, that characteristic was

> the ineluctable flatness of the support. . . . Flatness alone was unique and exclusive to that art. The enclosing shape of the support was the limiting condition, or norm, that was shared with the art of the theater; color was a norm or means shared with sculpture as well as with the theater. Flatness, two-dimensionality, was the only condition painting shared with no other art, and so Modernist painting oriented itself to flatness as it did to nothing else[4] ("Modernist" 69).

Therefore, the task of modernist painters was to purge the art form of all the characteristics it shares with other forms and produce paintings that emphasize two-dimensionality above all else. In Greenberg's view, this project began in the mid-nineteenth century with Manet and Courbet and found a radical expression early in the twentieth century with the Cubists. He saw the post-war American painters he championed, Pollock in particular, as pushing it still further.

Although Greenberg's reductionist concept of modernism in art has excited a great deal of critical reaction and remains both influential and provocative to this day, I am going to let it stand uncriticized here.[5] My main purpose is not to assess the usefulness or validity of Greenberg's analysis but, rather, to show parallels between Greenberg's way of thinking about painting and Nikolais' ideas about dance.

One starting point for this comparison is to ask: If Greenberg considered flatness to be the essential characteristic of modern painting, what did Nikolais consider to be the essential characteristic of modern dance? The crucial distinction he made between *movement* and *motion* seems to provide an answer. Nikolais defined dance "in its purest sense" as

> the motion of a neurologically and kinetically endowed body in which the purpose, meaning, or value of that motion is inherent in the motion itself. In ordinary circumstance movement is a means toward another end, and thus does not call attention to itself but rather to a point of interest or achievement beyond it. The unique character of dance is that motion itself is the end; reason is within it rather than beyond it. Dance accomplishes itself (Nikolais and Louis 6).

Nikolais' distinction between *movement*, which derives its meaning and purpose from something outside itself, and *motion*, which is entirely self-

1. Noumenom Mobilis *(1953). Photograph David S. Berlin, courtesy of the* Nikolais/Louis Foundation.

referential, is very close to the distinction Greenberg makes between painting or poetry, whose meaning derives from its reference to subject matter drawn from a world beyond itself, and modernist art, whose meaning lies entirely in the manipulation of distinctive formal means and the sensual appeal of such manipulation. Note that both emphasize purity of means, that which is unique to a particular art form, and self referentiality. One can easily imagine Greenberg seizing on Nikolais' final statement in this passage and gleefully paraphrasing it as "Painting accomplishes itself." There is a paradox, or at least a tension, inherent in this version of modernist formalism: the idea that the modernity of every art form resides in foregrounding its distinctive formal means simultaneously asserts and denies the specificity of different arts.

Nikolais shared with Greenberg both a commitment to the value of form over content and the sense that each art form has its proper means and norms.

For instance, Nikolais draws very much the same distinction between dance and mime as Greenberg does between representational and abstract art. For Nikolais, mime "focuses on motion for the purpose of descriptive, literal expression rather than on the values of motion itself"; he goes on to say that mime approaches the condition of dance when the mime's gestures exceed representation, and that dance starts to resemble mime when the dancer's gestures are illustrative and representational (Nikolais and Louis 6). In Nikolais' analysis, mime is similar to everyday action in that the referents of its movements and gestures reside outside of them, while motion in dance is meaningful in and for itself. If mime is inherently literal, dance is inherently abstract.

Nikolais and Greenberg's shared commitment to formalism led in both cases to advocacy of abstraction. Although it is evident that abstract art draws attention to its formal means more directly than representational art, Greenberg takes a different tack in his argument for abstraction:

> Abstractness, or the non-figurative, has in itself still not proved to be an altogether necessary moment in the self-criticism of pictorial art. . . . Representation, or illustration, as such does not abate the uniqueness of pictorial art; what does do so are the associations of the things represented. All recognizable entities . . . exist in three-dimensional space, and the barest suggestion of a recognizable entity suffices to call up associations of that kind of space. The fragmentary silhouette of a human figure, or of a teacup, will do so, and by doing so alienate pictorial space from the two-dimensionality which is the guarantee of painting's independence as an art ("Modernist" 70).

For Greenberg, then, abstraction is not an end in itself but a strategy by which the artist may direct the viewer's attention where it belongs: to the formal characteristics of the work. Representation is an obstacle to this goal because of the viewer's habit of associating depicted objects with their real-world correlatives.[6] As a result of this cognitive reflex, the viewer perceives the picture in three-dimensional terms rather than in two dimensions. Abstraction short-circuits this reflex by not giving the viewer anything to recognize.

The problematics of abstraction in dance do not revolve around the issue of two- and three-dimensionality, however; that issue is relevant only to a formalist account of painting (it does not even pertain to sculpture, for which existence in three dimensions is a limiting condition). But Greenberg's argument is not primarily about dimensionality. The fundamental problematic Greenberg addressed is *referentiality:* the question of whether the formal characteristics of a work deflect attention from themselves by allowing the audience to treat the work as representing something beyond itself rather than purely self-referential.

Nikolais framed the question of abstraction in dance in precisely the same terms. Like Greenberg, Nikolais does not simply dismiss representation qua representation. The problem with *movement* as opposed to *motion* is not that movement cannot be appreciated for its abstract qualities, but that the audience will not be able to perceive those qualities because it will inevitably treat staged movement as representational. In a comment on sculpture, Nikolais argues,

> The art of sculpture, the accomplishment of a three-dimensional structure, is to arouse interest by the particularly compelling quality of the shape itself. If the shape in any way assumes a literal suggestion rather than remains primarily within the experience of the shape itself, it does not meet the purist's definition of shape. For example, if one creates a form that begins to suggest a cat, then it is likely that the onlooker will begin to relate to his experiences of that animal. He is consequently distracted at least partly from the purer sculptural relation (Nikolais and Louis 188).

Like Greenberg, Nikolais points to the difficulty of using representation to create purely formal interest. Inevitably, both conclude, the audience will be unable to get past its own experiential associations with forms perceived as representational, thus making it impossible to advance a formalist project through representation.

Nikolais acknowledges that abstract dance encounters a problematic confronted by neither painting nor sculpture: the human body. The materials of painting or sculpture can be used readily either for abstraction or figuration because they have no intrinsic properties in this regard. Indeed, the recognition that a painting is made of paint is conducive to the kind of appreciation the formalist values, since it draws attention to the work's means. "When we come to dance," Nikolais avers, "we are indeed in a quandary. The dancer is a humanoid form and recognized as such" (Nikolais and Louis 188). It would not advance the formalist cause for the audience to focus on the materiality of dance, the fact that dances are so, to say, made of dancers, for as long as the audience perceives the dancers as human bodies, it will respond to them in ways derived from its responses to bodies in everyday life, not in terms of their formal aesthetic qualities.

A dance aesthetic that parallels Greenbergian formalism thus entails a certain negation of the body. The body must be defamiliarized to the point that it becomes possible to appreciate it as a pure, self-referential form that gives rise to no extrinsic associations *qua* body. (In other words, the audience's associations should derive from the perception of motion, not from reactions to the dancers' bodies as such.) Nikolais' first gesture in this direction, in 1953, was to use unisex costumes. Nikolais felt that, thanks to this deemphasizing of the dancers' genders, "Motion could more easily become the subject rather than being an adjunct of the dancer. . . . Dance became the art of motion, freed from literal subjects" (Nikolais and Louis 9). Although it is probable that by "subjects" here Nikolais meant subject matter, theme, or narrative, another sense of the word fits as well: the perception of dance as pure motion depends on the reduction of the dancer's presence as a subject. "Motion was no longer the servant of the individual; it became the master" (9). In this formulation, the dancer's status as a subject producing movement is deemphasized in favor of seeing the dancer as an object produced by motion.

Although I would not argue that this constitutes a complete reading of Nikolais' work, many of his choreographic and theatrical strategies can be seen to serve the purpose of reducing the body's recognizability as such, thus diminishing its capacity to evoke associations in the audience. I have already noted Nikolais' own comment on unisex costuming; Muriel Broadman points out some of the other ways his use of costume and lighting served to emphasize the formal aspects of the stage picture rather than the presence of human bodies:

> At times, Nik buries his dancers in costumes of his own design, that conceal their bodies and distort any semblance of "normal" movement. At other times his dancers are garbed in skin-snug leotards patterned with camouflage-like designs that break up their outlines and give the arms and legs an almost autonomous existence. Even when Nik clothes his people in starkly unadorned tights that could reveal every nuance of movement, he's likely to play lights across them that destroy the identity of the bodies and merge them into an overall production where they are one with the lights and shadows (8).

Nikolais deployed a range of strategies that included the concealment or distortion of the body or the melding of the human form into an overall visual composition in which it enjoyed no privilege over light, color, pattern, and shape. A number of his dances involve the fracturing and dismembering of the body into individual units, the better to perceive them as formal entities. *Crucible* (1985) is a particularly good example of this device: here, the dancers are seen only one piece at a time (hands first, then arms, then legs, and so on) and perform over a reflective surface such that each image they create is a symmetrical form made up of part of a body and its reflection. The lighting prevents the audience from clearly identifying individual dancers; at some points, the dancers serve as projection surfaces for lighting effects into which they disappear. Although the forms thus created are evocative (they sometimes suggest hieroglyphics, sometimes single-celled organisms, for instance), the associations a spectator might project onto them derive from the forms on display, not from the presence of human bodies. To put it a little differently, although a form might remind one of an amoeba, one does not understand what is going on as a dancer portraying an amoeba. Rather, one is aware of the formation of abstract visual images to which signification may be attached.

In an essay that examines the choreography of George Balanchine through the lens of Greenberg's theory of modernism, David Michael Levin argues that "the defining condition, or essence, of the ballet art" is "the pure classical syntax of the mobile human body" and that Balanchine's genius lay in his development of "a modernist formalism . . . adequate . . . to the . . . release and expression of this . . . essence" (126). Whether or not Levin is right about Balanchine, the formalism he describes is not the formalism of Nikolais.[7] (From a strictly Greenbergian point of view, it is difficult to see how the body could be the defining condition of dance, since it is a means that dance shares with mime and acting, for instance.[8]) For Nikolais, the essence of dance, its limiting condition, is not the mobile human body but a concept of mobility, or motion, that has its own identity as a formal entity apart from the body and of which the body can be a vehicle but is not the source. The difference between the formalism Levin sees in Balanchine and the formalism I am attributing to Nikolais is encapsulated in their respective choices of costuming. Because Balanchine arguably treated the human body as the essential aspect of ballet, he gravitated toward costumes that reveal the dancers' bodies. Nikolais, for whom motion is the essence of dance, preferred to disguise them. For Nikolais, it is through the body that motion becomes perceptible, but that process entails, as I have suggested, a suppression of the lived, organic body in favor of the body as an abstract form:

> Instead of designing himself as a human creature in space, [the dancer] must create the means whereby his literal state of being human is subdued. His body becomes, instead, an instrument that directly reveals the quality of his space idea. It's as if we don't see the piano being played, yet we hear the sound (Nikolais and Louis 159).

The metaphor of the invisible piano is very revealing of Nikolais' basic understanding of the relationship between dancer and motion. It deemphasizes the dancer's own agency—the dancer is the piano, not the pianist or the composer—and posits the dancer's disappearance as the condition of possibility for the manifestation of motion as an abstract entity.[9]

Levin further asserts that Balanchine's modernism was anti-theatrical. Here, Levin departs from Greenberg and derives from the work of his acolyte Michael Fried the claim that "theatricality and modernist formalism contradict one another" (129).[10] While remaining agnostic on the question of whether this is an accurate characterization of Balanchine, I will insist that it is another area in which Nikolais' formalism differs from the formalism Levin imputes to Balanchine. Far from purging his dances of theatricality, Nikolais reveled in using all the visual means available to the theater (though he repudiated dramatic narrative, insisting that "the art of drama is one thing; the art of theatre is another" [Nikolais 63]). Nikolais represented himself as anything but an ascetic formalist when it came to the purity of art forms. After describing how sculptural form, sound, and color capture his attention as much as motion, he concluded: "I am not a devoted husband to dance, for I choose to marry the lot of my inamorati rather than swearing fixed fidelity to one" (Nikolais 63).

How, then, to reconcile Nikolais' professed interest in purity of form with his equally strongly professed lack of interest in purity of means? Levin argues that as a consequence of Balanchine's use of "chromatically simple backdrop[s]" and lighting that did not produce chiaroscuro effects, "the dance events, instead of being enveloped and partitioned within an externally generated space, become the constitutive source at the interior of their own total space" (140). This observation derives from Levin's claim that Balanchine took the mobile human body as the limiting condition of dance: Balanchine's use of simple backdrops and nonsculptural lighting serve to reveal the body and make it seem as if the stage space is generated from the dancers' bodies rather than their seeming to be enveloped by an autonomous space. I have already shown that Nikolais, by contrast, considered motion, not the body, to be the essence of dance and that motion is best revealed as an abstract entity when the body is effaced to the degree that it does not distract by its referentiality. It follows from this premise that the stage picture must suppress the dancers' corporeal presence by *not* revealing the body and *not* making it seem as if the space derives from its presence.

In Nikolais' productions, the dancers' bodies frequently disappear into a visual environment of which they are a relatively undifferentiated part. This is apparent in both *Tent* (1968), where the dancers are lost in folds of fabric that serves, like their costumes and bodies, as projection surfaces for Nikolais abstract slides, and *Temple* (1974), in which masked dancers appear as sculptural forms emerging from and receding into a darkened space. It is tempting to suggest a parallel between these compositional strategies and what Greenberg called the "all-over" painting, in which "every element and every area of the picture is equivalent in accent and emphasis" ("Crisis" 156) thus undoing the "dramatic effect" created by traditional easel painting (154). By refusing the human form its normal focal position on the dance stage and making it equivalent to other visual elements, Nikolais undid the "drama" of corporeal presence.[11] Dance thus begins to achieve something of the opticality Greenberg ascribed to modernist sculpture.

> To render substance entirely optical, and form, whether pictorial, sculptural, or architectural, as an integral part of ambient space—this brings anti-illusionism full circle. Instead of the illusion of things, we are now offered the illusion of modalities: namely, that matter is incorporeal, weightless, and exists only optically, like a mirage ("New Sculpture" 144).

Nikolais's use of rich theatrical means to engulf his dancers, thus dematerializing their bodies by rendering them primarily as incorporeal, optical forms, was entirely consistent with his goal of revealing abstract motion as the essence of dance.

It is noteworthy that Nikolais, who was as concerned with dance technique and pedagogy as with choreography, mandated that the dancer's creative process be conducive to his notion of abstraction. Just as Nikolais sought stage images made of human bodies that would not stimulate normal bodily associations, so he wanted dancers to dissociate themselves from the meanings usually attributed to bodily movements and gestures:

> Downward is a direction, not an emotion. Yet we are so accustomed to associating downwardness with negative emotions and behaviors that it is difficult to sense going downward as simply a motional act. We must separate it from the negative behaviorisms that are often associated with it. Sadness, moroseness, weakness, or other submissive sensations must be set aside and gravity examined in its own terms (Nikolais and Louis 14).

Movements need to be understood and appreciated strictly in terms of their objective formal qualities, not as conventional representations of affective states. Or, in Nikolais' more mantralike formulation, "dance is the art of motion, not emotion" (Nikolais and Louis 10).

Consequently, Nikolais' dancers were not to derive their physical expressions from emotional states but from a sense of movements' formal properties understood in terms of visual aesthetics: "the dancer's art is motion, and dance training must stress the communicative values of motion—not those of mime or emotion. . . . Basically, the dancer does not practice sadness, madness, gladness, or the like. The dancer's language is instead the textures of light, heavy, thick, thin, soft, hard, large and small" (Nikolais and Louis 28). The meaning of motion must reside in motion itself, not only for the audience but for the dancer as well. In order to arrive at a movement, "the dancer does not imagine an emotional nostalgia (such as love)" but establishes a relationship with "the actual environment and what he is doing in it" (Nikolais and Louis 17).

The dancer, in other words, must focus on the objective reality of movement and its production rather than on the affective state or fictional character or world the movement might suggest.[12] Ideally, this approach to movement production becomes a closed system in which motion is the only point of reference: "The performer does not imagine an emotional state or conditioned environment such as fear, hate, nostalgia, love, or the like. It is a direct action devoid of any disagreement between mind, body, and environment. The feedback from the movement supplies the nature of the movement" (Nikolais and Louis 19). In a discussion of how a dancer may define space by acting as a sort of human pen or paintbrush tracing lines (as in the metaphor of the invisible piano, the dancer is imagined as an instrument), Nikolais argues that the dancer's objective is "to give the linear design a life of its own. Any weakness in these projections will seriously weaken the strength of peripheral design and call attention back to the body" (Nikolais and Louis 159). Like the painter who allows the hint of a human form or teacup into the two-dimensional space of the canvas, dancers who assert the presence of their bodies by failing to subordinate them to the formal design of the choreography risk drawing attention away from the abstract qualities of the work and to something the audience will construe as subject matter.

I have suggested that Nikolais' dance aesthetic parallels, at least at a theoretical level, the ruminations on the aesthetics of visual art in which Greenberg engaged as a major critical voice of the New York School. Like Greenberg, Nikolais was a formalist who championed an art of pure, self-referential abstraction. In both cases, the crux of their formulations is the issue of referentiality. Both perceived mimesis and representation as problematic not primarily in themselves but because they distract audience attention from its proper object: the work's formal means and values. A significant problematic specific to Nikolais's formalist aesthetic of dance is the presence of the human body as the basic material of the art form. Whereas paint or steel can readily be used to create either representational or abstract images, the body inevitably represents itself and evokes associations beyond those suggested by the work's formal properties. Therefore, an aesthetic of formalist abstraction in dance depends on the suppression of the body. Nikolais used a range of compositional and theatrical devices to deemphasize his dancers' presence as bodies and render them as self-referential abstract forms.

Since its inception in the early part of the twentieth century, nonobjective art has been accused of "dehumanization," and Nikolais was no exception—this criticism of his work was for him a *bête noire* to be denounced on every possible occasion. He characterized his critics as issuing "cries of 'dehumanization,' 'coldness,' 'puppetry,' and 'mechanicalness'. . . . The outcries were reminiscent of the early days of abstract painting. With no figurative or representational vision offered as a portal into the painting, literal-minded people failed to get the message" (Nikolais and Louis 11).[13] Nikolais did not deny that his interests lay beyond the physiological, psychological, narrative, or affective associations of the human body, but argued that this perspective constituted a positive philosophy, a version of ecological post-humanism: "I wanted man to be able to identify with things other than himself. This [1977] is the day of ecological and environmental visions. We must give up our navel contemplations long enough to take our place in space" (qtd. in Heimbuecher A-23).

José Ortega y Gasset, in his classic 1925 essay "The Dehumanization of Art," also noted that the majority of the audience "failed to get the message" of abstract art and attempted to explain why that was. He identified abstraction in visual and literary art with a trend toward dehumanization. Two of the issues this trend raised were the question of why artists had turned away from conventional representation of recognizable subjects and the anomalous position into which an audience used to nineteenth-century realism felt itself to be placed:

With the things represented on traditional paintings we could have imaginary intercourse. Many a young Englishman has fallen in love with Gioconda. With the objects of modern pictures no intercourse is possible. By divesting them of their aspect of "lived" reality the artist has blown up the bridges and burned the ships that could have taken us back to our daily world. He leaves us locked in an abstruse universe, surrounded by objects with which human dealings are inconceivable, and thus compels us to improvise other forms of intercourse completely distinct from our ordinary ways with things (21–2).

We can translate these reasons for the audience's discomfort with modern art into questions of *agency:* Why do modern artists employ their agency to create these hermetic worlds? And what kind of agency do audiences have in relation to them; how can we respond?

These critical questions certainly arose in response to both Abstract Expressionism and Nikolais' abstract dance. But in the context of dance, or any kind of performance, a third issue comes up as well, if only implicitly: the agency of the performer. I have shown that Nikolais consistently described his dancers by using metaphors of instrumentality and invisibility and that his emphasis on motion as a self-sufficient formal entity necessitated the subjugation of the performer's physical presence, which can only distract from it. Arguably, the problematic of the body makes performance a particularly provocative arena in which to experiment with formalist abstraction. Even those spectators who may feel at sea (to continue Ortega's metaphor) when confronted by nonobjective visual art do not usually trouble themselves over the agency of paint or steel. By contrast, the seeming dehumanization not just of images but also of human bodies as the material of an artwork is fraught because it transgresses boundaries that are sites of anxiety: between human being and thing, subject and object, autonomy and automatism.

By embracing an aesthetic of formalist abstraction and successfully adapting its terms to dance practice, Nikolais opened himself to the accusation of dehumanization that has haunted the modernist project from its inception. Although Greenbergian formalism is vulnerable to critique on the additional grounds of reductionism and essentialism (Fried 69), Greenberg and Nikolais both saw abstraction as extending agency by opening up new, more contemporary possibilities for artists. Rather than being locked into nineteenth-century canons of representation, artists were free to experiment with form as an end in itself. Both Abstract Expressionism and Nikolais' dance thus enacted the tension between the twin modernist desires to shake off the universal human subject as the referent of art and to celebrate a universalizing idea of form.

NOTES

1. If Greenberg emphasized the abstract side of Abstract Expressionism, critic Harold Rosenberg emphasized the expressionist side. In his 1952 essay "The American Action Painters," Rosenberg described Abstract Expressionism by saying, "A painting that is an act is inseparable from the biography of the artist. . . . The act-painting is of the same metaphysical substance as the artist's existence. The new painting has broken down every distinction between art and life" (216).

2. In terms of dance theory, I see strong parallels between Nikolais' formalism and that of Rayner Heppenstall, who said of ballet "it expresses only itself" (qtd. in Levin 141).

3. Nikolais and Greenberg also were nearly exact contemporaries: Nikolais was born in 1910 and died in 1993; Greenberg was born in 1909 and died in 1994.

4. As Ashton points out, many of the basic tenets of Greenberg's aesthetic theory, particularly the emphasis on the two-dimensionality of painting, came from the painter Hans Hofmann's teachings, a debt Greenberg acknowledged (Ashton 82).

5. For a brief discussion of the reaction against Greenberg in art criticism of the late 1970s and early 1980s, see Melville (87–9). Marshall Cohen argues that Greenberg's definition of modernism was inconsistent over time (170–2). For a sustained analysis and critique of Greenberg, see Kuspit (particularly 161–81).

6. Greenberg was not the first to arrive at this idea, of course; it has a long history in the discourse of modern art. José Ortega y Gasset, for example, in his 1925 essay on "The Dehumanization of Art," described the same problem: "Instead of delighting in the artistic object people delight in their own emotions, the work being only the cause and the alcohol of their pleasure. And such a *quid pro quo* is bound to happen whenever art is made to consist essentially in an exposition of 'lived' realities. 'Lived' realities are too overpowering not to evoke a sympathy from us which prevents us from perceiving them in their objective purity" (28).

7. Marshall Cohen argues that Levin's description and analysis of Balanchine's choreography are inaccurate (173–6).

8. Nikolais once commented that whereas "the dancer's art is motion . . . the actor's basic substance is emotion" (qtd. in Copeland 43). This is consistent with a Greenbergian approach. By implying that dancing and acting share the body as a means, Nikolais suggests that the presence of the body is not the defining condition of either form. That distinction lies in the *use* of the body. In Nikolais' view, the essential characteristic of dance is that the dancer uses the body as a vehicle for abstract motion, while the essential characteristic of acting is that the actor uses the body to express emotion and further a narrative.

9. There is, admittedly, a syntactical ambiguity in Nikolais' statement, such that it is not clear whether the piano and the one playing it both are invisible, or whether only the pianist is invisible. I have opted for the former reading, but either deemphasizes the agency of the dancer.

10. The reference here is to Fried's notorious essay "Art and Objecthood" (1967). For more on Fried's putative anti-theatricalism and its influence, see Auslander, "Presence."

11. In this respect, Nikolais' dance parallels Happenings, a form of art-world performance contemporaneous with his own work in the late 1950s through the mid-1960s. Michael Kirby suggests that Happenings also placed human bodies on

a par with other elements: "'acting' tends to exist on the same level as the physical aspects of the production . . . the performer frequently is treated in the same fashion as a prop or a stage effect" (19).

12. Willem Dafoe has expressed to me similar ideas about performing, whether in movies or Wooster Group performances. He sees his primary relationship while performing as being with the structure of the piece, the situation of performance, and the physical activity in which he is engaged, rather than with character or narrative. It is interesting that he compares his own work as a performer to dance: "I've always maintained that I'm more interested in dance than acting" (qtd. in Auslander, "Task" 100).

13. See also Nikolais (64), Copeland (41–3), and Heimbuecher (A-23).

WORKS CITED

Ashton, Dore. *The New York School: A Cultural Reckoning.* Harmondsworth: Penguin, 1972.

Auslander, Philip. "*Presence* and *Theatricality* in the Discourse of Performance and the Visual Arts." *From Acting to Performance: Essays in Modernism and Postmodernism.* London: Routledge, 1997, 49–57.

———. "Task and Vision Revisited: Two Conversations with Willem Dafoe (1984/2002)." *The Wooster Group and Its Traditions.* Johan Callens, ed. Brussels: P.I.E.—Peter Lang, 2004, 95–105.

Broadman, Muriel. "Nikolais Dance Theatre: Shedding Light on the Future of Dance." *Cue* 24 July–6 Aug. 1976: 8–9

Copeland, Roger. "A Conversation with Alwin Nikolais." *Dance Scope* Fall/Winter 1973–74: 41–6.

Copeland, Roger and Marshall Cohen. "The Dance Medium." *What is Dance?* Roger Copeland and Marshall Cohen, eds. Oxford: Oxford University Press, 1983, 103–10.

Cohen, Marshall. "Primitivism, Modernism, and Dance Theory." *What is Dance?* Roger Copeland and Marshall Cohen, eds. Oxford: Oxford University Press, 1983, 160–78.

Cohen, Selma Jeanne. "The Caterpillar's Question." *The Modern Dance: Seven Statements of Belief.* Selma Jeanne Cohen, ed. Middletown, CT: Wesleyan University Press, 1965, 3–14.

Fried, Michael. "How Modernism Works." *Pollock and After: The Critical Debate.* Francis Frascina, ed. New York: Harper and Row, 1985, 65–79.

Greenberg, Clement. "Avant-Garde and Kitsch." 1939. *Pollock and After: The Critical Debate.* Francis Frascina, ed. New York: Harper and Row, 1985, 21–33.

———. "The Crisis of the Easel Picture." 1948. *Art and Culture.* Boston: Beacon Press, 1961, 154–7.

————. "Modernist Painting." 1965. *The New Art (Revised).* Gregory Battcock, ed. New York: Dutton, 1973, 66–77.

————. "The New Sculpture." 1948. *Art and Culture.* Boston: Beacon Press, 1961, 139–45.

————. "Towards a Newer Laocoon." 1940. *Pollock and After: The Critical Debate.* Francis Frascina, ed. New York: Harper and Row, 1985, 35–46.

Heimbuecher, Ruth. "Versatile Nikolais Strives to Differ." *Pittsburgh Press* 17 March 1977: A-23.

Kirby, Michael. *Happenings.* New York: Dutton, 1966.

Kuspit, Donald. *Clement Greenberg: Art Critic.* Madison: University of Wisconsin Press, 1979.

Levin, David Michael. "Balanchine's Formalism. *What is Dance?* Roger Copeland and Marshall Cohen, eds. Oxford: Oxford University Press, 1983, 123–45.

Melville, Stephen. "Postmodernism and Art: Postmodernism Now and Again." *The Cambridge Companion to Postmodernism.* Steven Connor, ed. Cambridge: Cambridge University Press, 2004, 82–96.

Nikolais, Alwin. "No Man From Mars." *The Modern Dance: Seven Statements of Belief.* Selma Jeanne Cohen, ed. Middletown, Ct: Wesleyan University Press, 1965, 63–75.

Nikolais, Alwin and Murray Louis. *The Nikolais/Louis Dance Technique: A Philosophy and Method of Modern Dance.* New York: Routledge, 2005.

Ortega y Gasset, José. "The Dehumanization of Art." 1925. Helene Weyl, trans. *The Dehumanization of Art and Other Essays on Art, Culture, and Literature.* Princeton, NJ: Princeton University Press, 1968, 1–54.

Rosenberg, Harold. "The American Action Painters." 1952. *American Art 1700– 1960.* John W. McCoubrey, ed. Englewood Cliffs, NJ: Prentice-Hall, 1965, 213–22.

CHAPTER 10

Period Plots, Canonical Stages, and Post-Metanarrative in American Modern Dance

MARK FRANKO

> *"The historical moment of the disciplines was the moment when an art of the human body was born, which was directed not only at the growth of skills, nor at the intensification of its subjection, but at the formation of a relation that in the mechanism itself makes it more obedient as it becomes more useful."—Michel Foucault*

This chapter assumes that any reevaluation of the critical reception of Alwin Nikolais' work has to account for the discourse of modernism and its role in canon formation. What allows choreographic work to achieve and sustain visibility in the modern-dance field pertains both to the choreographer's efforts at self-promotion and to the discourse the work does or does not elicit. You don't exist unless people talk about you, and they don't talk about you unless your work continues to be performed. What can be said—what it is possible to say at a particular time and place—affects the ability of choreography to engage the circuits of criticism and publicity, and to consolidate itself in historical accounts.[1] All these discursive phenomena have been dominated in the United States since the 1930s by the precepts of esthetic modernism.

Since many practitioners continue to draw distinctions between dance and discourse, let me flesh the idea out a bit further. Once a dance is performed— delivered into public space—it elicits responses that can take the form of talking or silence, writing or not writing, and further dancing or not dancing. At the moment of performance the dance enters into or becomes part of something we could call discourse, and it is also revealed as having itself emerged from discourse. I am describing a state of affairs that I believe to be that of dance in modernity, but one that exceeds the discourse of modernism itself. It would be particularly unacceptable to the dance-modernist position to say that a dance engages in/with discourse that occurs openly, publicly, and in an open-ended way. Instead, the modernist would ascribe to an "organicist" view of choreographic innovation, in which dance occurs before language and remains autonomous from it because the corporeal sources of creativity are considered to be constitutionally separate from discourse.[2] Just as it is a modernist article of faith that the body is the "absolute" material of artistic creation, so the body is construed as divorced by that very fact from language. Against this view, I am positing continuity between dance and all that circulates around and "outside" it, before it and after it: notably, discourse.[3] What an artist says or does not say—does or does not do—enters into the discourse that dances manifest, but also call forth about themselves and other things. Yet there is a discourse of modernism that upholds the separation of dance and discourse, and which has dominated the discourse that it is possible to have of dance. One important effect of the discourse of modernism is the canon; one role of the canon is to safeguard the continuation of the discourse of modernism.

The art that a culture, or a given professional class within the culture, believes *should* be seen again (even if revisiting it is not practically feasible) constitutes the canon. In twentieth-century theatrical dance history the canon was largely determined by the discourse of modernism. A new awareness of the undue influence of canonical works in culture emerged in the 1980s, prompted by vituperative debates about the canon raging in the fields of literature, music, and visual culture. That these debates took place in the academic milieu indicated that the contents of the disciplines were under attack. These debates brought to general awareness how canonical works do more than just monopolize the networks of dissemination: they actually *constitute* the "curriculum" in the form of texts, scores, museum exhibitions, and repertories.[4] One of the most important effects of the canon is, in other words, exclusion. Canonical works are deemed the cultural objects most worthy of sustained and repeated attention, and are thus best positioned to merit rearticulation across time. In other terms, they are the most likely candidates to be anthologized, reread, reheard, and reseen. In this way, canonical works establish a certain cultural hegemony within any given field of study or cultural pursuit.

I evoke this debate to ask why no debate has taken place over the dance canon comparable to that in neighboring fields. Perhaps it is because choreographers, failing to grasp objectively the way canon formation functions, have worked in cooperation with its mechanisms, continuing to hope it would one day include them.[5] What form would such a debate applied to dance take? First, it would have to revisit the old differences between modern dance and ballet from a new perspective. This distinction has been proverbially drawn on the esthetic differences between modern and classical techniques. But another distinction emerges in the light of the canon. Given the relative homogeneity of ballet technique worldwide, ballet companies can and do collect repertory, and have greater latitude in mounting retrospectives than most modern companies.[6] The ballet company that brought this most clearly to our attention some time ago was the Joffrey Ballet. In a series of unprecedented reconstructions of important but forgotten twentieth-century works— Kurt Jooss's *The Green Table* (1932, reconstructed in 1967), the Picasso/Satie *Parade* (1917, reconstructed in 1979), and Vaslav Nijinsky's *Rite of Spring* (1913, reconstructed in 1987)—the idea of repertory as a vital reflection on history became a reality this company performed. By contrast, the Martha Graham Dance Company, although it has extended its retrospective scope to a few works by choreographers who influenced Graham, such as Ruth St. Denis and Ted Shawn, generally limits its revivals to works its founder created between 1926 and her death in 1991.[7] Most modern-dance companies specialize in performing the works of the founding choreographer and therefore operate from within their own choreographic and dance-technical "archive," whereas most ballet companies work with a wider and more eclectic repertory.[8] Consequently, the ballet world is less dependent upon the modernist metanarrative than the world of modern dance. "A canon is an idea; a repertory is a program of action."[9]

What drives this difference between repertory or, to borrow Diana Taylor's term, *repertoire*, and archive, is the status of technique.[10] Ballet technique is international and thus parochial, whereas modern techniques are highly differentiated from one another and thus more specialized.[11] This is not to deny that different ballet choreographers cultivate different understandings of ballet technique, but the single-choreographer ballet company has been more unusual than the single-choreographer modern company, and it is worth noting that the works of ballet choreographers such as George Balanchine, Jerome Robbins, and William Forsythe are in the repertory of a number of ballet companies. There is, of course, a parallel ballet modernism whose cycloid is Nijinsky-Nijinska-Balanchine with its arbitrarily neglected figures (Goleizovsky, Jacobson, Tudor, etc.). But despite the balletic metanarrative, ballets are normally performed in a substantially less "archival" context.[12] Evidence for this can be found in the variety of interpretations permitted, and even expected, of the nineteenth-century classics.

There is another aspect of modern-dance technique that historically favored the exclusionist character of the modern-dance company. Modern techniques in both Germany and America presented themselves as nativist and bore the ideological burden of reflecting national identity. The exclusivity of modern techniques is also a direct result of the discourse of modernism that maintained the importance of technical innovation as a criterion for creative accomplishment. It is a well-known fact that until at least the 1950s any self-respecting modern-dance choreographer was expected to invent and transmit by teaching their own unique dance technique, which was understood to be the matrix of their choreographic activity. The fact that Nikolais did not focus on the codification of a movement vocabulary as much as on a technique for improvisation that would answer choreographic problems places him in some important sense outside the discourse of modernism, but within the framework of the twentieth-century avant-gardes. The Bauhaus is noteworthy in this context.[13]

These reflections were generated by the question of what the debate on canonicity would look like should it have occurred in the dance field. So here we could ask ourselves what the equivalent of the canonical reading list is for the university dance curriculum. Its equivalent is technique as taught in the studio. Technique classes offered in many university dance departments tend to be either in modern dance or ballet. The modern techniques have until recently been those of canonical modernist figures: notably Graham and Cunningham. Thus, to ask how the canon became "academicized" in the university curriculum involves inquiring into the universal value of modern and ballet techniques. Currently the demand for a change in educational emphasis toward world dance cultures is putting the universal value of these canonical techniques into question. The fact remains that technique and training are media of canon formation in the university. In this sense, the canonicity of modern dance is supported by techniques, which from this angle take on the status of the archive. A connection thus begins to emerge between technique, the archive, the canon, and dance as a discipline. This connection begs the question of the institutionalization of dance and the historical grounding of its appearance in the academy. It merits a short digression.

The relationship between dance and academe in America began at the University of Wisconsin in 1926 under the auspices of dance educator Margaret H'Doubler.[14] This was the beginning of what became known as dance education. A professionalized relationship to the university was initiated when prominent modern-dance choreographers took up summer residency at Bennington College in Vermont in 1934, where they taught their dance techniques and developed new choreography for the New York concert scene with professionals and apprentices.[15] This was the beginning of modern-dance pedagogy within the humanities and arts curricula. Both the educational and professionalized discourses of university dance hinged on the modern. What distinguished the late nineteenth- and early twentieth-century European forerunners and innovators of modern dance (François Delsarte, Emile-Jacques

1. Gladys Bailin and Bill Frank in Runic Canto *(1957). Photograph David S. Berlin, courtesy of the Nikolais/Louis Foundation.*

Dalcroze, Rudolf von Laban, and even Isadora Duncan, whose career was primarily European) from the European ballet tradition of the nineteenth century was their implicit or explicit educational mission. Moreover, given the emphasis of Central European modern-dance pedagogy on composition over training—a trait largely disseminated in America too—modern dance suited the liberal arts curriculum better than could classical ballet.[16] Although the modern dancer's creative horizon did not exclude technical proficiency, the ultimate horizon of her skills was less performance per se than the creation of original dances to perform. By contrast, the ballet dancer was generally viewed as a (pyro)technician in a theatrical spectacle, placing little value on research and creativity.[17] Thus, thanks to the disciplinary formations of dance education and modern-dance pedagogy, choreography acquired the status of a liberal art in the context of American universities, whereas classical dancing was disparaged as a strictly vocational pursuit. As dance became an academic discipline, it tended to undermine the disciplinary practices (in Foucault's sense of useful obedience) of dance in favor of self-exploration and self-discovery, from which dance therapies also stem. This trend is at odds with the European system, in which the formation of the dancer for the professional world of dance performance takes precedence over secondary cultural considerations. State-supported conservatories that constitute the professional "art field" in dance back the European system. The disciplinary standards of such institutions are unmistakable. In both Europe and America the existence of choreographers is still at a premium with relationship to the formation of dancers, and lacks, for the most part, official and formally sanctioned rites of passage. What is institutionalized in the American academic world as choreographic practice is in the professional dance world the least trainable function.[18]

Another aspect of the canon at stake in the curriculum of university dance is the teaching of dance history and theory. Sali Ann Kriegsman noted in her keynote address to the conference "Dance Reconstructed" in 1992: "Dance is still a young art in terms of collecting its history. A dance canon does not really exist as yet."[19] I think it is a familiar gesture of such assessments from within the dance field to defer the encounter of dance with its own past. But if a literary scholar believes left-wing women authors of the 1930s need to be studied, she first rediscovers the important texts and then gets them published or republished. Analogous operations occur in dance. A myth of the unrealizable totality seems to inhibit thinking about and acting on the past.[20]

The digression into the history of dance's institutionalization in the university brings us back to the issue of the canon. The canon can be camouflaged as such in the disciplinary knowledge web. I have two additional caveats with respect to the supposed nonexistence of the canon. First, the field of dance studies, since its inception in the 1980s, has been concerned with either challenging the idea of the dance canon or with substantially broadening it. This has occurred with the rehabilitation of lesser-known or unknown choreographers and movements as well as through the rediscovery of minoritized dance communities and dance subcultures. Such critiques indicate that a certain concept of the canon does exist in dance, and that dance studies, like ethnomusicology, which began in the 1950s, has radically different views from those of traditional dance history as to what the canon is and/or how to treat it in historical and contemporary contexts.[21] In fact, dance studies wages a battle for the interpretation of history against the canon itself.[22] Dance studies is the first major departure from the discourse of dance modernism and, as such, is to be distinguished from the dance history that preceded it. As it struggles to establish itself as an academic discipline, dance studies poses an epistemological challenge to neighboring disciplines in the humanities and social sciences, thus demonstrating that its assault on the canon is also potentially an assault (albeit of a neighborly sort) on the disciplinary structure of academic knowledge, which the canon itself, in its various academic manifestations, is designed to underwrite.[23]

Apart from the scholarly community, the world of dance practice has recently been obliged to engage with canonical issues from the perspective of documentation and preservation.[24] The institutions concerned primarily with dance practice seem motivated by an effort to shore up a failing historical infrastructure. The millennial divide is rife with calls for heritage conservation and at the threshold of digital translation of existing archived moving images, as well as beset by thorny issues of public access to such resources; canon formation has been displaced from live performance to the visual archive. This archive consists of photographs and other ephemera, but most importantly of films of lost works and performers, as well as of more recent videos of reconstructions. Access to a broad range of archival materials and reconstructions constitutes an impetus to widen the idea of the canon, and Kriegsman was doubtless foreseeing this in her 1992 remarks. With reduced resources for live performance, the importance of reconstruction has diminished, but the potential of dance to survive in new media technologies has increased. Thus, in a slightly paradoxical sense, dance studies emerged at the dawn of the digital age, presaging the parallel emergence of a visual archive that would support its vision of noncanonical proliferations.

Debates that did occur in the dance scholarly community in the 1980s about the reconstruction of dances, from the Renaissance and the Baroque periods to lesser-known aspects of historical modern dance, brought dance's past into contact with contemporary performance practices. In this context, issues of authenticity, academicism, reinvention, and reinterpretation superceded the prerogative of techniques. Kriegsman may mean by *canon* a sort of dance museum where valued works of the past would be consistently reperformed; this indeed does not yet exist. Yet given the disciplinary functions of the museum, could we expect such a utopian concept of the dance museum to come about?[25] I think reconstruction was a significant part of *contemporary creative* practice in the 1980s. I would like to claim that it constituted, in fact, the debate over the canon in the dance field, albeit a debate that appeared less polemical than in other fields. I shall return to this shortly in the context of a counter-history of modernist canonicity.

Let us dwell further on the sense of the canon, which I take to mean a social-critical compact that silently and effectively determines whose work can be seen and for how long. For musicologist Marcia J. Citron "the controversy boils down to a struggle over power: who will decide what is studied, which in turn becomes emblematic of society itself."[26] It seems to me that dance culture has long languished under the threat of innovation, a direct result of the discourse of modernism. Those choreographers who can expose their work, shown with the frequency necessary to keep them visible and marketable, are all presented as innovating, as doing "new" work. This is a fundamental tenet of modernism: to outdo the predecessor in refining the stakes of their game.[27] The premium is on aesthetic innovation, and the ideal is an apolitical, aesthetically articulated progress toward new frontiers.[28] The progress in question historically concerned the reduction of dance's dependence on extrinsic elements such as narrative. Its goal was the autonomy of dance as an art form through the reduction of subject matter to the essence of its own medium: movement. This is a speculative, or in some sense idealist, project. I have proposed that the American modern-dance canon has been emplotted in the course of the twentieth century from the cycloid: Duncan, Graham, Cunningham. In this cycloid, what is important is not that we can still see the works of these choreographers today, but that the rejection of Duncan occasions Graham, just as the rejection of Graham occasions Cunningham. The rejection of a predecessor acts as the warrant for the visibility of the successor. The plot is woven from the most radicalized dramas of rejection, which can simultaneously preserve the organicist prejudice in dance making. This prejudice consists in placing the highest value on innovation in the reformulation of techniques. I do not believe the authenticity debates of

1980s reconstruction were part of the narrative essential to canon formation. Reconstructions were quite the opposite, because they hinted at an untamed value in past (even forgotten) work. Reconstructed works could make a contribution to the contemporary world not as surpassed predecessors *to* it but as active participants *in* it. To my mind, this was disturbing to the idea of canonicity, because with the unsettling returns heralded by reconstructions different historical accounts of origins were being implicitly proposed. Even if these performances were not in themselves polemical, they pinpointed the possibility of thinking canonical history not through its confirming end point but through odd revisitations that were anything but dogmatic. Historical reconstructions had the effect of pluralizing histories of origin. Ultimately, this amounted to a competing, nonlinear concept of history at odds with the modernist narrative of successionist progress.

One such return was that of the founding mother, Isadora Duncan herself; with the plethora of reconstructions since the 1970s came the realization that Duncan's choreography had not disappeared, but was preserved. This shifted notions of technique and institutionalization away from the founding era of the 1930s and introduced an anachronistic sensibility into the metanarrative. Duncan was no longer a forgotten origin, but a newly relevant figure—relevant in particular to nascent feelings that were coalescing around cultural feminism. Duncan's position as an origin was counteracted by several factors that complexified our grasp of dance history and its role in contemporary performance practices. Indeed, Duncan suddenly appeared to stand at the origin of a counter history through the multifaceted representations reconstructions afforded of her dancing. Canons are, in short, always constructed with respect to particular conceptions of history: they are always retrospective inasmuch as they are effects of periodization. Periodization is a function of what Hayden White has called emplotment—the creation of plots adequate to the representation of history.[29] Different sorts of emplotment bring with them different tropes governing narrative structures as well as different ideological presuppositions.

Here is a plot: the decade of the 1930s is the foundational decade of modern dance. It is a period when the discourses of criticism take hold—most notably the influential voices of John Martin at the *New York Times* and Louis Horst at the *Dance Observer*—as well as the sense that modern dance was a new art form engaged in a self-legitimating process. We see the debate over dance and politics as well as the first, albeit short-lived, federal sponsorship of dance. In sum, the decade of the thirties offers us what Jean-François Lyotard called the metanarrative of twentieth-century culture as emancipa-

2. Tim Harling in Liturgies *(1983). Photograph Peter Koletzke, courtesy of the Nikolais/Louis Foundation.*

tion: the left-leaning emancipation of the working class as well as the emancipation of American dance from European and class-oriented models.[30] Alongside this unifying principle is the speculative one that Lyotard also identifies
as legitimating scientific knowledge.[31] The idea of disinterested truth in the
scientific sphere finds its correlate in the purity of movement that underwrites modernist succession, legitimating artistic innovation as authentic. The
narrative of dance modernism consolidates self-consciously into a canon, however, only in the 1940s, when the connection between individual and collective identity is achieved both artistically and critically. This was the period of
Martha Graham's Americana works from *American Document* in 1938 to *Appalachian Spring* in 1944, when modern dance became widely accepted for its
thematic and aesthetic ties to national identity. More than any other choreographies, Graham's Americana established this connection in the public mind,
and thus brought great popularity to modern dance.[32] The forties also witness
the consolidation of techniques, which Randy Martin has identified as central to the institutionalization of modern dance both on the stage and in the
university, in the form of dances that supported nationalism while still retaining aspects of popular-front ideology.[33] The popular front shifted the ethi-
cal burden of humanism from economic and social egalitarianism to resistance to fascism. In this context, the nation was valued as an important factor
in individual identity, while the ability to criticize it remained lively and alert.

From the end of World War II until the late 1950s, the model for modern
dance making changed radically in that, as with the visual arts, myth became
the preferred antidote to the popular-front aesthetic.[34] In this way, modern
dance became more preoccupied with the unconscious and less interested in
the ethics and politics of emancipation. The political repression of the Mc-
Carthy era consolidated the apparently apolitical stance of choreographers
who had rejected popular-front aesthetics. By the mid-fifties some dance was
used for international cultural export, as a tool of American foreign policy:
modern dance, like abstract expressionist painting became branded as an indigenous American art that emblematized the artist's freedom in Western
culture. Privileging certain choreographers as cultural ambassadors meant
that the canon would now be determined on the basis of international consumption.[35] As Randy Martin has noted, even the radical destabilization of
dance technique by the pedestrian body of the early sixties—a phenomenon
that was hardly thought to fit the cultural requirements of foreign policy—
could still be paradoxically subsumed, if not crassly instrumentalized, within
a desire for global hegemony.[36] The very neutrality of this body in its most ob-
jectivist moment could be mapped onto a new version of universality, one

whose national characteristics were submerged, yet nonetheless all too evident. My narrative of canonicity concludes a bit earlier with Cunningham, whose choreographic career begins in the 1940s, but who accedes to prominence in the sixties. Following White's theory of historical emplotment, one could say that the modernist metanarrative is "contextualist": "The Contextualist insists that 'what happened' in the field can be accounted for by the specification of the functional interrelationships existing among the agents and agencies occupying the field at a given time."[37] The contextualist mode of emplotment is satirical (hence the critical edge to succession), and its mode of ideological implication is liberal.

What I have just proposed is a period plot that sketches the reasoning behind the canonical formation of dance modernism. Of course, it leaves out a lot. For example, it does not take into account Agnes DeMille's *Bloomer Girl* (1944), Katherine Dunham's *Southland* (1951), Paul Sanasardo and Donya Feuer's *Laughter After All* (1960), or, for that matter, the work of Alwin Nikolais during the 1950s and 1960s.[38] But that is just the point; canons are exclusionary. We can note that the cycloid as such only crystallizes in the mid-sixties with the ascendancy of Cunningham as the modern-dance choreographer who finally succeeds in perfecting the stakes of self-referentiality in movement through aleatory procedures and the noncorrespondence of music and choreography. Weak versions of this plot also exist, such as that of Mark Morris taking up the project of choreography wed to music that Balanchine started, and adding to this claims to apoliticalness. My purpose here is not to revisit all the vicissitudes of the metanarrative, but to point out instead the nonprogressive or "nonnarrative" position of the fifties within this period plot. In any period plot the decade of the fifties occupies an anomalous position. If we can agree that the thirties represents the initiation of the canon, that the forties witnesses its institutionalization, and that the sixties has been interpreted as fully accomplishing its cyclical trajectory, what are we to make of the fifties?

In the seventies Don McDonagh wrote that the fifties was a fall between two rises. "Modern dance," he wrote in *The Rise and Fall and Rise of Modern Dance*, " the only form of serious, indigenous theatrical dance developed entirely outside the tradition of classical ballet, reached a pinnacle of acclaim in the 1930s."[39] The very critical voices that championed the rise of modern dance in the thirties—Martin and Horst—fell, McDonagh shows, out of sympathy with the fifties innovators whose work would only take on its full significance in the sixties. McDonagh ascribed the anomalous position of the fifties to a significant generation gap between young choreographers and es-

tablished critics. One could add to this the phenomenon of anomaly the si-
lencing of dissent as a result of the McCarthyism of the early fifties, and the
subsequent new role of modern dance choreographers as cold-war cultural
ambassadors. Both factors required what Serge Guilbaut has labeled "political apoliticism."[40] The standards of legitimacy become more enmeshed in
extra-artistic considerations and became simultaneously less ethically and
politically based. These are all symptoms of anxiety over the canon in the
dance field of the fifties. McDonagh's history was, according to White's ter-
minology, "formist": "the depiction of the variety, color and vividness of the
historical field is taken as the central aim."[41] Each chapter in McDonagh's
book is devoted to an individual choreographer's work. To pursue White's
schema, McDonagh's mode of emplotment is romantic, and its mode of ideological implication is anarchist.[42] It was no longer possible to embrace new
developments as direct results of the modernist canon of the preceding
decades, nor was it possible to debate the political tenor of new and ongoing
work in the cold-war climate that showed itself favorable to the survival of
dance in some respects. Thus, the two conditions that presided over the
thirties—critical advocacy and political controversy—became unavailable to
the fifties. Cunningham marks this collapse of the metanarrative even though
he has also been used to shore it up.[43] Modern dance survived fascism, World
War II, and McCarthyism, and was poised by the fifties to develop outside the
metanarrative that had prevailed since the thirties and forties. This was the
seed of what became known by the late sixties as the dance boom.

The modernist reappropriation of the sixties that eventually took hold—
that of Sally Banes starting with *Terpsichore in Sneakers*—recuperated the
work that McDonagh perceived to be in a state of free float—yet again—to
the modernist metanarrative. But decidedly something else was at work here,
something that might begin to be illuminated with reference to Lyotard's
idea of the postmodern condition as "incredulity toward metanarratives."[44]
Even though Cunningham's work was painstakingly interpreted in such as way
as to accommodate the modernist metanarrative of succession, no successor
to Cunningham could be found.[45] The point here is not to ask whether Cunningham completes that narrative or takes off in another direction in spite of
itself (it is well known that he does both), but to point out that by the sixties
we find ourselves in the domain of the "post." The postmodern is also the
post-metanarrative. Indeed, the period between the 1950s and the 1980s, while
named as the dance boom, is more pertinently the period the modernist metanarrative can no longer adjudicate. It is "post" with respect to this narrative
rather than with respect to a style called modernism. Dance studies emerges

in the eighties as a means to open the dance field to another sort of proliferation, which is the historical and critical revisioning of the entire history of (modern) dance. In other terms, dance studies emerges at the moment when the rejection of the metanarrative becomes a self-conscious historical reality. Dance studies signals a discursive shift away from the modernist metanarrative. Choreography since the fifties motivates this discursive shift. With the loss of the autonomy of the modern, the loss of the imperative to innovate technically if not choreographically, and the loss of a formal linear narrative regulating emplotment, we witness between the fifties and the end of the eighties the explosion of many different modernisms and postmodernisms, we also witness the concurrent burgeoning of new dance programs in the academy and the development of other "studies" programs (cultural, performance, American, Africanist) within which dance also found a place, as well as the multiplication of new dance companies and of independent choreographic projects; we further witness the consideration of dance as a self-sustaining business and a vital sector of the economy, especially during the Reagan era.

The assault on the NEA foreclosed the period of noncanonical dance. The dismantling of the NEA sealed the delegitimation of metanarative with the delegitimation of dance *tout court*, making subsequent debates over the canon unnecessary.[46] With the dance bust, canon formation became a strictly retrospective question. Revisiting this moment of disenfranchisement from the perspective of the new millennium, one can see that the ultraconservative assault was aimed at the entire period from the 1950s to the 1980s: the "postmodern" period. In this nonnarrative terminus to the modernist metanarrative we can perceive the politically risky potential of canonical deregulation. Perhaps this last bit of emplotment I offer here may be helpful in situating the heretofore-unrecognized values of Alwin Nikolais's choreographic output and new ways of historicizing those values.

NOTES

1. The choreographic event is a *discursive event* in the Foucauldian sense. See Michel Foucault, *The Archaeology of Knowledge,* translated by A. M. Sheridan Smith (London, Tavistock Publications, 1972).

2. Roger Copeland has identified this set of modernist assumptions about dance as primitivism, and located the repudiation of primitivism in avant-garde choreography since the 1960s. I think the discursive practices of modernism are also policing the disciplinary boundaries of dance. From this perspective, primitivism might be too restrictive a term where it is an issue of innovating while respecting

the disciplinary boundaries that sever movement from speech. See Roger Copeland, "Postmodern Dance and the Repudiation of Primitivism," *The Partisan Review* (1983), 101–121.

3. For a more developed statement of this position, see Mark Franko, "Dance and Figurability," *The Salt of the Earth: On Dance, Politics, and Reality*, edited by Steven de Belder (Brussels: Flemish Theater Institute, 2001), 33–57.

4. See Keith Moxey, "Motivating History," in Art Bulletin 77/3 (September 1995), 392–401; Katherine Bergeron and Philip V. Bohlman, editors, *Disciplining Music: Musicology and its Canons* (Chicago and London: University of Chicago Press, 1992); and the "Canons" issue of *Critical Inquiry* 10/1 (September 1983).

5. I am indebted to Cynthia Jean Cohen Bull for this insight. One day, as I entered her studio for a meeting of the New York Study Group in the eighties, she greeted me saying: "Mark, do you realize you will never be part of the canon?"

6. The Frederick Ashton retrospective performed at Lincoln Center in the summer of 2004 by several ballet companies was a case in point.

7. Influences on Graham are nonetheless denied as such in the name of her revolt from predecessors. The most recent title of a Graham retrospective is "Prelude and Revolt: Denishawn to Graham." See my remarks in what follows on the narrative of succession in modernist canon formation. On this most recent retrospective, see Jack Anderson, "Stepping Gracefully Through a Memorable History," *New York Times* (July 1, 2005), section E, page 5.

8. That the companies of canonical modern choreographers do view their repertory as an archive is attested to by the recent initiative to license the performance of their works. Licensing works to companies not specialized in a particular modern style is becoming a source of revenue that can support the survival of the repertoire. The Anna Sokolow Archive Company is a case in point.

9. Joseph Kerman, "A Few Canonic Variations," *Critical Inquiry* 10/1 (September 1983), 107.

10. Diana Taylor has described distinctions between the archive and the repertoire as parallel to the distinction between recorded and embodied knowledge. See her book *The Archive and the Repertoire. Performing Cultural Memory in the Americas* (Durham, NC: Duke University Press, 2003), 19–23.

11. An interesting illustration of this point is to be found in the film *Probe Sacre*, which documents Pina Bausch teaching the role of the Chosen One in her *Rite of Spring* to a Japanese dancer who was evidently trained in Graham technique. Although the result is ultimately successful, the process of translating movement across techniques, as the filmed rehearsal shows, is excruciating.

12. Unless, of course, an archival attitude is adopted by the choreographer, as with Pierre Lacotte's productions of nineteenth-century ballets at the Paris Opera in the 1980s.

13. Debra McCall's reconstruction of Oskar Schlemmer's "Bauhaus dances," which were performed extensively between 1981 and the early 1990s, brought this alternative avant-garde tradition to our attention. It could be described as broadly as "mechanical" or "technological" in opposition to the "organicist" lineage. McCall's reconstructions forged a link between the Bauhaus, Nikolais, and 1960s minimalism. But, similar to another technological innovator of historical modern dance—Loie Fuller—Schlemmer is difficult to integrate into the modernist canon. On this alternative noncanonical tradition in modern dance, see Felicia McCarren, *Dancing Machines: Choreographies of the Age of Mechanical Reproduction* (Stanford, CA: Stanford University Press, 2003). On the connection between Schlemmer and Nikolais, see Marc Lawton, "Du Bauhaus au Playhouse," in *Oskar Schlemmer et la figure d'art* (Paris: Centre national de la danse, 2001), 131–144.

14. See Janice Ross, *Moving Lessons: Margaret H'Doubler and the Beginning of Dance in American Education* (Madison: University of Wisconsin Press, 2000). H'Doubler was a pioneer of dance education in the American university: "[She] saw herself as giving students the power to link emotional and physical understanding in order to become better adjusted and more efficacious individuals in the world" (ibid., 4).

15. See Sali Ann Kriegsman, *Modern Dance in America. The Bennington Years* (Boston: G. K. Hall & Co., 1981).

16. The emphasis on composition derives in part from German modern dance of the Weimar era, which placed pedagogical emphasis on individual and group improvisation in the development of choreographic composition.

17. See Leila Sussman, "Recruitment Patterns: Their Impact on Ballet and Modern Dance," in *Dance Research Journal* 22/1, 21–28. Sussman notes the close alliance between modern dance and women's colleges, which "enabled modern dance to survive" between the 1930s and the 1960s (page 25).

18. This situation is beginning to change, at least in Europe. The analysis, it should be clear, is limited to the Western perspective.

19. Sali Ann Kriegsman, keynote speech, *Dance Reconstructed. Conference Proceedings* (New Brunswick, NJ: Rutgers University, October 16–17, 1992), 9.

20. See Mark Franko and Annette Richards, editors, *Acting on the Past: Historical Performance Across the Disciplines* (Middletown, CT: Wesleyan University Press, 2000).

21. See Philip V. Bohlman, "Ethnomusicology's Challenge to the Canon: the Canon's Challenge to Ethnomusicology," in Katherine Bergeron and Philip V. Bohlman, editors, *Disciplining Music: Musicology and its Canons* (Chicago and London: University of Chicago Press, 1992), 116–136.

22. One can note as well within the university dance curriculum a potential split between technique, choreography, and history/theory. In a proposal for an MFA in dance commissioned by the School of the Arts, Columbia University, I recommended a program in choreography and critical studies, one that would effec-

tively exclude technique. Such a program would instate choreography into the research university as an interdiscipline without the canonical links to techniques.

23. I plan to guest edit an issue of *Dance Research Journal* on dance and inter-disciplinarity.

24. See the pamphlet *America's Irreplaceable Dance Treasures: the First 100* (Washington, DC: Dance Heritage Coalition, 2000).

25. See Tony Bennett, *Birth of the Museum: History, Theory, Politics* (New York: Routledge, 1995).

26. Marcia J. Citron, *Gender and the Musical Canon* (Cambridge: Cambridge University Press, 1993), 1–2.

27. I discuss this at length in Mark Franko, *Dancing Modernism/Performing Politics* (Bloomington: Indiana University Press, 1995). See also Gay Morris, *Games for Dancers* (Middletown, CT: Wesleyan University Press, 2006).

28. On the way, politically oriented dance has constituted a brand of antimodernism in the twentieth century; see my book *The Work of Dance: Labor, Movement and Identity in the 1930s* (Middletown, CT: Wesleyan University Press, 2002).

29. "Emplotment is the way by which a sequence of events fashioned into a story is gradually revealed to be a story of a particular kind." Hayden White, *Metahistory: The Historical Imagination in Nineteenth-Century Europe* (Baltimore and London: Johns Hopkins University Press, 1973), 7.

30. Jean-François Lyotard, *The Postmodern Condition: A Report on Knowledge*, translated by Geoff Bennington and Brian Massumi (Minneapolis: University of Minnesota Press, 1984).

31. Lyotard refers to these two language games that establish the legitimacy of knowledge as "humanist and idealist": the first is prescriptive, the second is denotative. Ibid., 46.

32. See Mark Franko, "L'utopie antifasciste: *American Document* de Martha Graham," *Etre ensemble*, edited by Claire Rousier (Pantin: Centre national de la danse, 2003), 283–306.

33. See "Between Technique and the State," in Randy Martin, *Critical Moves. Dance Studies in Theory and Politics* (Durham, NC: Duke University Press, 1998), 151–179.

34. "Specifically between 1945 and 1946 the intellectual elite of New York turned to the analysis and use of myth as a way to move beyond the aesthetics of the Popular Front." Serge Guilbaut, *How New York Stole the Idea of Modern Art: Abstract Expressionism, Freedom, and the Cold War*, translated by Arthur Goldhammer (Chicago and London: University of Chicago Press, 1983), 110.

35. See Naima Prevots, *Dance for Export: Cultural Diplomacy and the Cold War* (Middletown, CT: Wesleyan University Press, 1998).

36. See Randy Martin, "Modern Dance and the American Century," *A Modern*

Mosaic. Art and Modernism in the United States, edited by Townsend Ludington (Chapel Hill and London: University of North Carolina Press, 2000), 203–226.

37. White, *Metahistory,* 18.

38. On these unorthodox but important works, see Liza Gennaro, "Agnes de Mille: Dance Modernism in the American Musical," M.A. thesis, Gallatin School of Independent Study, New York University (2005); Constance Valis Hill, "Katherine Dunham's *Southland:* Protest in the Face of Repression," *Dancing Many Drums. Excavations in African American Dance,* edited by Thomas F. DeFrantz (Madison: University of Wisconsin Press, 2002), 289–316; and Mark Franko, *Excursion for Miracles: Paul Sanasardo, Donya Feuer, and Studio for Dance (1955–1964)* (Middletown, CT: Wesleyan University Press, 2005).

39. Don McDonagh, *The Rise and Fall and Rise of Modern Dance* (New York: Outerbridge & Dienstfrey, 1970), 1.

40. Guilbaut, *How New York Stole the Idea of Modern Art,* 2.

41. White, *Metahistory,* 14.

42. Ibid., 29.

43. For an account of the attempt to keep Cunningham within this metanarrative, see Mark Franko, "The Readymade as Movement: Cunningham, Duchamp, and Nam June Paik's two Merces," in *Res: Anthropology and Aesthetics* 38 (2001), 211–219.

44. Lyotard, *The Postmodern Condition,* xxiv.

45. I have argued that it is actually Yvonne Rainer whose work signals the final collapse of the metanarrative in "Some Notes on Yvonne Rainer, Modernism, Politics, Emotion, Performance, and its Aftermath," *Meaning in Motion. New Cultural Studies in Dance,* edited by Jane Desmond (Durham, NC: Duke University Press, 1997), 289–303. Interestingly, and scandalously, Rainer is not mentioned in *America's Irreplaceable Dance Treasures.*

46. For a compelling narrative of the rise and fall of the NEA from the perspective of the visual arts, see Michael Brenson, *Visionaries and Outcasts: The NEA, Congress, and the Place of the Visual Artist in America* (New York: New Press, 2001).

Documents

Before Henry Street

ALWIN NIKOLAIS

I was discharged from the army in 1946[1] and was soon in New York City tramp-
ing around the streets looking for a place to live. Martha's, Hanya's, and Doris'
and Charles' studios were all in the village and this was where I was determined to be. I don't remember much about the ordeal of searching except
that there seemed to be no "for rent" signs out and mostly one scanned the
windows to see if a flat looked empty. Or you looked for the super in some de-
crepit building hoping that you'd hit on something—and I did—on Carmine
Street. The New York City law permitted walk-ups of only four flights and my
living treasure was on the fifth. But after a clean up and paint job it was a
delight—a living-room-bedroom with two windows and a fireplace, a medium-
size kitchen with a high bathtub with a porcelained tin cover that served as
a kitchen table—and a toilet in the hall. All for $16 a month. I needed no
more to move in immediately except a bed. I don't remember how Ed Ely, a
Southington school buddy, got into the act. Three blocks away on Bleecker
Street I found the bed and mattress. I also found I could rent a push cart for
fifty cents an hour, and in no time flat Ed and I were pushing the cart through
the village streets feeling devilishly self-conscious and bohemian hoping no
one we knew would spot us in the un–New Englandy act. My first home in
New York City. Soon I was cooking, inviting friends to dinner and fast becoming a real villager. But best of all—at last I was dancing—with Martha, Doris
and Charles, and Hanya—and studying choreography again with Louis. It
was all too much—like having four desserts and consequent aesthetic indi-
gestion. I was on the G.I. Bill so I had money not only to pay for classes but
also to live.

All during the army I had been working on my notation and had somewhat
rediscovered the German technique. Dance notation required an analysis of
space and its relativity to the body. So in exploring all this I had at least an in-

[1]Nikolais misremembers the year of his discharge. His discharge papers are
dated November 5, 1945. The activities he describes occurred in the winter and
spring of 1946. He spent the intervening year in Connecticut.

tellectual knowledge in the von Laban-Wigman technique, which employed the same analysis in dance technique. Because of my congeniality to the German method I dropped all other study and devoted myself to Hanya. This proved to be a most rewarding choice.

Hanya was scheduled to teach for eight weeks in Colorado College in that wonderful beautiful mountain and ghost-town area surrounding Colorado Springs. Hanya had selected four of us from the studio to be a sort of professional nucleus. She had choreographed a quartet for us which was ghastly fast. We managed it OK in New York City, but in Colorado Springs at 6000 foot elevation the dance seemed impossible until after one week we finally adjusted to the altitude. Pikes Peak seemed within spitting distance and a desert area nearby led to the Garden of the Gods—justly named. In the other direction was the honky-tonk town of Manitou Springs where we would go to dance. There was the old gold road—a wonderfully mad, dangerous, cliff-hanging, one-track, snaky road that led to the old gold town of Cripple Creek. Oliver Kostock and Glen Tetley appeared that year. Oliver had a jalopy that frequently stopped and let off steam on our mountain excursions.

Oliver, Glen and I were Hanya's "boys," and she would brook no deflection of focus from her hierarchical heights. This caused no end of difficulties because we, with others, liked to go out to paint the town red, or other suitable innocent hell-raising colors, to places which Hanya had no affinity. Hanya would invariably learn of our escapades. She would then direct a nasty undercurrent of wrath—not directed at us but all those whom she discovered were part of our entourage. Hanya was very possessive of me. She, Ollie, Glen and I lived in Hamlin House along with the Budapest string quartet, the musicologist Nicolas Slonimsky and his Christian Science Monitor art critic wife, Dorothy Adlow. Sometimes we spent the evening together in our parlor, and Nicolas would entertain us with mad technical exhibitions on the piano—like playing thirteen notes against seventeen. He also sang ridiculous songs he made up, like "Babies Cry for Castoria," which he thought was devastatingly hilarious.

The big dance event of my last summer with her was Hanya's reconstruction of one of her pieces from "Trend." Nicolas was to conduct the orchestra, which included sirens and special percussion instruments. The score was Varese's "Ionization" and was most complicated—particularly the percussion part. The Denver Symphony percussionist was unable to master it, so Nicolas was obliged to dismiss him. The difficulty that arose from this was that with the percussionist's exit, his instruments went with him and no others were available. Nicolas ransacked the kitchen of all its huge pots and pans and assembled a seemingly adequate collection to substitute for the real stuff. But our difficulties weren't over. The dancers knew the counts but were unable to identify them with the music. So Hanya put herself in the down-stage wing on one side and I on the other. Each with score in hand we shrieked out the counts above the din of the music. Nicolas however got too excited and conducted the piece at twice the expected speed. It was over before it began, but the reception was a cacophonous ovation that suitably followed the tin pan din of the Varese score, so in was repeated at a more reasonable speed and all was well.[2]

[Nikolais describes two other summers in Colorado and his life in the East where he studied with Holm and held several teaching jobs. One was at Hartt School of Music in Hartford, Connecticut, where he choreographed operas. He recounts amusing episodes in the staging of two of them. By 1947 Nikolais was teaching at Holm's studio and when in 1948 she was invited to choreograph an episode of the Broadway bound *Ballet Ballads,* he took over most of her classes. His account continues:]

. . . This season, 1948, was without a doubt the most significant year because it proved to be a new beginning for me. Through Hanya I got a call from Grace Spotford, the director of the Music School and Playhouse of the Henry Street Settlement. I was asked to start a dance department at the Playhouse. The Playhouse was on the Lower East Side—one of the shabbiest and most dangerous sections of New York City.

[2]The episode Nikolais recounts occurred in 1949. He assisted Hanya Holm at her summer school at Colorado College from 1946 to 1949. Other dancers who were present confirm the unusual circumstances of the 1949 concert. See Claudia Gitelman's *Dancing with Principle: Hanya Holm in Colorado, 1942–1983* (Boulder: University Press of Colorado, 2001), 48–49.

"On Nikolais"

MURRAY LOUIS

Excerpted by the author from *Inside Dance: Essays by Murray Louis*
New York: St. Martin's Press, 1980

I met Alwin Nikolais during a dance summer session at Colorado College. I had been discharged the previous year from the navy, and after a period of working road company musicals and an unmentionable night club stint, I was on my way back to New York. I was looking for a career with vision, and vision I got indeed during that inspiring summer with Nik. So filled was I with the endless possibilities of the art, my concern then became whether I would have enough time in my life to do all the things in dance I could now envision.

I returned with Nik to become a student at the Henry Street Playhouse. In my long and widely traveled career, he is the only genius I have ever met, much less known. When people ask me to talk about Nikolais, I often find myself at a loss for words; for to me, who probably knows him more intimately than anyone else in the world, he often remains a mystery. Although Nik was a product of earlier values, he is today a statement of the future.

At the Henry Street Playhouse, we had two studios. The larger could handle fifteen dancers and the smaller ten. If there were more than twenty-five people in class, including the company, we would join forces and use the stage if it were available to us. Today, all of that studio space would fit in our large studio alone, and a class of less than forty students seems unattended.

After warm-ups and pliés Nik would go to the piano and accompany the class as we went across the floor. And could he play. I mean, sweet Jesus could he play. And did we dance our asses off. We all lived for that hour of going across the floor. After class it was not perspiration that poured from our bodies, it was exhilaration.

As students in those days, we were not the ideal raw material upon whom an innovator of his caliber could evolve and shape theories. As a matter of fact we were a pretty motley crew. Most of us had little in common with each other, apart from our absolute devotion to Nik. What made the chemistry work in those years was that he called upon us to contribute to, not simply take class. He made it clear to us that he had to see us do what he was calling for before he could see where he was going next. And did we work. Gladys, Phyllis, Dorothy, Bill, Beverly, Coral, and myself. We were black and white, tall and short, nervous and sedated, heavy and thin, wiry and phlegmatic, but we all had a common focus: Nik.

On thinking back, I realize now how our diversity was probably the best thing that could have happened to him; the odds were with him. With this cross-section someone was bound to understand what he was saying and once one of us materialized what he wanted, then we all knew what he wanted of us, and we put out. By learning to identify motion, we sealed our individual bond with the art of dance, because now we knew what dancing meant for ourselves. We would never need to wear someone else's shoes, not need to follow in the footprints made by someone else's feet.

One day much later I said to Nik, "Do you realize you don't depend upon a cult or a coterie? How do you expect to be a success?" "Yep," he answered, "but I have an audience." I don't believe there is another artist involved with theater today who knows audiences as Nik does. Sitting in the back of the house with direct inter-communication to his stage manager backstage, he starts the house lights down when he feels the audience is settled. He sets the overture levels to match the audience's pre-curtain hub-bub. He keeps his finger on the audience's pulse through out the entire performance. He adjusts lights when it becomes necessary and important (This becomes a godsend to his stage manager, who must set up and light a show in as many as three or four different houses a week throughout a tour.) Audience reaction, the direct response during the performance, is the only criticism to which he'll respond. "How did it go tonight?" I'll ask. If he is satisfied he'll say, "The audience liked it."

The first time I saw a Nikolais production was in 1972. I had danced in everything he'd choreographed since 1949, and left his company in 1969 to devote myself to my own company. For the following three years I was never in New York City when he was giving his seasons; but in 1972 at his Broadway season at the ANTA Theater, I sat out front and watched his work for the first time.

In all honesty, I had no idea of what that total stage looked like when I was dancing his pieces. I was staggered, simply staggered. It created a world so completely of its own that for a moment I felt I didn't know the man who had created it. I knew some of those dances inside out, having danced them myself for years, but to see them now through his eyes, I found myself in awe of him, and this time I saw him objectively, for the genius he is.

Jovial as he appears, he is never without tension, nor can he stop working. He has often made me ponder the fine line between the driven and the dedicated. Preparing food and swimming in Peconic Bay are the only times he can or ever does relax. He is big boned and has heft. He cannot be confined and needs space, and if he can't get space, he'll settle for grandeur.

Critical Reception of the
Choreography of Alwin Nikolais

. . . .

compiled and edited by NAIMA PREVOTS

This compendium of critical responses to Alwin Nikolais' choreography spans a forty-year period, from 1953 to the year of the artist's death in 1993. Casting an eye over the extensive critical attention to Nikolais' productions in the United States, I made a good faith effort to represent the range of attitudes toward his work. I also looked for reviews that describe. Respecting stylistic differences of publications, such as italics or quotation marks for titles of works, and different constructions of the possessive of the choreographer's name, I save the reader from the interpolation [*sic*] in rare cases of misspelling and insignificant mistakes of fact.

Louis Horst, founder and editor of the influential journal *Dance Observer*, wrote in the August-September 1953 issue of the magazine: ·

> Under the direction of Alwin Nikolais, the Henry St. Playhouse Dance Group gave its annual spring program on May 23, and 24. A feature of the performance was the presentation of Charles Weidman's *Lynchtown*, a well-known success of the modern dance repertory of a decade or more ago.
>
> The opening number was *Theme and Improvisations*, choreographed by Mr. Nikolais and danced by six members of the group. This was a bright, rhythmic and well made composition that evidenced a fine sense of musicality. *Antechamber*, a theatrical solo by Murray Louis, created a tense atmosphere of anticipation and displayed an effective employment of silhouette and shadow. Then followed Gladys Bailin's *Harlequinade*, which had been performed at an earlier concert at the Y.M.-Y.W.H.A., and is reviewed in another column of this issue. Miss Bailin gave this work a superb performance, but it still suffers from an unsatisfactory music score.
>
> Phyllis Lamhut's *Periphery of Armor*, constituted an interesting essay in the psychology of fear. Luke Bragg's *The Juggler*, which was a character dance, the title of which was not clear, and the transitions of which were too abrupt. Also disappointing was *Little Man*, danced by Mr. Louis and choreographed by Miss Bailin and Mr. Louis, although it seemed to be

liked by the audience. *Noumenom,* choreographed by Mr. Nikolais and danced by Beverly Schmidt and Dorothy Vislocky, employed two large tubes of material which enveloped the bodies of the dancers. This proved to be a highly interesting and effective projection of designs in space; a sort of surrealistic avant garde version of Martha Graham's *Lamentation.*

Mr. Nikolais' *Aqueouscape,* for four dancers, was another work concerned with space design, and employed stylized props suggesting two boats. This brought forth some interesting linear patterns; however, the overall effect was too romantic.

After an intermission Mr. Nikolais presented his longest work, *Forest of Three,* a ballet of fantasy and theatricality. Although presented as a fairy tale, it contained many passages of fine choreography and received an excellent performance from the company. Gladys Bailin, as the Princess, was, as usual, outstanding.

It was interesting to again see Mr. Weidman's *Lynchtown,* but at this performance, despite its strong dramatic situations and fine choreography, it showed evidences of dating.

P.W. (Phyllis Winifred) Manchester, managing editor and principal critic of *Dance News,* reviewed the Playhouse Dance Company performance of Masks — Props — Mobiles December 10, 1955. She wrote in the February 1956 issue of the journal:

> Not all the items in this experimental program came off successfully, but enough of them did to make the evening a fascinating one. In all but one of the numbers the dancers were completely impersonal, and in several they disappeared into a deliberate dehumanization as they manipulated their props or materials.
>
> In *Noumenom Mobilis,* for example, Beverly Schmidt and Dorothy Vislocky were encased in oblong sheathes of jersey in scarlet and white. By movements of their limbs, the torso and head, the casings assumed all manner of sculpturesque shapes, grotesque or weirdly beautiful. At first sight they looked like two somewhat malevolent wing chairs which then proceeded to rock themselves into other resemblances, evanescent but each one sharply defined in turn.
>
> In *Belonging to the Moon,* to some other-wordly sounds devised by Alan Hovhaness, Murray Louis choreographed and danced a strange, faceless being, drawn by the moon's spell as the tide must respond, helplessly attracted. *Web* had Beverly Schmidt, Dorothy Scott, Luke Bragg, and Murray

Louis skillfully manipulating long streamers in intricate designs which miraculously never became entangled, while in *Tournament* to music by Chavez, the colored cloaks of the dancers made the joust as formal as a display of heraldry and as fierce as a game of chess.

Dorothy Vislocky was both choreographer and dancer of *Paraphernalia* in which, to a series of evocative percussive noises, she maintained a marvelous imperviousness to her gradual total embroilment with a couple of hoops and two cylinders which turned her finally into an automaton. This was a small triumph of observation and comment on this mechanized age.

The exception to this approach to movement came with *Aqueouscape* to a charming excerpt from the incidental music to *Pelleas and Melisande* by Sibelius. Two slender masts were held by Luke Bragg and Murray Louis, while Beverly Schmidt and Dorothy Scott moved round them. The masts, ropes and the net coverings of the dancers, combined with the gentle smoothness of the rhythmic movement, had all the mystery and romance of the sea shore by night.

Other numbers were not so successful but there was none that did not have some interest, for idea or costuming or lighting effects. These last played a great part in a rather exciting evening.

Alwin Nikolais, co-director of the Playhouse, who choreographed five of the nine items and directed the whole program, has certainly made an unusual contribution to the dance field.

The Henry Street Playhouse Dance Company had its first national exposure at the Ninth Annual American Dance Festival at Connecticut College in August 1956. Doris Hering, critic and editor of *Dance Magazine*, reviewed Nikolais' choreography as she reflected on the festival as a whole. Her piece in the October 1956 issue of the magazine reflects the dominant dance esthetic of the mid-twentieth century.

In its choice of contributing artists, the American Dance Festival was more imaginative this year than in recent seasons. The companies of Anna Sokolow and Alwin Nikolais supplemented the Doris Humphrey-José Limón nucleus. And Swedish modern dancer Birgit Akesson and Wigman exponent, Margaret Dietz, were on hand to contribute their special flavor.

But despite this wider range of styles, the dominant impression was one of surface complexity—of urgent energy and stamping feet—streaming tresses shaken and tossed around faces and shoulders—people climbing on people or swaying in circles polarized by overhead light—wisps of cloth and discs and gongs and drums upon drums and violins upon violins.

Time and again we found ourselves watching eagerly for those all-too-rare moments when form and content came into close harmony, when there was a simple, natural flow between the originating emotion and its dance-shape.

In only three works did we find this balance unbroken. They were Anna Sokolow's *Lyric Suite*, Birgit Akesson's *Winter*, and José Limón's *Emperor Jones*. In the others, we had to be content with occasional flashes—Margaret Dietz melting through parted upstage curtains in *Of Burden and Of Mercy*; José Limón curved like an embryo in *"There is a Time"* or with his arm extended generously toward the audience in the opening of *Symphony for Strings*; and the women in Doris Humphrey's *Ritmo Jondo* suddenly aware of their emptied arms.

While in most of the dances the over-weighting of form was accidental, or perhaps part of an unwritten trend in today's modern dance, in Alwin Nikolais' ingenious group work, *Kaleidoscope*, it was deliberate. In fact, there was virtually nothing but form.

The dance was like a giant mobile, a play of bright objects in space. But air currents move mobiles, while the dancers were the anonymous force in *Kaleidoscope*. And to accentuate their anonymity, Mr. Nikolais had them paint their faces in the same bright tones as their costumes.

Each section of the eight-part dance improvised about an object or set of objects—discs fastened to the dancers' feet; a pole balanced between the two dancers; skirts, hoops, straps, capes. The accompaniment was colorful, if at times bombastic, variety of ethnic and composed material with an emphasis on percussion.

Kaleidoscope was an extension of shorter works presented by Mr. Nikolais this past winter. But in stretching his original idea, he has still not proved his basic premise, that there can be valid art without emotion. Actually the most successful parts of *Kaleidoscope* were those incorporating an extra non-visual element. In *Skirts* it was humor and surprise; in *Straps* it was the precariousness of physical tension; and in *Bird* it was a sense of mystery. The other sections were clever. But cleverness can be dry, especially when clothed in excessive length.

Mr. Nikolais' diligently trained company consisted of Gladys Bailin, Murray Louis, Beverly Schmidt, Phyllis Lamhut, Dorothy Vislocky, Coral Martindale, and William Frank.

The Festival Committee often showed poor judgment in programming. One example of this was to follow Mr. Nikolais' hour-long work with another of similar length, Anna Sokolow's turbulent *Rooms*. And unfortunately, *Rooms* received an off-key performance. But the company more than redeemed itself two days later in *Lyric Suite*.

In the medium of music it has always been quite natural to compress emotional content into abstract form. But in the dance, this kind of balance is tantalizingly hard to achieve. Miss Sokolow has spun it in *Lyric Suite*. And through repeated performances, the company has achieved just the right personal-impersonal state. Although the entire company was inspired, Judith Coy was especially touching in the rounded softness of her arms and the innocent lift of her head. And Jeff Duncan and Eve Beck found new tenderness in their duet.

Other members of Miss Sokolow's company were Jack Moore, Beatrice Seckler, Annelise Widman, David Gold, and Paul Sanasardo. and for *Lyric Suite*, Rhoda Levine, Patricia Christopher, and Betsy Hamerslag were added.

Like Anna Sokolow, Birgit Akesson is a deeply honest choreographer. But with Miss Akesson, the honesty is sometimes a campaign, rather than an underlying quality.

Her first solo, *Winter* (Vivaldi), most tellingly expressed her artistic intent. Encased in a whitish suit, Miss Akesson stood quietly upstage, hair loose, face radiant, as though bathed in winter sunshine. She lifted her arms slowly, hands lightly joined. There were dainty circles about the stage, with feet lightly patting the floor. She sat quietly, foot soles together, arms up, head turning slowly. Then the arms fell wide, the body took a V-shape, and she slowly lowered her head to the floor.

Unlike so many dancers on the Festival, Miss Akesson was not afraid of stillness—the stasis sometimes after only a tiny movement. But hers were not poses. They were pauses, as though the movement were going on innerly and would soon again quietly manifest itself on the outside.

But Miss Akesson has not conquered the problem of monotony. In the quest for honesty, her choice of choreographic material is sometimes too paired down, too limited. In her remaining three solos, *Music for Strings, Percussion and Celeste* (Bartok); *Movement* (unaccompanied); and *Persephone Dance* (to a lovely score by Blomdahl) there were often similar materials, similarly used.

On the same program with Miss Akesson (another example of unimaginative programming) was the German-trained dancer, Margaret Dietz. She premiered a solo called *Of Burden and of Mercy* (Benjamin Johnston).

Looking regally feminine in a long purple gown, Miss Dietz created a formal image of tragedy. And although her style, with its full gestures and open, spiraling turns, was quite dissimilar to Miss Akesson's, she, too, possessed the quality of "inner listening"—of keeping the flow of feeling fresh and simple.

Sometimes, as in Pauline Koner's case, brilliant technique can impose imitations. In her premiere of *The Shining Dark* (Quartet No. 1, Leon Kirchner), based upon incidents in the life of Helen Keller, she began with a touchingly understated image of anguish. Like an insect trying to escape from its cocoon, she plucked at an obscuring curtain of gauze. But with the arrival of the two other dancers, Lucy Venable and Elizabeth Harris, the prevalent dichotomy began to set in. The emotional impact was engulfed in elaborate dancing.

By way of compensation, Miss Koner and her companions turned in wonderfully relaxed performance of her *Concertino in A Major* (Pergolesi). The easy flow of their pretty dresses and the lightness of their uplifted torsos made the dance a welcome interlude on a Festival marked by much, much dancing intensity.

Funny dances are hard to make, and Ruth Currier's new *Triplicty* (Ricardo Pick-Mangiagalli) was not successful. It attempted to satirize the competing predatory and experienced lady (Betty Jones) and a predatory and inexperienced lady (Miss Currier) over a not-very-bright male (Richard Fitz-Gerald). But while there were amusing moments, especially in a slapstick procession with a pseudo-corpse, the choreographer always seemed to be laboring to fill the score.

The Festival also featured two minor revivals, José Limón's *The Exiles* and the Desert section from Doris Humphrey's *Song of the West*. The latter has a clean vitality, a pleasure in movement and in the conquest of space, that were nicely conveyed by Miss Humphrey's Repertory Class.

With Adam and Eve as its protagonists, *The Exiles* tells of the death of innocence and the awakening into maturity. Ruth Currier, new in the role of Eve, was radiantly beautiful. And the ever-gracious Mr. Limón surrounded her with a frame of solicitous male strength. If only the structure of *The Exiles* had been as consistent as its performance.

Like the Sokolow company, Mr. Limón's group displayed wide variations in dancing quality. The opening night performance of *"There Is a Time"* had a disturbingly high-minded intensity. But a subsequent performance achieved the quiet glow that one remembers from the premiere last spring.

This problem of intensity, of how much energy to use for dancing, seems especially to plague the male members of Mr. Limón's company. (Lucas Hoving, Richard Fitz-Gerald, Michael Hollander, Harlan McCallum, Chester Wolenski, and José Gutierres). They often seem to be trying too hard, to be over-accentuating the individual rhythms and shapes so that the long phrase lines are disturbed. For some reason, the distaff side (Betty Jones, Ruth Currier, and Lavina Nielsen) dances with more ease and rhythmic elasticity.

The Limón company was also seen in a powerful performance of Doris Humphrey's *theatre Piece #2*. But despite rapier moments of satire, Miss Humphrey's indictment of theatrical insincerity terminates in the very quality she condemns.

The Festival also offered an "extra" in the form of a "dress rehearsal" of José Limón's new work, *Emperor Jones*. Danced after the closing matinee, it was in every way a finished and clean-edged performance.

Emperor Jones was commissioned by the Empire State Music Festival and premiered at Ellenville on July 12. The lush score is by Heitor Villa-Lobos, the spare and suggestive set by Kim Edgar Swados, and the inspired costumes by Pauline Lawrence.

Mr. Limón conceived the Eugene O'Neill theme in a mood of tempestous anger and fear. And the mood sustained itself without break.

Never have we seen Mr. Limón so sinisterly beautiful as in his opening solo. His tigerish strut was in brilliant contrast to the shifty, steely gait for Lucas Hoving as the nemesis. Together they immediately established the pulse of destruction.

The dance careened from one grim fantasy to another—a harsh auction block scene—a voodoo dance with gleaming, sweaty male bodies—and a crushing finale with the dead hulk of Jones tossed like a rag doll onto his meaningless throne. Mr. Limón and his male dancers performed as through transfixed. If only the whole Festival could have revealed the power of *Emperor Jones*, the directness of *Lyric Suite*, the quietude of *Winter* . . . and the simplicity inherent in all three!

P. W. Manchester, wrote in the April 1964 issue of *Dance News:*

Alwin Nikolais' latest work is magnificent; so sure, so completely developed and presented to the tiniest detail that it becomes an experience at which one ceaselessly marvels.

It has seemed as each of his works succeeded one another that he must have reached the furthest stages of what could be achieved with form, shape, color, design and bodies in space. *Sanctum* finds him soaring far beyond anything that has preceded it in assurance and imaginative flights.

He lays a spell on us from the moment the curtain rises and the lonely figure on its trapeze is hit by a blaze of deep red light as he turns slowly, high above the amorphous mass that only gradually reveals itself as being composed of individuals. The figure puts out a hand as though to find a contact with what must be his fellows and then withdraws it, not yet ready to leave his isolation. But when he does, dropping slowly, slowly, he is immediately swallowed up in the huddle of figures.

He has left the security in that moment when he joins the mob and he returns to it only at the very end when, the trapeze having fallen unobtrusively into place, he makes his unexpected escape. Have we watched the cycle of birth, life and death? Whether we have or not is not important because it happens not to be germane to *Sanctum* as it pursues its way.

There is a scene where all of the dancers carry long, flat, lathes. They are any color Nikolais chooses as he pours his lights on them, and in the end they send off iridescent sparks. But as the dancers move about the stage, bathed in a misty half light, they might be on some unknown shore at the very edge of the world and, as they move, they move into infinity.

Another time, the trim bodies move within the casing of material that binds them at head and feet, and the light hits them and changes the strange shapes they assume into hollowed jewels, until they stand up, still and white, like mummies lined up in a forgotten tomb.

Towards the end there is a fabulous grouping of Murray Louis, Phyllis Lamhut, Bill Frank, Ray Broussard, Ann Carlton and Roger Rowell, and it is like some marvelous formation of coral, gleaming and pink.

And there is an episode, funny and terrible, in which two puppets, hideous with silent laughter, turn upon their masters with the weapons that have been put in their hands, and then set upon the laughing audience and finally, with no one else in sight, set about destroying each other, with the same meaningless, dreadful mirth.

Murray Louis and Phyllis Lamhut are wonderful here, as they are throughout, though Louis is the key figure. He has the other chilling moment when, dancing casually to the tinny sounds of a piano with an occasional blast from a whistle, like the accompaniment of an old Keystone comedy, he does not notice that the figures surrounding him are gradually closing in, tighter and tighter, until he is trapped and can no longer move. It is part of the Nikolais magic that we do not notice this either until we share the identical feeling of helplessness.

As always the sound track is also created by Nikolais, and George Constant is the color consultant who helps to make the whole fantasy possible. The dancers wear leotards and tights, but the three principals, Louis, Lamhut and Frank, wear an incredible variant of these, transparent and tight fitting as an extra skin. Is Nikolais saying, naked came we into the world, and telling us that no one can escape life?

Is he saying anything except that he has found an engrossment in one particular way of art which it will take him a lifetime to explore? What does it matter, when the result is as exciting a theater experience as *Sanctum* proved itself to be.

Clive Barnes, dance critic of *The New York Times*, wrote on February 21, 1967:

Alwin Nikolais's "Imago" is a remarkable work, as much theater as dance and an experience not to be missed by anyone interested in either. This revival of "Imago," which has been made possible through a grant form the National Council on the Arts, opened at the elegant, little Henry Street Playhouse which still shows its admirable resistance to conformity by remaining at 336 Grand Street last Thursday.

It is scheduled for a month's season, with performances Thursday, Friday, Saturday and Sunday evenings and a matinee on Sunday, through March 12. Performances are not quite sold out for the season, but if experience is any guide, they will soon be.

"Imago," created four years ago, is perhaps the most important of all Nikolais' full evening works, and it is good news indeed that after closing at the Playhouse it is going on a national tour for six weeks. No one interested in the arts of the theater can afford to ignore Mr. Nikolais, who combines the roles of poet and showman in a strangely meaningful way. Mr. Nikolais suggestively offers a subtitle "The City Curious," which presumably is intended to propose some insight into his purposefully abstract work.

Under this title Mr. Nikolais has grouped 11 separate, yet clearly linked dances, and his intention appears to be to show to the vaguest, yet most suggestive manner possible, man as a social animal.

This of course, is merely the shadow-play to his vital purpose. His carefully controlled and always spectacular images move across the stage, and at times we see things apparently connected with everyday life.

Here, diagramatic and abstractly symbolized, may be people rushing along a subway, or bouncing along a city street, but this is at any rate dimly perceived, and the vital thing is not the original purpose, but the theatrical result.

Theatricality is the key and essence of Mr. Nikolais's art. In "Imago" he takes responsibility for not only the choreography, but also for the costumes, the screen-projected settings, the lighting and, assisted by James Seawright, the sound score.

What Mr. Nikolais is accomplishing is a total theatrical effect; this is the Wagnerian dream of the gesamskunstwerk—the complete theatrical concept of one artist.

At times Mr. Nikolais achieves results of startling beauty. Enormous, threatening shadows are cast across the backcloth; bodies, all but submerged in all-over tents, bounce up and down; mysterious men enter bearing immobilized Calder-like mobiles and figures, subtly, yet defiantly, balance off-balance. There is humor here and at times more than a hint of menace.

Mr. Nikolais's failing is to be easily seduced by the obvious effect—the clearly anthropomorphic, and therefore humorous, electronic sound, the engagingly pretty symmetrical effect, the slightly too obvious bout of humor and the susceptibility to the merely effective.

Sometimes his ideas are beautiful—such as when three boys have triangular shapes fitted to them, and by their movements, make the triangles dance across the proscenium. This is an effect both cute and lovely.

Elsewhere the spatial, the purely sculptural, the purely painterly results of the theater-piece are a shade too obvious.

Clearly Mr. Nikolais is a pioneer in a new form of theater, or, at least, a new form of theater-dance. But he leaves me wanting more, which I suppose is the surest indication of his successful pioneering.

He apparently objects to his dances being described as "Martian," yet there is a rather banal space-fiction element to his work, a basic tinsel touch that not even his brilliance can disguise.

My attitude to Mr. Nikolais is, I realize, sadly ambivalent. Obviously he is one of the most important men ever to hit theater-dance, and even if, at present, his ideas are more significant than the way he executes them, a work such as "Imago" is not only breathtakingly interesting, it is also mysteriously beautiful.

Mr. Nikolais has proposed a whole new arena of sight, sound and sense that dance can enter. At present, and just at present, he has limitations, I would say, of taste, but the arena itself is limitless. After all, the limitations of taste may well be mine—not his.

Marcia B. Siegel reviewed a five-year retrospective at the Brooklyn Academy of Music in November 1968. Siegel titled her January 13, 1969 review in *New York Magazine* "Deus ex Machina."

If you go to the theatre several times a week and have a speaking acquaintance with light plots, cue sheets, and all the backstage machinery that makes the theater work, it's hard to believe in magic. But Alwin Nikolais flips me out every time. Nikolais, of course, is the choreographer-composer-designer who made words like mixed media and total theatre obsolete, and whose company gave its only New York performances this season a few weeks ago at Brooklyn Academy. Nikolais is visual, funny, nonliteral, and absolutely unique.

His work is always evolving, and the Brooklyn season covered a five-year span that I think represents very great progress indeed, from the full length *Imago* (1963), a suite of dances in which the dancers are at different times merged with their environment, dominated by it, and aloof from it; to *Tower*, a section of the longer 1965 work *Vaudeville of the Elements*, in which the dancers, chattering inanely, build a sort of Tower of Babel out of aluminum pipe, with suitably apocalyptic results, to *Somniloquy* (1967) and *Tent* (1968), where, with consistent and concentrated imagery, the dancers appear in an almost ecological relationship to their dreamlike environment.

Nikolais is traditional about one thing: he confines his theatre to the stage. None of this audience-participation, break-down-the-barriers, we're all-performing-together sort of thing for him. The Nikolais' theatre is carefully planned and controlled, but it is at the same time wide open to interpretation by the viewer.

Within the playing area, Nikolais achieves great spatial flexibility, often breaking down the dimensionality and perspective that the proscenium stage imposes on our understanding of a theatre event. In *Imago*, for instance, in the section called "Fence," bands of tape are stretched horizontally across the stage, creating two narrow upstage corridors through which the dancers pass in a seemingly endless stream. Our orientation to the stage as a boxlike enclosure is destroyed, and we can then imagine the horizontal corridors and the dancers in them traveling an infinite distance out into the wings.

This extension of the imagination through a restructuring of space is carried even further in *Somniloquy*, where the entire dance takes place in several horizontal planes across the stage. Action occurs sometimes in front of a scrim, sometimes behind it, sometimes in both places simultaneously. Colored lights and projections can make the overlapping spaces appear and disappear. Like the spaces, the people in them materialize in a variety of ways: as silhouettes growing larger and smaller on the scrim, as disembodied faces or limbs, as figures that suddenly appear out of the darkness and then fall away into the void, or as complete bodies weirdly lit by projections. The people sometimes cross from one dimension to another, by leaping through shafts of colored light, or by drawing up the scrim. Viewed through these layers of perception, the dance is a play on the degrees of reality and unreality, and the thin line that divides the two.

In *Tent* the playing space expands and contracts around a womblike shelter to which the dancers relate in various ways. When they bring the tent out at the beginning, furled like a sail, they inspect the stage and the audience jauntily, like circus performers coming into a new town. But as soon as the tent is pitched, no other space has any meaning for them. They gather inside it, venture out—but not very far, arrange it into new shapes, dance underneath it, and finally are crushed by it. Nikolais' gorgeous lighting and projections intensify the idea of the tent as the center of a growing and shrinking universe by sometimes focusing on the tent against a blacked-out background, sometimes adding light so that we can also see the area around it.

Nikolais' movement style, from which all his choreographic ideas have developed, is highly spatial. His dancers are trained to move in relation to space, not according to arbitrary demands of body alignment or motor strength. Soloists Phyllis Lamhut and Murray Louis, in their subtle, virtuosic duet in *Somniloquy*, show the discovery of space, and of the self in space. They feel and explore the space around the body, and when they touch, they become part of one another's space. When they embrace, the feeling is not so much one of contact as of enclosure.

In *Imago* there are still traces of the "dehumanization" for which Nikolais is, wrongly, I think, sometimes condemned. Even when his dancers are the most disguised, the most subservient to props, costumes, and effects, even when they become objects, they relate to each other in human ways. The cumulative effect of ten depersonalized dancers in *Tower*, alternately at voluble cross-purposes and in inexplicable harmony, building their aluminum fortress, is both very funny and very human.

But with *Somniloquy* and *Tent*, I think, Nikolais has reached the most impressive and meaningful realization of his contention that man and his environment are inseparable. For some people this may mean that man is diminished. For me, the human spirit comes off immeasurably enriched.

Nikolais collaborated with composer Gian Carlo Menotti on a one-act opera. Arlene Croce reviewed one of the New York City performances for a February 1970 issue of the London-based publication *The Dancing Times*.

Gian Carlo Menotti's latest one-act opera was inspired, he tells us, by the theatre of Alwin Nikolais, "which has fascinated me since its very beginning with its unique combination of eeriness and humor." *Help, Help, the Globolinks!* billing itself as "an Opera for Children and Those Who Love Children", was staged over the Christmas holidays at the City Center for Music and Drama, and it is, as you might imagine, a work of suffocating archness, concerning some Martian-type invaders who, accompanied by electronic beeps and burbles, descend on an American school and are put to rout only when the teachers and children play conventional musical instruments at them. What is really dismaying about it, however, is its demonstration of the incapacity of a fully developed "art" theatre like that of Alwin Nikolais to function in a commercial context, not because its resources of expression are too many, and thus inhibited by that context, but because they are too few, and thus exposed by it.

To create the Globolinks, Menotti got Nikolais himself, and though the electronic music that is used to identify them is apparently by Menotti, it sounds exactly like the scores Nikolais creates for his own work, or perhaps I should say score, since the synthetic blurgellating which is Nikolais' rather comfy idea of electronic music hardly ever varies in its effects from one Nikolais work to another. The same, transposed to traditional vocal and orchestral composition, might be said of Menotti, and, indeed, Nikolais might be thought of as the avant-garde Menotti in more than the musical sense. Both men are showmen who seem to suffer from the same exacerbated pride in their own seriousness as artists. Menotti's operatic ventures are generally accompanied by polemical outbursts against the musical establishment. (In the present case, the polemics are in the libretto). Nikolais's tack, on the other hand, has been to over-extend his talents drastically in even longer, more repetitious and pretentious extravaganzas that seem designed to shore up a reputation as an all-purpose avant-garde genius. What Menotti sees as "eeriness and humor" are there, of course, but less and less frequently in combination; they've become separable and increasingly unstable elements in the media compound that the Nikolais "sensorium" uses nowadays to impress us with its abstract beauty. It's odd that what Menotti tries to make ridiculous and villainous in his little parable about the crises in modern music should show up on the stage as nothing more harmful than Nikolais' familiar bag of tricks incorporated all but whole—odd, not because the Globolinks are about as detestable as the Blue Meanies in *The Yellow Submarine*, but because they're really nothing at all; the eeriness and the humor latent in what Nikolais has devised, but neither he nor Menotti has bothered to make these elements dramatically suggestive or exciting in terms of the story that is being told. The show is just an abstract parade. What we get for a Globolink horde is only a typical Nikolais corps de ballet, the men this time looking like concertinas in top hats, the girls like unsprung paratroopers; and what we get for choreography in the action scenes is a simple business of diddling around in these costumes.

No effect is ever so magical on the stage that it can't destroy itself in seconds by giving away its secrets too soon, or worse, by failing to have any. Children's entertainment it seems to me, owes its audience a standard of invention as high as, if not higher, than entertainment for adults simply because children are prepared to believe in and therefore question what they see. A lot of what passes for children's entertainment in New York—generally it's presented around Christmastime and generally it centers on dance of some sort—doesn't survive imaginatively beyond the barest presentation of its materials, and I suspect the children know it even if their parents don't. *Help, Help, the Globolinks!* was preceded by *Amahl and the Night Visitors*, Menotti's now classic Christmas variation on the story of the Three Magi. It has parts for dancers but its biggest part is for a crippled boy soprano—it's that kind of classic. Coming out of the theatre afterward, a little girl asked her mother, "Which one did you like better, Mommy?" "Well," said this buck-passing Mommy, "I guess the first one was a little sad. *You* liked the second one better, didn't you?" "Well," said the child, "Well . . . yes, I guess so." This child knew she had been let down by *Globolinks*, and I think I know just when it happened. Like most of Nikolais' pieces, it had opened splendidly, with Menotti interrupting his overture, Welles-style, for an almost-for-real loudspeaker bulletin announcing the arrival of the Globolinks. Following this were five minutes of sheer enchantment; Ming Cho Lee's radar towers revolved in the pulsating void of Hans Sondheimer's lighting, and Nikolais' dancers alighted in shadow projections. Then the dancers emerged (as always thereafter from stage right—the girls' 'chutes must have been hooked up there somewhere), and, after the first giggle or two, the rest was that questioning silence which tells us that no answer will suffice. Nor was any answer offered; this host of Globolinks had nothing further to show us, no demonstration beyond the minimality of being. After that we were in Menotti-land, with its static, puppet-like recitatives in which people call attention to feelings they can't otherwise express: "Where am I? What's happening? I feel so funny. How strange!"

I'd gone to this dull entertainment of Menotti and Nikolais because I had expected something from it, more on Nikolais' part than on Menotti's.

Nikolais, I thought, would survive commercial pressure very well. Liberated at last from his experimental art for art's sake lab, he might turn out effects in support of Menotti's gassy little fable that would be the making of him as a popular artist. Nikolais' real business is, unless I mistake him profoundly, neither choreography, nor décor, nor lighting, nor sound-engineering, but the amalgamation of all of these arts (which other men have mastered better than, or at least as well as, he) in a plastic, totally manipulatable palette of effects that could service popular theatre if a popular theatre worthy of him, and worthy of the name, could exist. Nikolais evenings are not in themselves theatre but brilliant suggestions of what a new theatre might consist of; they're trips into dimensions of sight and sound that are like a perennial World's Fair of possibilities; they're spectacles en route to an experience to which Nikolais, as playmaker or theatre poet, cannot take us because he thinks like a technician, not a poet. A poet dominates, whereas a technician is dominated by, his materials, and it's one of the absurder tenets of avant-garde propaganda that we're all so victimized by technology we have to accept art, too, as a passive victim of the environment. Absurd: because it isn't a theory, it's an apologia with a wearying way of being presented to you *after* the fact of creation; it has the ring of all desperate philosophies made up to suit shabby conditions and failed art. If you believe in Nikolais' genius, for example, you have to believe in its dramatic promise, and in its steady etiolation from lack of exposure to circumstances that would have nourished it. You have to believe, in other words, in the difference between a poet of the theatre and a technician who's hypnotized by his own inventions, who is obliged to reinvent and repeat himself endlessly because the novelty wears off almost as quickly as the novelty of colour TV. Nikolais by himself has no staying power—it's great the first time but never so great again—and his wizardry is increasingly self-absorbed and remote because no broad avenue of expression has been offered it. Promise is not the same as opportunity.

There is always a crisis of definition at the point where art and commerce intersect. The last man of comparable stature and gifts to survive this crisis was Busby Berkeley, but now that movie musicals are dead (and Berkeley is an "artist"), his successor, whoever he may be, has no place to go. Nikolais has always done well on television, and before the debacle of *Globolinks* I would have thought he'd go down extremely well at a place like Radio City Music Hall. But the Music Hall is committed to enervated, dim spectacles fifty years behind the taste of the vast audiences who patronize it. Even if it weren't, Nikolais has himself overdrawn his account with the avant-garde. All those rarified evenings at the Henry Street Playhouse—what have they come to? A few weeks before the Menotti event, the City Center presented Nikolais' own company in a week of performances, and it was revealing and dispiriting to see. There were undeniable marvels: stages made magically high, wide, and deep by tricks of lighting, darkened to pinpoints or irradiated with a suddenness that took the breath; dancers made to appear or vanish in a flash, or to loom four times their natural size, or to inhabit ghostly, inhuman forms; dead materials made to animate; static elements (scenery, props) made liquid and evanescent. One also saw fantasy without depth, visions without majesty, poetic energy without poetic purpose. The new work, *Echo,* used the Moog Synthesizer (as if that made any difference) and dealt at interminable length in optical paradoxes of number and scale, with dancers constantly filing off and on, between and around their own images, and audiences constantly wondering whether they were here or there, or two or twenty (and finding out, alas, long before the dance was finished). The engagement was well attended and obediently sat through and prestigiously acclaimed, but the only real excitement was caused by two excerpts from a very early work, *Masks, Props and Mobiles* (1953). In one, three dancers sheathed in red stretch fabric made like teeterboards, and in the other, the company, manipulating long cords, rocked the stage in a brilliant series of cat's cradles. These dances, both very famous, were wildly, and I mean wildly, applauded. Their logic and charm were perhaps the last clang of Bauhaus functionalism in American theatre art, but they started Nikolais on his way, and his way now seems to have become irretrievably lost.

One can only dream. Nikolais needs someone to produce him, yes, but producers of latitude and zest and sound commercial instinct are as unemployable as the avant-garde. A Diaghilev, a Ziegfeld, a Disney, even a Billy Rose or Mike Todd might have found vehicles that could have changed Nikolais' life and our own. Maybe another director would have gotten more out of the Menotti-Nikolais collaboration than Menotti himself did. (Menotti always seems to be directing in a church basement). But that would have been sheer luck, and out of phase with the times. What we have today in the American theatre is a bleak middle ground where dandified art meets "elevated" commercial intentions—it's not even vulgar with conviction—and you can't grow upward from either. In his latter-day films like *Neptune's Daughter* and *Jumbo,* Busby Berkeley was still able to make complicated, grand gestures without the pop songs that had always been his springboards, but Nikolais hasn't been able to get enough life and force out of avant-garde freedom to hit Broadway. As an initiation into his kind of theatre art, the ballet of the Globolinks isn't even fun the *first* time. The failure hasn't anything to do with the isolation or passivity of art in a technological age. People who say so love also to speak of the shrinking audience for genuine art, but it's not the audience that's shrinking, it's their heads.

Note: Croce goes on to review Balanchine's *Nutcracker,* Taylor's *Churchyard,* and American Ballet Theatre.

Marcia B. Siegel wrote in the *Boston Herald Traveler* March 29, 1971:

> People are probably going to think Alwin Nikolais' new dance, *Scenario,* is a radical departure for the great abstracter and "dehumanizer" of movement, but it isn't. *Scenario* does use emotions — or the physical properties of emotions — in a more specific way than Nikolais has done during his mature career, but it uses them in the same way and for the same purposes that he previously used color, the shape of natural forms, and the sound of words.
>
> Nikolais long ago outdistanced the myth that he doesn't make works for dancers, that his people are the servants of props and devoid of individual expression. As far back as *Tower* (1965) he was working with the pop-art, collage effect of many people talking, moving and emoting at the same time. *Tent* (1968) is as pure-dance a work as anyone has ever made; Nikolais' stunning concept of a circus tent that can change shape, color, and design was meant to—and did—enhance the dancers rather than override them.
>
> The works that followed *Tent* — *Echo, Structures* and now *Scenario* — all concentrated on the dancer as the main event in a potentially threatening landscape, the dancer laughing, whistling, jigging, with a corner of his eye on the shadowy distance.
>
> *Scenario,* premiered February 25 during the Nikolais company's ANTA Theater season, sets out four emotional territories or weathers that the dancers create with their voices and movement, and intersperses them with a diagrammatic commentary of slide projections.
>
> The dancers start out in a lineup, pinned against a dark backdrop by projected cubicles of diminishing sizes and then by straight and wavy stick figure designs. In a jagged lightning-split background the men punch and yell at each other. Girls spar with ghostly figures in the dark. There's a hysterical orgy of crying and another one of laughing. People grope around a

brightly lit stage as if they can't see, and frighten each other into scream-
ing fits with the slightest move.

At the end they mix up their fight, fright, laughter and tears at random
in a madhouse of temperament, and finally they line up again and shuffle
toward the audience, holding little speakers that emit scratchy mechanical guffaws.

I found *Scenario* disturbing, and I'm not sure why. Though there are
some dazzling visual effects, the piece isn't primarily an essay in sensual
images, as many Nikolais works are. It doesn't flow smoothly from one idea
to another, or sustain ideas; it's constantly being broken up by blackouts
and by the dancers freezing in a posture, their faces twisted in mid-shout.

The dancers handle the technique of sobbing or giggling with great fa-
cility, yet I balked at the idea of such strong emotional manifestations
being under such tight control. Is Nikolais saying here that emotions are
just another theater element, to be turned on and shut off at will? He's
often stated as a keystone of his whole aesthetic that "Art is motion, not
emotion."

Somehow, while I can buy that joyfully in his other work, it seems contradictory and even cynical when the subject of the work is emotion itself.
If anything, *Scenario* seems more dehumanized than its decorative predecessors, not less.

Alan M. Kriegsman wrote in *The Washington Post* November 9, 1974:

Alwin Nikolais, that Merlin of the dance stage, was at it again last night
at Lisner Auditorium, where his small but superb company (10 dancers
minus one due to injury) cast forth its accustomed spells and marvels.

Nikolais, in case you haven't yet caught up with this most polydexter-
ous and inventive choreographer of our time, has been mesmerizing audiences with his wonder-filled dance theater creations since the early '50's.
He's 62 now, still devising his own tape music, lightplots, scenic effects
and choreography, and his imagination seems as vivid and prolific as ever.
Last night's program began with the U.S. premiere of his latest opus,
"Temple," premiered on his recently concluded European tour. It deploys
three triplets of dancers, lined in a row across the stage and often suggesting pillar-like formations in the gymnastic configurations they assume. In
typical Nikolais fashion, projected backdrops and ingeniously shifting
lights and colors add aspect to the visual implications of the shapes.

The movements themselves are mostly loose and bobbing, giving the
dancers the look of dangling rubber dolls. Aside from the columnar for-

mations, the only other apparent reference to the title of the piece comes in the cruciform poses of the closing moments, struck and held in an ominous red glow. "Temple" was performed as part of an opening assortment which also included excerpts from such earlier works as "Somniloquy" (1967), "Grotto" (1973) and "Masks, Props and Mobiles" (1953).

The highlight of "Foreplay," a rambling work dating from 1972, is an uproarious section featuring the simulated rigidities and immobilized expressions of mannequins. Most winning of all is a mock pas-de-deux, in which the short-statured Suzanna McDermaid plays out a balletic fantasy with her tall, "dummy" partner, Bill Groves.

The program ended with "Cross-Fade" (1974), seen earlier this year at Wolf Trap. In its masterful manipulation of illusion and semblance this complex composition ranks as one of the master's most astonishing, mystifying works. Nikolais takes the most advanced optical innovations of film and video and turns them into living tableaux before your unbelieving eyes.

Deborah Jowitt, critic for the *Village Voice* titled a review "How Do You Tell If It's Human?" She wrote in the July 14, 1975, issue:

It's easy to be dazzled by Alwin Nikolais's light-spangled dances and see the dancers principally as moving surfaces to receive and manipulate color and pattern. But Nikolais is not a magician to whom all rabbits may be the same; his choreography is shaded by the dancers in his company at any given time. In the early Henry Street days, the dancers on whom he worked out his first ideas—Murray Louis, Phyllis Lamhut, Gladys Bailin, Beverly Schmidt, Bill Frank, and the others—became expert at the dynamic subtleties of movement. Their collective style seemed soft and buoyant, but they could twitch as well as glide, lash out as well as undulate; and often they could do all these things at once. Few of them had slim, high-kicking ballet bodies. But they could easily look like insects, blobs, stone idols, rays of light.

As members of the original company broke away and were replaced by less experienced dancers, Nikolais made works like the magnificent "Tent" and "Somniloquy" in which the remaining old pros were the "stars" and everyone else was ensemble. (This is all an oversimplification). Although it was in "Somniloquy" that the long, cool contortionist Carolyn Carlson made her first notable appearance—wrapping her legs like resilient pincers around a surprised-looking partner. At one point, Carlson was almost the only vivid performer Nikolais had, and he built "Echo" completely around her. I know that other dancers had important things to do, but my memory of the dance is that everything in it—projected silhouettes, the other people—seemed like echoes and shadows of Carlson. When Carlson left, Nikolais buried his dancers in a city of brilliant screens ("Structures" 1970) or set them walking, running, laughing, howling in a relatively simple crowd dance ("Scenario" 1971).

Over the past few years, Nikolais has been evolving another kind of company. These dancers are strong, and he displays their strength. Many of them have long, lithe bodies and pretty young faces; he presents them unclothed—or nearly so—glamorously made up and often bathed in pink and amber light. In "Crossfade," they pose in front of huge nude photographs of themselves.

The new two-act "Tribe," which Nikolais premiered during the company's recent people-packed season at the NYU School of Education Auditorium, shows these dancers moving from a sci-fi prehistory through various scenes of exploration, social encounters, and common rituals. (Like most Nikolais dances, it's structured in suite form, so you have trouble feeling a progression). In the beginning, the men swim miraculously through a red glow; actually they're belly-down on skateboards. A little later, the women straddle the men and ride with them; some of them stand in rigid positions looking like stone goddesses aboard sacred alligators. The dancers at first wear pale, form-fitting suits that cover their heads and show you dark, jagged eyeholes, but later they appear in briefs (the men) and body stockings (the women). Suzanne McDermaid—strong and strongly built, but very fluent and now dancing magnificently—has a solo that by Nikolais' standards is almost Dionysiac, full of a kind of dramatic tension, broad sweeps of movement, and reaching gestures. There's an acrobatic duet for Gerald Otte and James Teeters—fine when they hang off each other in peculiar counterbalances, not so hot when they sit facing each other, link legs, and rock back and forth in Tweedledum-Tweedledee complacency.

When the second part begins, the small translucent, jagged cloud-things that hang above the stage have been augmented by similar vertical ones. The company, shrouded again, pair up and work partly hidden between the panels, so that, instead of couples, you see a single two-headed being with both "its" legs floating in space. The quality of this second act is more quizzical, the actions more exploratory. Although throughout "Tribe," the dancers look about them excitedly, warily—as if the woods were full of enemies or hidden treasure. (Bill Groves is good at this). In his busy solo, Rob Esposito keeps miming something that looks like stepping into different rooms or opening Pandora's box. The extremely interesting dance that Gerald Otte performs is slow, often stops completely. In some way, it's painful too, as if it had to do with the learning of a sad truth. He bends and feels the ground; several times he constricts his body and crumples over. Several of the group dances are resoundingly athletic—you see bodies plunging through the air or being swung and hurled by others; sometimes they're giddy and a bit silly—the dancers prance and clap in unison (or divide up into "the boys" and "the girls").

The other new Nikolais dance, "Temple," looks like a Nikolais experiment of the '50s, almost more like someone else's imitation of Nikolais than the real thing. Three groups of three work on separate islands, each consisting of a tall stool and shorter round pedestal. In each group, one person is the apex, and the other two mirror each other. They all wear horrid pink, feature-smashing masks with eye gashes. Painted on the torsos of their leotards are huge black spots outlined in green. They look as if their chests have been ripped open and their hearts removed. That's the way they dance too. I don't think there is a single move that's not symmetrical and very few that aren't slow and stretchy. The dancers never leave their pedestals, just negotiate careful designs with their limbs, seldom turning their hollow gazes away from the audience. They may be meant as celebrants of an extraordinarily rigid religion, congealing into the pyramids they erected.

Perhaps "Temple" was created to flesh out the programs of excerpts and shorter works that Nikolais exhibits these days. But one of the most provocative small works shown during the NYU season was the triple duet from last year's "Grotto." Like "Temple," it involves three equally spaced groups, all doing the same dance, but the members of the couples share a single enveloping striped garment. Only their heads protrude. The third couple wears flesh-colored leotards and tights. When you watch the shrouded couples, you see the stretching fabric emphasize the tensions that the movement sets up between the dancers. The unshrouded dancers show you a quiet storm of limbs twining and separating. In one case, you are forced to concentrate on the forces that hold a structure together and those that threaten to separate it; in the other case you watch individual actions whose implications are less obvious. For instance, the man of each couple bends forward and makes a circle of his arms while his partner sinks to a squat within that circle. The unshrouded couple shows you a protective embrace. But the women of the shrouded couples sink into a pit of fabric and completely disappear.

I wish I'd seen "Grotto." This fragment of it raises interesting dance questions; it also brings out a particularly Nikolaisian dilemma. Which is more "human"—the elegant groping limbs or the physical tensions that motivate their groping? Are the leaping, scampering, muscle-flexing youths of "Tribe" really more "human" than the three quietly stretching and re-forming blob women of "Noumenon" (1953)? Or more profound? I don't like to think of a man like Alwin Nikolais responding—even unconsciously—to those who claim his work is "dehumanized."

Nikolais' company had a two-week-long season at the Beacon Theatre in 1978. Clive Barnes wrote of the second program in the *New York Post* April 21:

Nowadays, the Dance Theater of Alwin Nikolais makes no demands whatsoever upon the emotions or intellect of its spectators. The dances seem to go in one eye and out the other. It was not always so.

Nikolais, who offered the second program of his two-weeks' season at the Beacon Theater last night, is obviously one of dance's master showmen. Unfortunately more and more, the showman has become infinitely more important than the dance. We are expected to ooh and ah at his devilishly clever effects, and gasp appreciatively at his banal gurgles of electronic sound, but the choreography that all this aural and visual paraphernalia surrounds now seems to have been reduced beyond an irreducible minimum.

With Nik it is not the Emperor's New Clothes that are invisible—they at least are all too evident—it is the Emperor himself. The Nikolais company has tried to make packaging into an art form. And apart from the technical cleverness of it all, the esthetic standards bear a visual comparison with wall paper, the more arty type of Christmas cards, and those peculiar lamps, which you can buy in the cheaper forms of furniture stores, that are all oily bubbles and colored lights.

Last night's program opened with a world premiere which was commendably brief. It was called "Castings" and it had men and women in mixed doubles, dressed as if prepared for an encounter of the fourth kind, and performing gymnastics with a bar. It proved monotonous and beautifully lit.

But where was the dancing gone? Take the second number, "Guignol (Dummy Dancers)." This was a movement essay on the subject of dolls, puppets and mannequins. The back projections, of doll faces, or statues, or, at one point, a mad pattern of spare arms and grasping hands, proved exquisite.

The drama however—there really was no dancing at all worth speaking of—was simply naïve. Puppets going beserk and attacking their masters with slapsticks, a marionette controlled by electric hands, a group of people dancing with, and later assaulting, a group of similarly dressed dummies.

Such expressionist devices have their place, but to trot out such simplistic clichés, one after another, seemed almost self-defeating.

The evening ended with Nikolais' 1976 work "Triad" and this is Nikolais at his most magical. Yet, surely, once you have seen it, you have seen it. Three caverns of light, with magic lantern effects, and a group of apparently not unduly talented dancers.

In the past when dancers like Murray Louis, Phyllis Lamhut and Gladys Bailin, were still in the company Nikolais choreographed technically extremely demanding choreography. No longer. In "Triad" when the dancers break out of their light-cocoons, and come downstage to actually dance, the choreography is repetitious (at one point deliberately so) and unimaginative. The dancers, even so, look clumsy.

The sheer theatrical qualities of Nikolais are not to be denied. He is a pioneer in a new theater of visual wonders. Yet over the years he seems to have paid a price for this. And to see his programs is, I feel, to be made subject to that Draconian artistic law of diminishing returns.

If you have never seen Nikolais, pray go. And even if you have seen him a lot, you will still find new tricks to marvel at. Moreover, I am sure that other programs are less dazzlingly bland than this presumably atypical combination of works. Yet I do wonder whether Nikolais is being fair to his talents. Not so long ago he was offering us evenings of theater to think and feel about as well as just to watch. At present, we could do with more matter and less art.

The Alwin Nikolais Dance Theatre appeared at City Center Theater from February 16 to 26, 1984, presenting old and new works. Arlene Croce wrote in the *New Yorker* March 12:

> In Alwin Nikolais's new piece *Persons and Structures*, the curtain goes up and you see at the right of the stage what looks like a phone booth covered in white cloth. The cloth goes up and there's a two-story glass box mounted on metal legs about a foot high. Inside the two cubicles are two men, one up and one down, who look completely naked and who squirm uncomfortably. The cloth comes down and a moment later goes up again, and this time two men are crammed together in the top box and two women are below. The cloth cover keeps rising and descending all through the piece,

which is set to one of Edgar Varèse's most disquieting compositions, the *Poème Électronique,* and we never lose our dread of what we will see stuck and writhing in there. The content is always different; once it's just one man on top with an empty box below him. Inside the boxes, the people are either desperate to get out or determined to perform; they do slow tumbling acts, displacing each other with enormous difficulty. In the meantime, the stage is full of background and foreground motion. Numbers of dancers are constantly crossing behind the box, which is open at the back, and, of course, some of them get in and out while it is draped. Perhaps to divert us, the foreground action consists of a sequence of dances. I shall have to see the piece again to say what these were like; after the first one, a pas de trios in which two men lifted a woman between them by pressing their heads against her rib cage (her feet dangled in the air like a doll's), I stopped looking. The box was too fascinating.

Nikolais has often shown a flair for the freak show, but these spectacles of his seldom sustain themselves beyond the first few minutes. A good example is *Gallery* (1978), which the Nikolais company was also presenting this season (at the City Center). It's "gallery" as in "shooting gallery." A row of fluorescent green skulls floats in black air. Pop, pop, and they disappear. They rise and sink, they change places, they appear in clusters, but soon enough we've seen it all, and Nikolais isn't able to renew our interest. He also is surprisingly careless with the mechanics of his illusions. In the same piece, two clowns come out wearing bags that have a clearly defined illuminated front and a black velvet back. This makes convincing two-dimensional plastic shapes in the dark, and when the clowns take their feet off the ground the shapes contract to squiggling blobs in the air. But if Nikolais is so concerned to keep that two-dimensional front before us why does he have the two clowns turn sideways again and again, exposing their "nonexistent" rears? Although the dance goes on and on, we never again can see the original illusion. Some essential part of the Nikolais spectacle is constantly being undermined by imprecision or by laxity in planning and development; we wonder why he is showing us these things. And sometimes in the more horrific numbers there seems to be a reluctance to go the route—an emotional holding back, as if the dispenser of these grim and grisly treats wanted us to see him as really a harmless old fuff who wouldn't hurt a fly. In another of the new pieces, *Liturgies,* two men carry a third (Joy Hintz, the shortest woman in the company, made up as a little bald man), who hangs between them on a pole. There are ropes tying the third figure to the pole, but if you think you're going to see anything made of that you don't know Nikolais. The whole apparatus drags its unexamined possibilities around the stage a few too many times and vanishes. In another section, he experiments again with a rope and a hanging body and again goes nowhere. The man is either a terrible tease or a self-satisfied conjurer whose least soap bubble must be preserved for posterity.

The boldness and succinctness of *Persons and Structures* therefore come as a surprise. Nikolais doesn't shrink from the logic of the pattern he has set in motion, and he even dramatizes it. When the people outside the box rush to it and flatten themselves against it while the ones inside peer out, they instantly double the emotional power of the image, which has been steadily rising. It's as if they, too, were helpless animals. The dancers don't act this moment; they state it and trust us to respond. This trust is something I am not used to in Nikolais's work. The lack of drama in so many of his pieces had made me see him as a displaced person—a fine-arts designer with no great theatrical appetite. Infinitely delicate and painstaking with his designs, he has often directed with a heavy touch. His dancers not only act, they overact. Not content with being clever, they are also cute, forever capping some tricky bit with a dead stare out front, prompting our reactions. When they play for laughs, they play for keeps. (The same pedantic humor was seen in Debra McCall's recent revival of the dances of Oskar Schlemmer, the director of the Bauhaus theatre workshop and a forerunner of Nikolais. Form followed function, all right, and fun *had* to follow form). In the new piece, the pathos is greater for not being pushed out at us. Nikolais's theatre sense here has a leaping, charged quality I'm also not accustomed to. Maybe his using another composer's score instead of having to compose one of his own helped him find a dramatic focus. The costumes, too, which effectively imply total nudity, were inspired by another designer, Lindsay Davis. *Persons and Structures* is a most untypical Nikolais production, yet it's the production many of us have long wanted from him—the piece he has often promised but never quite delivered. He builds it to an unforgettable climax. The last time we see them, both of the boxes are filled to bursting with bodies—a jumble of hands, feet, faces. The rising cloth that reveals this horrid sight keeps on rising and uncovers a man standing erect on top. Before we can decide how he got there and who he is, the scene blacks out and the piece is over.

Nikolais's theatre has lately become less illusionistic—concerned less with costumes and props than with the exposed bodies of dancers dancing. When he makes a nifty piece of choreography these days (like the opening of *Liturgies*, which churns out a great froth of insect visualizations, from beetles to centipedes), his conceits are likely to be purely anatomical. The company is trained to this kind of expression, and it's no longer as good at disappearing into the décor as it used to be. An old piece like *Noumenon* (1953) loses its point, because the dancers, who are completely enclosed in stretch fabric, let us see, in between the triangles and pentagons and trapezoids and whatnot, the outlines of *persons,* and the intent of the choreography is that we not see this until the very end, when the fabric falls about the heads and shoulders of those within, defining them as so many draped but unmistakably human statues. Looking at the older pieces in the current repertory—three out of four were revivals from the fifties—I was struck by how often they seemed to require (as much of their audience as of their maker) a hermetic concentration on form and no interest in the real world. We are seldom taken beyond the manipulation of design elements into an understanding of where the design impulse comes from. In Nikolais's work then and for a long time to come, a decorative object that looked like an onion or a trumpet was never used to remind us of onions or trumpets, because, I suspect, references of that sort were thought to be at best utilitarian and at worst anti-art and just too Disney. Though Nikolais's abstractions may have corresponded to the mood of the fifties—particularly to the ethos of some Abstract Expressionists—their lack of resonance makes them look pointless and trivial today. Whereas Disney (to invoke the archfiend of those years) has started to look really bright and consequential. Right after the Nikolais matinee, I saw *Fantasia,* which was playing just across the street, and I kept thinking of Nikolais— of his affinities with Disney and his lack of interest in them.

Note: The remainder of the review is about the film *Fantasia.* Croce does not continue any comparisons with Nikolais.

Lewis Segal's review in the *Los Angeles Times,* May 5, 1988, was titled "Alwin Nikolais' Latest Samples of Legerdemain."

It's all done with mirrors: the latest example of legerdemain by that genial wizard of modern dance, Alwin Nikolais. But it's also something of a sly joke at his own expense.

Introduced locally in Royce Hall, UCLA, Thursday evening as the opening work of a three-week engagement by Nikolais Dance Theatre,"Crucible" (1985) hides 10 dancers beneath low mirror panels. Sometimes they raise only a single finger above the top edge of the looking glass, sometimes a leg or two, eventually whole, bare upper torsos.

Early on, the piece is exclusively whimsical, as hands behave like puppet-creatures and the reflections below merely embellish the playful confrontations. But with the addition of colored lights and slide projections—and the development of horizontal limb-motifs that merge perfectly with their mirror images—Nikolais takes "Crucible" into the realm of awesome kaleidoscopic abstraction.

The joke comes from Nikolais' identification over the past 40 years with a style of movement based on intricate muscular isolations—an emphasis on body parts rather than full-body statements. "Crucible," of course, may be the ultimate essay in that style, since it reduces the Nikolais dancers to disembodied pieces.

A joke of another sort is the 1987 parody "Blank on Blank" (pun definitely intended), which pretends to be the kind of piece that Nikolais has always said he'll never, ever do: the gesture-based contemporary social and psychological expose. Here are 10 very unpleasant urban types, dressed in white versions of streetwear, picking their noses, lumping indolently against one another, posing inanely for snapshots, lashing out in spasms of anger (the action sometimes runs backwards and forwards like a loop of film), all to a documentary sound-score: dripping water, demolition noise, etc. The work fairly oozes contempt for people who take such pretensions seriously.

In contrast to this nasty novelty, the familiar "Graph" (1984) offers classic Nikolais values: scenic metaphors (grids resembling giant spider webs), dancer metamorphoses (washes of colored light that isolate cast members in shifting, individual auras), electronic music (by David Gregory this time, instead of Nikolais himself) and special effects (a strobe-lit finale). Plus dancing of meticulous control—especially the fearsome contortions performed by Sheila Lehner and Sara Hook against plastic panels.

More dance gymnastics (a relatively recent Nikolais preoccupation) turn up in "Contact" (1985). It begins with rhythmic walking and movement flurries against that rhythm whenever dancers connect. Soon, however, it settles into an exploration of complex partnering gambits, capped by a demanding, lift-laden duet for Alberto Del Saz and James Murphy.

Lehner, however, gets the hardest, most unorthodox showpiece: a solo in which she's seated on the floor, leaning back, and her legs drift upward as if they had a life of their own, forcing her body into increasingly impossible contortions. Quite amazing—and it's NOT done with mirrors.

George Jackson saw a performance at the Kennedy Center. His review ran in the *Washington Post* September 21, 1988.

A surprise was in store for those who only knew the Alwin Nikolais of yore and his reputation for reshaping human anatomy. Last night, the first half of the Nikolais Dance Theatre's opening program at the Kennedy Center's Terrace Theater focused on the body. Men's bodies, women's bodies—unaltered and practically unadorned—were the instruments for much of the choreography. And flesh showed not just in a matter-of-fact way, but as part of a new Nikolais titillation.

All the pieces before the intermission were made in the '80s and were given their Washington premieres last night. "Crucible" begins in semi-darkness as 10 brightly lit fingers poke up over the edge of a mirrored plane. Other fingers, palms and wrists follow, and for a long while it seems that we see not only each hand—there are 10 pairs in this piece—but also its reflection joined to it. Hands, though, don't become a fetish. Suddenly legs shoot up over the edge of that shiny inclined plane, and then there are bodies, almost naked bodies that rise and fall and bend. The dancers do, in a sense, become dressed. Nikolais bathes them in pattern and color— rainbow spectra and organized shapes of austere hues. Always, though, the dancer's reflections are part of them, and before the piece ends, these Siamese-twin physiques have come to seem almost natural.

"Contact" is even more different from old Nik. There is lots of everyday dance movement, beginning with processional crossings of the stage in which the bodies are held at a low center of gravity and growing into all sorts of contact—collisions, lifts, supported tumbling. There's also less anonymity here. A male duet singles out Alberto del Saz and James Murphy; Nikolais uses them athletically for falls and catches as if they were clones of each other, though Murphy is long-legged and streamlined and del Saz long-chested and built squarely. Sheila Lehner, however, is made to seem truly unique. It's not just that she dances a solo, one that looks akin to Hindu contortion, or that she displays intense concentration and exhibits great control, but there are signs of emotion. Another dimension is implied here.

"Persons & Structures" is perhaps the best of Nikolais' new works. Throughout, the movement continues to surprise. There are lots of bodies, dressed in a film so thin and luminescent that it shows more detail than would mere nakedness. Some of the bodies are confined in glass cubicles, and it's fascinating to see the difference between their actions and those of dancers performing freely in space. The idea of the work alludes to Leonardo da Vinci's analysis of planes and anatomies, and balletic arabesques appeared briefly.

Concluding the program was some vintage Nikolais. The 1963 "Imago" is surgery, done with choreography and costuming, in which the dancers are given long, vertebral arms and then limbless bodies, billowing torsos and other mutations. Their heads are expanded to terminate in tubular knobs. "Tensile Involvement" from 1953, begins with normal anatomies but these become distorted as the dancers involve themselves with long streamers.

Whether he works with real bodies or not, Nikolais will attract some people and repel others. Those who like him mention his wild ideas. Those who don't say that the movement corollaries he draws from his ideas are too uniformly light in tone, more like cartoons than sculptures. His fans love his logic; his detractors complain that no revolution ever occurred during the course of a Nikolais dance. He himself claims that there are enough other choreographers to delve into deep feelings. Concepts, though, can also be heroic or erotic, and if that one contorted solo is any sign, Alwin Nikolais may one day be telling love stories in his dances.

A few months before Nikolais died in May 1993, colleagues and pupils gathered to honor the ailing artist. Anna Kisselgoff wrote in the *New York Times* January 24, 1993:

There was a time when modern dance was an art of new beginnings, a concept that was brought home with special force at a tribute to Alwin Nikolais's teaching and artistry earlier this month. The evening, a benefit for the school directed by Mr. Nikolais and his longtime collaborator, Murray Louis, had a family atmosphere and included performances plus reminiscences from alumni.

Now 82 years old, Mr. Nikolais has so accustomed us to the delights of his mixed-media universe that it is hard to recall how strange it once looked. Nowadays we take for granted that his dancers' bodies are disguised by sacks, masks, cylinders, props, and slide projections.

Known as Nik throughout the international dance world, Mr. Nikolais hit his stride as a choreographer in the 1960s when the gorgeous colors and designs of his light shows were considered in tune with the psychedelia of the day. But Mr. Nikolais was no fad; his work signified a sharp break with the prevailing dance esthetics of the 1950s. Since then, he has given the public a new vision of dance. There has always been depth behind the dazzle.

Above all, Mr. Nikolais has remained true to his belief that modern dance must be rooted in what he calls the "unique gesture," creativity that stands out in its originality. Current dance experimentalists, by contrast, may be ingenious, but they tend to resemble one another and fall easily into categories.

Mr. Nikolais, for his part, had witnessed the seminal growth of American modern dance when he studied from 1937 through 1939 at the Bennington School of Dance in Vermont. His teachers were pioneers who hammered out the art form's distinctive idioms — Martha Graham, Doris Humphrey, Charles Weidman and Hanya Holm.

Yet even though Mr. Nikolais became Holm's assistant after World War II in Colorado Springs, he used her teaching as a springboard for a new departure. Instinctively, he sensed that the postwar period called for a different approach to dance. He turned toward abstract form and away from the psychological dance-drama that had been dominant through the 1940's. The idea that dance could be seen as pure movement rather than as body language was shared by choreographers as different as George Balanchine, Merce Cunningham and Erick Hawkins. Dance is "motion, not emotion," Mr. Nikolais likes to say.

Nonetheless, he plays with formal elements in his own way, making dance only one component of a nonrealistic total theater. Typically, his works lack narrative and stress visual abstraction. (An elongated dancer in his "Aviary" suggests the essence of "birdness" just like a wingless Brancusi sculpture). As decorative as it may seem, Mr. Nikolais's dance theater is also intended to convey a philosophical idea.

Imaginatively distilled, this message says that man has made a mess of things and does not deserve to be viewed as the center of the universe. Instead, Mr. Nikolais shows us man as inseparable from his environment. This allegory is retold in virtually every Nikolais work, in which light plays upon the dancers' bodies and they literally become the scenery. A vivid example is the 1985 "Crucible," which was performed at the tribute, on Jan. 13, at the Marymount Manhattan Theater.

These were hardly the kind of pieces that Mr. Nikolais composed at the start of his career. In 1939, he co-choreographed an overt social-protest piece, "Eight Column Lines," with his first teacher, Truda Kaschmann. Two years later, he seemed headed for a conventional dance career and directed a small touring company, called Dancers En Route. But in 1948 he was appointed dance director of the Henry Street Settlement Playhouse. It was the perfect venue to explore new dances for new times. The tribute celebrated these beginnings, and the program was billed as an homage to Mr. Nikolais as "an artist and a master teacher."

Mr. Nikolais and Mr. Louis (who was co-host of the evening with Phyllis Lamhut, another leading dancer in the original Nikolais troupe) remained at the playhouse until 1970, before expanding into other locales. One remembers how audiences from all parts of the city flocked to this veritable hothouse of creativity on the Lower East Side. Mr. Nikolais's first major success was "Masks, Props and Mobiles" (1953), followed by "Kaleidoscipe" and "Prism" (both from 1956).

A continuing favorite with the public is "Noumenon" from "Masks, Props and Mobiles": three dancers encased in jersey sacks evolve from blobs into figureheads and sculptured altar figures. No matter how disguised or unsung, the Nikolais dancers are always dancing: the precision required for unison work by three bodies in jersey tubes is nothing short of virtuosic.

People no longer talk, as they did for two decades, about "dehumanized" Nikolais dancers. The truth is, the world has caught up with Mr. Nikolais. Astronauts in space helmets or young people in trendy constructed clothes by Japanese designers do not look any stranger than Nikolais dancers with disks attached to their feet.

Remarkably, Mr. Nikolais's dance theater has never dated. This does not mean all of the choreographer's pieces are successful. But he has worked in an amazing variety of ways within his unique style. A retrospective season planned for July at the Joyce Theater is bound to point up his two major themes: man's evolution and man's folly. The first can be defined by an image as simple as froglike figures on skateboards rising from the primordial ooze in his "Pond." The second can be as direct as the mushroom-shaped cloth billowing upward in "Tent." The secret of Mr. Nikolais's appeal lies in our recognition of his subject — the human condition. The Martians on stage look familiar: They are us.

Chronology of the
Choreography of Alwin Nikolais

. . . .

researched and compiled by JANA FEINMAN

To compile this chronological list of works choreographed by Alwin Nikolais I consulted programs of first performances. A complete run of programs has been hard to come by. Some were lost during relocations of the Nikolais/Louis foundation and it appears that some were not brought back with the company from foreign tours. That existing programs are filed in different categories in various libraries and archives was another handicap. Relying on available documentation and reasoned judgment, I compiled what I believe to be the most accurate chronology it is now possible to create. My list both amplifies and diverges from the chronology posted on the website of the Nikolais/Louis Foundation for Dance.

Occasionally a work was performed first in one venue and claimed as a premiere in another venue shortly after; I give the date of the second, reckoning that the earlier performance was a try-out or preview. Dancers report that Nikolais often substantially revised works after a premiere. That being a common practice among choreographers, I leave it without remark. I also leave without remark the appropriation of material from one choreographed work to another, knowing that this, too, is a frequent practice among choreographers. That said, I have noted name changes in titles of works.

The Jerome Robbins Dance Division, New York Public Library, has extensive, but incomplete program files dating from 1946 to 1978. With the help of Judith Connick, archivist of the Nikolais/Louis Papers at University Libraries, Ohio University, Athens Ohio, I found some additional programs and press coverage that helped to clarify the record. Murray Louis allowed me access to photocopies of programs at the Nikolais/Louis Foundation for Dance in New York City. I owe thanks to Gerald Otte for help in accessing other material and to Teresa Cuevas for assistance in library research. Ann Brandwein at the Wadsworth Atheneum in Hartford, Connecticut, and archivists Ethel Bacon and Margaret Mair at the University of Hartford (the Julius Hartt School of Music when Nikolais taught there in the 1940s) were helpful in filling in the record of works premiered at those institutions.

Sabine Women
    Play by Leonid Andreyeff
    12/15/36, Palace Theater, Hartford, CT
    The Charles Gilpin Players of Hartford, Negro Unit of the WPA Theatre
    Music: speaking chorus
World We Live In
    Play by Josef and Karel Kapek, also called "The Insect Comedy,"
    12/13/37, Avery Memorial Theatre, Hartford, CT
    WPA Federal Theatre Negro Unit
    Choreography and percussion treatment by Alwin Nikolais
Eight Column Line
    Choreography by Tuda Kaschmann and Alwin Nikolais
    5/19/39, Avery Memorial Theater, Hartford, CT
    Music: Ernest Krenek
    Settings and costumes: A. Everett Austin
    With support of Trustees of the Wadsworth Atheneum and the Friends
        and Enemies of Modern Music
Birthday of the Infanta
    Play by Oscar Wilde
    5/27/39, Avery Memorial Theatre, Hartford, CT
    Dance movement by Alwin Nikolais
American Greetings
    1/19/40, Avery Memorial Theatre, Hartford, CT
    Music: Louis Horst
The Jazzy 20's
    1/19/40, Avery Memorial Theatre, Hartford, CT
    Music: Beatrice MacLoughlin
Opening Dance
    5/29/41, Hartt College Auditorium, Hartford, CT
    Music: Joaquin Turina
American Folk Themes
    5/29/41, Hartt College Auditorium, Hartford, CT
    Music: David Guion
Pavanne
    5/29/41, Hartt College Auditorium, Hartford, CT
    Music: Esther Williamson
Evocation
    5/29/41, Hartt College Auditorium, Hartford, CT
    Music: Wallingford Riegger

Ten Maidens and No Man
>   Comic Opera in One Act by Franz Von Suppe
>   5/13/42, Hartt College Auditorium, Hartford, CT
>   Dance direction by Alwin Nikolais

Character Sketches
>   [In the suite titled *War Themes*]
>   5/15/42, Avery Memorial Theatre, Hartford, CT
>   Music: Sergei Prokofieff

Popular Themes
>   Choreographed with Olga Dzurich
>   5/15/42, Avery Memorial Theatre, Hartford, CT
>   Music: George Gershwin

Martha
>   Opera by Friedrich Von Flotow
>   5/6/46, Hartt College Auditorium, Hartford, CT
>   Dance direction by Alwin Nikolais

Fable of the Donkey
>   8/17/46, Fine Arts Center, Colorado Springs, CO
>   Music: Freda Miller
>   Script: Lillian de la Torre

The Barber of Seville
>   Opera by Giovanni Paisiello
>   2/17/47, Hartt College Auditorium, Hartford, CT
>   Choreography by Alwin Nikolais

Romeo and Juliet
>   Opera by Charles François Gounod
>   2/18/48, Hartt College Auditorium, Hartford, CT
>   Dance direction by Alwin Nikolais

The Princess and the Vagabond
>   Folk opera in four scenes by Isadore Freed
>   5/13/48, Hartt College Auditorium, Hartford, CT
>   Choreography by Alwin Nikolais

Dramatic Etude
>   8/13/48, Fine Arts Center, Colorado Springs, CO
>   Music: Marshall Bialosky

Extrados
>   5/26/49, Henry Street Playhouse, New York City
>   Music: Alfred Pew (pseudonym for Alfred Brooks)

1. Phyllis Lamhut with Griffin and Mock Turtle in The Lobster Quadrille, *a children's dance play created by Nikolais in 1949. Photograph Davis S. Berlin, courtesy of the Nikolais/Louis Foundation.*

The Lobster Quadrille (from "Alice Through the Looking Glass")
    11/19/49, Museum of Natural History Auditorium, New York City
    Music: Freda Miller
Shepherdess and the Chimney Sweep (from Anderson)
    12/16/49, Henry Street Playhouse, New York City
    Script: Dorthy McFadden
    [No music credit. Music compilation credited to Florence Moed Deutsch
       on later programs.]
Opening Suite
    3/18/50, The Brooklyn Museum, New York City
    Music: Malcolm Waldren

Starbeam Journey
> 12/27/50, Henry Street Playhouse, New York City
> Music: Improvised
> Script: Alwin Nikolais and Murray Louis

Sokar and the Crocodile
> 12/28/50, Henry Street Playhouse, New York City
> Music: Freda Miller
> Script: Alwin Nikolais and Murray Louis

Heritage of Cain
> 4/30/51, Henry Street Playhouse, New York City
> Music: Eugene Nicolait

The Invulnerables
> 5/2/51, The Brooklyn Museum, New York City
> Music: Rex Wilder

The Committee
> 5/25/51, Henry Street Playhouse, New York City
> Music: Sergei Prokofiev

The Vortex
> A movement drama with timing and dynamic growth improvised
> 5/25/51, Henry Street Playhouse, New York City
> Music: Recordings

Romeo and Juliet
> Opera by Charles François Gounod
> 6/30/51 Central City Opera House, Central City, CO
> Fencing choreography by Alwin Nikolai [*sic*]

New England Suite
> 11/9/51, The Cooper Union for the Advancement of Science and Art, New
> York City
> Music: Douglas Moore

Aqueouscape
> 11/9/51, The Cooper Union for the Advancement of Science and Art, New
> York City
> Music: Jean Sibelius
> [Integrated into the concerts titled *Etudes II: Masks, Props, and Mobiles,*
> 1/26/53, and *Masks — Props — Mobiles,* 12/10/55]

Noumenon
> 11/9/51, The Cooper Union for the Advancement of Science and Art, New
> York City
> Music: Percussion

[Retitled *Noumenom Mobilis* and integrated into the concerts *Etudes II: Masks, Props, and Mobiles*, 1/26/53, and *Masks — Props — Mobiles*, 12/10/55]

Theme and Improvisation
11/9/51, The Cooper Union for the Advancement of Science and Art, New York City
Music: Freda Miller
[Retitled *Theme and Improvised Variation* and integrated into the concert titled *Etudes II: Masks, Props, and Mobiles*, 1/26/53]

The Indian Sun (From an American Indian legend)
2/16/52, Woodmere High School, Woodmere, NY
Music: Percussion and piano

Merry-Go-Elsewhere (The Story of a Merry-Go-Round)
12/28/52, Henry Street Playhouse, New York City
[Music credited to Freda Miller on later programs]

Forest of Three (A Fairy Tale with One Character)
5/23/53, Henry Street Playhouse, New York City
Music: Percussion

Kaleidoscope
5/27/53, Henry Street Playhouse, New York City
Music: Percussion
[This short group work for nine dancers differs from the 1956 work of the same title]

Farm Journal
7/18/53, Sturbridge Village Theatre, Sturbridge, MA
Music: Douglas Moore
Commissioned by Sturbridge Village Theatre

The Devil and Daniel Webster
A Music Play
7/18/53, Sturbridge Village Theatre, Sturbridge, MA
Music: Douglas Moore
Script: Stephen Vincent Benét

St. George and the Dragon
1/1/54, Henry Street Playhouse, New York City
Music: Freda Miller

Legend of the Winds
12/22/54, Henry Street Playhouse, New York City
Trumpet improvisations by Don Ferrara

Web

2/13/55, Henry Street Playhouse, New York City

[Premiered on the concert titled *Village of Whispers,* integrated into the concert *Masks — Props — Mobiles* (12/10/55), and later reworked as a full company dance titled *Tensile Involvement*]

Music: Percussion

Tournament

2/13/55, Henry Street Playhouse, New York City

[Premiered on the concert titled *Village of Whispers,* and integrated into the concert titled *Masks — Props — Mobiles* (12/10/55)]

Music: Carlos Chavez

Three Kings

12/17/55, Henry Street Playhouse, New York City

Music: Percussion

Battle

12/17/55, Henry Street Playhouse, New York City

Music: Carlos Chavez

Kaleidoscope

5/25/56, Henry Street Playhouse, New York City

[Untitled at this time, sections of the work follow exactly the dance presented 8/17/56 at the Connecticut College American Dance Festival, New London, CT.]

Music: George Antheil, Carlos Chavez, Alan Hovhaness, Edgard Varèse, Heitor Villa Lobos, ethnic sources, and Playhouse Percussion Group.

Prism

12/27/56, Henry Street Playhouse, New York City

Music: Percussion recordings by the Playhouse Percussion Group, ethnic sources Alan Hovhaness, George Antheil

The Bewitched—A Dance Satire

3/26/57, University of Illinois Auditorium, Urbana-Champaign

Music and book: Harry Partch

Commissioned by the Fromm Foundation, the University of Illinois School of Music, and the Dance Division of the Department of Physical Education for Women

Runic Canto

8/16/57, Connecticut College American Dance Festival, New London, CT

Music: Arranged by Alwin Nikolais, assisted by David Berlin and Margaret Dietz, from "Music Concrete" sources and original recordings

2. Murray Louis and his shadow leap from the cyclorama in Prism *(1956).*
Photograph David S. Berlin, courtesy of the Nikolais/Louis Foundation.

Commissioned by Connecticut College for the Tenth American Dance
Festival

New Dances [also known as *Cantos*]

12/27/57, Henry Street Playhouse, New York City

Music: Playhouse Percussion Group, Eddie Sauter, Bill Finnegan, Pierre
Henry, Pierre Schaeffer, Michael Phillipot, Daniel Pinkham, Henry Brandt

Mirrors

An improvised dance fantasy designed and directed by Alwin Nikolais

5/16/58, Henry Street Playhouse, New York City

Music: Alwin Nikolais

Allegory

1/30/59, Henry Street Playhouse, New York City

Music: Alwin Nikolais assisted by Robert Mason

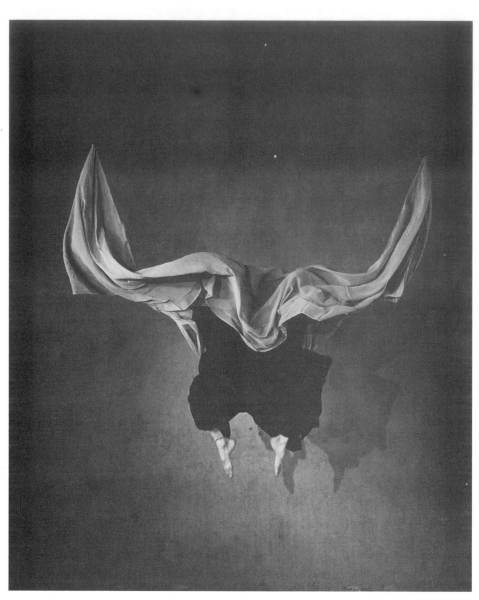

3. The Bewitched, *a 1957 collaboration with composer Harry Partch, shown here in the 1959 premiere at the Henry Street Playhouse. Photograph David S. Berlin, courtesy of the Nikolais/Louis Foundation.*

Kites

    5/31/59, *The Steve Allen Show*, NBC-TV

Pavanne

    9/28/59, *The Steve Allen Show*, NBC-TV

Ritual

    10/19/59, *The Steve Allen Show*, NBC-TV

Seascape

    12/28/59, *The Steve Allen Show*, NBC-TV

Totem

    1/29/60, Henry Street Playhouse, New York City

    Music: Alwin Nikolais

Paddles

    3/21/60, *The Steve Allen Show*, NBC-TV

Eight Compositions of Abstract Dance

    11/30/60, Caspary Auditorium, New York City

    Music: Alwin Nikolais

    Contemporary Music Society Concert

Stratus

    1/27/61, Henry Street Playhouse, New York City

    Music: Alwin Nikolais

Nimbus

    1/27/61, Henry Street Playhouse, New York City

    Music: Alwin Nikolais

Création

    8/5/61, Comedia Canadienne, Montreal, Canada

    Music: Alwin Nikolais (Some sounds in the score were created on a new elec-
        tronically controlled piano by Dr. Richard Evans of Salt Lake City, Utah)

Illusions

    8/7/61, Comedia Canadienne, Montreal, Canada

    Music: Alwin Nikolais

    Twenty-sixth annual season of the Montreal Music and Drama Festival

Divertissement

    7/7/62, Teatro Nuovo, Spoleto, Italy

    [This was the first time *Divertissement* appeared in a program. Over the
        years Nikolais used this title to present a variety of short dances
        selected from his entire repertory.)

Peacock

    7/23/62, Teatro Caio Melisso, Spoleto, Italy

    Music: Alwin Nikolais

Imago (The City Curious)
  2/24/63, Hartford Jewish Community Center, Hartford, CT
  Music: Alwin Nikolais and James Seawright. Sounds produced on the
     RCA synthesizer of the Columbia-Princeton Electronic Music Center,
     New York City.
Sanctum
  2/20/64, Henry Street Playhouse, New York City
  Music: Alwin Nikolais. Sounds were produced at the Columbia-
     Princeton Elecronic Music Center, New York City.
Galaxy
  3/19/65, Henry Street Playhouse, New York City
  Music: Alwin Nikolais. Some sounds in the electronic scores were produced
     at the Columbia-Princeton Electronic Music Center, New York City.
  Commissioned by the John Simon Guggenheim Foundation
Vaudeville of the Elements
  12/10/65, Tyrone Guthrie Theatre, Walker Art Center, Minneapolis, MN
  Music: Alwin Nikolais. Portions of the electronic scores were produced
     at the Columbia-Princeton Electronic Music Center, New York City.
  Commissioned by the Walker Art Center
Somniloquy
  2/9/67, Solomon R. Guggenheim Museum, New York City
  Music: Alwin Nikolais
  Commissioned by the Contemporary Music Society
Fusion
  Film in collaboration with Edmund Emschwiller
  3/28/67, Hilton Hotel, New York City
  Music: Alwin Nikolais
  Commissioned by Spring Mills, Inc.
Premiere
  A multi-media event
  3/28/67, George Abbott Theatre, New York City
  Music: Alwin Nikolais
  Sound consultants: Robert Moog and Robert Lamarche
  Film projections: Edmund Emschwiller
  Introduction: Steve Allen
  Commissioned by Spring Mills, Inc.
Triptych
  11/30/67, Henry Street Playhouse, New York City
  Music: Alwin Nikolais

4. *Carolyn Carlson, Anne Carlton, and Susan Buirge in premiere performance of* Vaudeville of the Elements *(1965). Photographer Eric Sutherland for the Walker Art Center, Minneapolis.*

Tower
   [Third act of *Vaudeville of the Elements*]
   7/5/68, Theatre Auditorium, University of South Florida, Tampa, FL
   Music: Alwin Nikolais
• *Tent*
   7/5/68, Theatre Auditorium, University of South Florida, Tampa, FL
   Music: Alwin Nikolais
   Commissioned by University of South Florida
Limbo
   [An electronic experiment created for television]
   7/20/68, CBS-TV

Help, Help the Globolinks (An opera for children and those who love children)
   12/21/68, Hamburg Opera, Hamburg Germany
   Music and libretto: Gian-Carlo Menotti
   Commissioned by Hamburgischen Staatsoper
Echo
   12/3/69, City Center Theater, New York City
   Music: Alwin Nikolais
   Made possible by a grant from the National Endowment for the Arts
Structures
   4/29/70, City Center Theater, New York City
   Music: Alwin Nikolais
   Commissioned by Chimera Foundation for Dance
Scenario
   2/25/71, Anta Theater, New York City
   Music: Alwin Nikolais
   Made possible by a grant from the National Endowment for the Arts
The Relay
   [Created for TV]
   6/71, BBC, London, co-production with National Educational Television
   Music: Alwin Nikolais with Moog synthesizer
Foreplay
   1/22/72, Brooklyn Academy of Music Opera House, New York City
   Music: Alwin Nikolais
   Rehearsal period funded by the New York State Council on the Arts
Chrysalis
   [Film in collaboration with Edmund Emschwiller]
   3/9/72, Buffalo, NY
Grotto
   2/17/73, Brooklyn Academy of Music Opera House, New York City
   Music: Alwin Nikolais and James Burton
   Made possible by a grant from the National Endowment for the Arts
Kyledx I
   2/9/73, Hamburg Opera House, Hamburg, Germany
   Music: Pierre Henry
   Commissioned by Hamburgischen Staatsoper
Cross—Fade
   2/5/74 Lyceum Theater, New York City
   [Previewed with the title *Fixations* on 12/8/73 at the Wisconsin Union
      Theater, University of Wisconsin, Madison]

Music: Alwin Nikolais

Made possible by a grant from the National Endowment for the Arts

Scrolls

2/2/74, Middletown, High School, Middletown, New York

Music: Alwin Nikolais

Funded by The Greater Middletown Arts Council, Inc. with assistance
from the New York State Council on the Arts

Temple

9/20/74, Teatro Zarzuela, Madrid, Spain

Music: Alwin Nikolais

Commissioned by: The Rockefeller Foundation

Tribe

5/3/75, Teatro Colón, Buenos Aires, Argentina

Music: Alwin Nikolais

Made possible by a grant from the National Endowment for the
Arts with additional funding from the New York State Council
on the Arts

Styx

8/3/76, Beacon Theatre, New York City

Music: Alwin Nikolais

Made possible by a grant from the National Endowment for the
Arts with additional funding from the New York State Council
on the Arts

Triad

8/4/76, Beacon Theatre, New York City

Music: Alwin Nikolais

Made possible by a grant from the National Endowment for the Arts

Guignol (Dummy Dances)

2/9/77, Beacon Theatre, New York City

Music: Improvised by the Paul Winter Consort with the exception of the
electronic sounds created by Alwin Nikolais

Made possible by a grant from the National Endowment for the Arts

Arporisms

2/11/77, Beacon Theatre, New York City

Music: Alwin Nikolais, and improvisations by the Paul Winter consort
(dance #7)

Poetry: Jean Arp

Commissioned by the Contemporary Music Society of New York and
Mrs. Madeleine Chalette Lejwa.

5. Gallery *(1978). Photograph © Tom Caravaglia 2007.*

Gallery

    4/19/78, Beacon Theatre, New York City

    Music: Alwin Nikolais

    Made possible by a grant from the National Endowment for the Arts

Castings

    4/20/78, Beacon Theatre, New York City

    Music: Alwin Nikolais

Aviary "A Ceremony for Bird People"

    12/7/78, Union Theater, University of Wisconsin, Madison, WI

    Music: Daniel Harris and Les Thimmig

    Commissioned by the University of Wisconsin, Madison. Additional
        support provided by the Wisconsin Arts Board, the Wisconsin
        Foundation for the Arts, and the Evjue Foundation

Countdown

    5/7/79, Palacio de Bellas Artes, Mexico City, Mexico

    Music: Alwin Nikolais

    Commissioned by George Soros with partial funding from the National
        Endowment for the Arts and the New York State Council on the Arts

The Mechanical Organ

    6/4/80, Gaillard Municipal Auditorium, Spoleto Festival, Charleston, SC

    Music: Score improvised by David Darling Ensemble under Alwin
        Nikolais' direction. Tapes compiled and edited by Alwin Nikolais.

    Commissioned by George Soros with partial funding from the National
        Endowment for the Arts and the New York State council on the Arts

Schema

    12/18/80, Palais Garnier, Paris, France

    Music: Improvised by David Darling Ensemble under the direction of
        David Darling and Alwin Nikolais. Tapes compiled and edited by
        Alwin Nikolais.

    Commissioned by the Paris Opera

Five Masks

    A suite of five dances from *Schema*

    2/12/81, City Center Theater, New York City

    Music: Improvised by David Darling Ensemble under the direction of
        David Darling and Alwin Nikolais. Tapes compiled and edited by
        Alwin Nikolais.

Talisman

    2/12/81, City Center Theater, New York City

    Music: Improvised by David Darling Ensemble under the direction of

David Darling and Alwin Nikolais. Tapes compiled and edited by
Alwin Nikolais.

Funded by the New York State Council on the Arts

Pond

5/18/82, Grand Auditório Gulbenkian, Lisbon, Portugal

Music: Alwin Nikolais

Made possible by funds from The National Endowment for the Arts

Mechanical Organ II

6/22/82, Théâtre de la Ville in the Théâtre de Paris, Paris, France

Music: Electronic scores by Alwin Nikolais. Additional music
improvised by the David Darling Ensemble.

Commissioned by George Soros with partial funding from the National
Endowment for the Arts

Liturgies

3/29/83, Teatro Municipal, Caracas, Venezuela

Music: Alwin Nikolais

Commissioned by Venezuelan National Cultural Council for the Simon
Bolivar Bicentennial

Lenny and the Heartbreakers

12/22/83, Public Theater, New York City

Music: Scott Killian (orchestrations)

Direction and choreography by Alwin Nikolais and Murray Louis

Produced by Joseph Papp Public Theater/New York Shakespeare
Festival

Persons & Structures

2/16/84, City Center Theater, New York City

Music: Edgar Varèse (*Poem Electronique*)

Commissioned by the Electronic Music Center, Columbia University, as
part of the School of the Arts' "A Varèse Celebration."

Video Game

4/16/84, Olympics Arts Festival, Pasadena, CA

Music: David Gregory

Commissioned by Olympic Arts Festival

Graph

7/18/84, American Dance Festival, Durham, NC

Music: David Gregory

Golden Commission by the American Dance Festival

Illusive Visions

3/2/85, Wacoal Art Center, Tokyo, Japan

6. Persons and Structures *(1984) in a 1993 reconstruction. Lower box: Joelle VanSickle, Eric Dunlap, Clarence Brooks; upper box: Kay Anderson and Karen Safrit. Photograph © Johan Elbers 2007.*

Music: Alwin Nikolais

Commissioned by Wacoal Art Center, Tokyo, Japan

Crucible

6/13/85, American Dance Festival, Durham, NC

Music: Alwin Nikolais

Commissioned by the American Dance Festival

L'Homme Oisseau

7/85, Aix en Provence, France

Music: Alwin Nikolais

Commissioned by Aix en Provence Festival

Contact

7/8/85, Pavillion Vendome, Aix en Provence, France

Music: Alwin Nikolais

Commissioned by La Danse à Aix & Le Festival des Nuits de l'Esterel

Velocities

12/22/86, Joyce Theater, New York City

Music: Alwin Nikolais

Made possible by a grant from the National Endowment for the Arts
with additional funding from the New York State Council on the Arts,
and the Andrew W. Mellon Fund.

Arc en Ciel

5/29/87, Paris Opera, Paris, France

Music: Alwin Nikolais

Commissioned by the Paris Opera

Eruptions and Entanglements

12/15/87, Joyce Theater, New York City

Music: Alwin Nikolais

Blank on Blank

12/23/87, Joyce Theater, New York City

Music: Alwin Nikolais

Zones One-Two-Etcetera

6/1/88, Midland Center for the Arts, Midland, MI

Music: Alwin Nikolais

Commissioned by the Matrix Midland Festival

Oracles

7/20/89, Herod Atticus Theatre, Athens, Greece

Commissioned by Surdna Foundation and the Athens Festival

Intrados

10/25/89, Joyce Theater, New York City

7. Blank on Blank *(1987). From left, Pamela Aarons, Alberto Del Saz, and Shiela Lehner.*
Photograph © Tom Caravaglia 2007.

Music: Alwin Nikolais

Made possible by a grant from the National Endowment for the
Arts with additional funding from the New York State Council
on the Arts

Seque

Choreographed with Murray Louis

10/29/89, Joyce Theater, New York City

Music: Alwin Nikolais

Commissioned by the Surdna Foundation

The Crystal and The Sphere

4/3/90, Terrace Theater, the Kennedy Center, Washington, DC

Commissioned by the Kennedy Center for its community outreach
program *Imagination Celebration*

Hollow Lady

4/24/91, Joyce Theater, New York City

Music: Alwin Nikolais

Commissioned for the dancer Nina Watt to celebrate her artistry and
commitment to the José Limón aesthetic over the last two decades.
Made possible, in part, with commissioning funds from the New York
State Council on the Arts.

Aurora

1/28/92, Joyce Theater, New York City

Music: Jon Scoville

Made possible by funding from the National Endowment for the Arts
with additional support from the Harkness Foundation for Dance

Log of Company Performances

. . . .

compiled by CLAUDIA GITELMAN

Once established at the Henry Street Settlement in the Lower East Side of Manhattan in the fall of 1948, Alwin Nikolais began showing choreography in the New York City area on joint programs at such venues as the Dance Center of the 92nd Street YMHA, Hunter College, Adelphi University, and at the settlement house theater, called the Henry Street Playhouse, although it stood on Grand Street, a short distance from the settlement complex. His company was a fluid group of students and professionals. In November 1949 the group acquired the name the Playhouse Dance Company, sometimes the Henry Street Playhouse Dance Company. This list of performances will begin at that date. Gladys Bailin, Phyllis Lamhut, and Murray Louis formed the core of the company and remained with Nikolais for many years. These three and William Frank, Coral Martindale, Beverly Schmidt [Blossom] and Dorothy Vislocky (sometimes listed as Locke) are considered the original Playhouse Dance Company, although other dancers also appeared. Many early performances at the Henry Street Playhouse and other venues were of children's dance dramas scripted and staged by Nikolais. Programs through 1955 often included choreography by company members as well as by Nikolais.

The log of company bookings that follows is based on an itinerary list provided by the University Libraries at Ohio University, the repository of the Alwin Nikolais and Murray Louis Papers. The list was crosschecked with programs filed there and in the Jerome Robbins Dance Division of the New York Public Library, as well as with facsimiles stored at the Nikolais-Louis Foundation for Dance in New York City. Press coverage and programs kept by some dancers were consulted in an effort to fill gaps in these collections. Dudley Brooks, Alberto Del Saz, Marc Lawton, Lynn Lesniak Needle, and Agnes Preissel were helpful here. The following log of performances is as complete and accurate as available documents allow.

.1949–1950

Nov.19	Museum of Natural History, New York City
Dec. 16–19	Henry Street Playhouse
Feb. 22	Kaufman Concert Hall, YMHA, New York City

1. *Original Playhouse Dance Company: Murray Louis, Beverly Schmidt, Bill Frank, Coral Martindale, Phyllis Lamhut, Dorothy Vislocky, and Gladys Bailin. Photograph: David S. Berlin courtesy of the Nikolais/Louis Foundation.*

	Mar. 5, 18	Henry Street Playhouse
	Apr. 29	Henry Street Playhouse
	May 24	Henry Street Playhouse
	Nov. 28	Henry Street Playhouse
	Dec. 22	Henry Street Playhouse
1951		
	Jan. 15	Henry Street Playhouse
	Apr. 30	Henry Street Playhouse
	May 1, 5, 12	Brooklyn Museum, Brooklyn, NY
	May 23, 25	Henry Street Playhouse
	Nov. 9	The Cooper Union, New York City
	Dec. 31	Henry Street Playhouse

2. *From left: Murray Louis, Dorothy Vislocky, and Beverly Schmidt, in* Tensile Involvement, *created by Ruth Grauert in 1953. Nikolais used Grauert's concept for his quartet* Web *(1955) and expanded it to a full company work, again titled* Tensile Involvement *(1968). Photograph David S. Berlin, courtesy the Nikolais/Louis Foundation.*

1952

Feb. 16	Woodmere High School, Woodmere, NY
Feb. 29	University of Pennsylvania, College Park
Apr. 30	Kaufman Concert Hall, New York City
May 21	Brooklyn Museum, Brooklyn, NY
May 28	Henry Street Playhouse
Dec. 28	Henry Street Playhouse

1953

Jan. 26	Henry Street Playhouse
Feb. 14	Henry Street Playhouse
May 23, 24, 27	Henry Street Playhouse
July 18	Old Sturbridge Village, Sturbridge, MA
Dec. 26–28	Henry Street Playhouse

1954

Note: Programs of concerts for children often did not indicate name of venue.

Jan.1–3	Henry Street Playhouse
Jan. 8	Montclair, NJ
Jan. 22	Westchester
Jan. 25	The Cooper Union, New York City
Jan. 28, 30	Henry Street Playhouse
Feb. 5	Bronxville, NY
Feb. 6, 7, 12, 13	Henry Street Playhouse
Mar. 5	Huntington, NY
Mar. 11	Rockville Center, NY
Mar. 12	Freeport, NY
Mar. 15	Garden City, NY
Mar. 19	Mountain Lakes, NJ, and Ridgewood, NJ
Mar. 21, 22	Henry Street Playhouse
Apr. 2, 6	Henry Street Playhouse
Apr. 22	Plainfield, NJ
Apr. 23, 24	Henry Street Playhouse
May 8	Rye, NY
May 21, 22, 27	Henry Street Playhouse
Oct. 23	Henry Street Playhouse
Oct. 24	Kaufman Concert Hall, YMHA, New York City
Oct. 30	Henry Street Playhouse
Nov. 6	Locust Grove School, Syosset, NY
Nov. 11	Hempstead, NY
Nov. 20	Lawrence High School, Lawrence, NY
Dec. 22, 27, 30	Henry Street Playhouse

1955

Jan. 8	Montclair, NJ
Jan. 30	Henry Street Playhouse
Feb. 5	Bronxville, NY
Feb. 6, 7, 13	Henry Street Playhouse

Mar. 8	Rye, NY
Mar. 26	Academy of Music, Philadelphia, PA
Apr. 23, 24	Henry Street Playhouse
May 26	Henry Street Playhouse
Oct. 27	Keene Children's Theater, Keene, NH
Oct. 29	Rhode Island School of Design, Providence
Nov. 5	Henry Street Playhouse
Nov. 14–19	University of Cincinnati, Cincinnati, OH
Dec. 4, 10, 11	Henry Street Playhouse
Dec. 17, 18, 20, 21, 27–30	Henry Street Playhouse

1956

Jan. 7	Great Neck, NY
Jan. 8	Henry Street Playhouse
Jan. 14	Westfield, NJ
Jan. 15	Henry Street Playhouse
Jan. 22	Henry Street Playhouse
Feb. 17	The Cooper Union, New York City
Mar. 31	Metropolitan Museum of Art, New York City
May 25–27	Henry Street Playhouse
Aug. 17	American Dance Festival, New London, CT
Nov. 3	Wesleyan University, Middletown, CT
Dec. 1	Eastern Avenue Junior High School, White Plains, NY
Dec. 27–29	Henry Street Playhouse

1957

Mar. 26	University of Illinois, Urbana-Champaign
Apr. 1, 9	Southern Illinois University, Carbondale
Aug. 16	American Dance Festival, New London, CT
Oct. 11–13	Henry Street Playhouse
Nov. 8 10	Henry Street Playhouse
Dec. 27–29	Henry Street Playhouse

1958

Jan. 24–26	Henry Street Playhouse
Feb. 14–16	Henry Street Playhouse
Mar. 14	The Cooper Union, New York City
Mar. 28	Pennsylvania State University, University Park
May 16–18	Henry Street Playhouse
Apr. 9	Southern Illinois University, Carbondale

	Apr. 18–20	Henry Street Playhouse
	May 16–18	Henry Street Playhouse
1959		
	Jan. 30–Feb.1	Henry Street Playhouse
	Mar. 22	*The Steve Allen Show*, NBS Television
	Apr. 25	Wesleyan University, Middletown, CT
	May 17	*The Steve Allen Show*, NBC Television
	May 31	*The Steve Allen Show*, NBC Television
	Sept. 28	*The Steve Allen Show*, NBC Television
	Oct. 16, 17	Douglass College, New Brunswick, NJ
	Oct. 19	*The Steve Allen Show*, NBC Television
	Nov. (date not available)	*A Time to Dance*, WGBH-TV, Boston, MA
	Nov. 20	The Cooper Union, New York City
	Dec. 8	Smith College, Northampton, MA
	Dec. 28	*The Steve Allen Show*, NBC Television
	(date not available)	CBC Television, Montréal, Quebec, Canada
1960		
	Jan. 29–31	Henry Street Playhouse
	Feb. 5–7	Henry Street Playhouse
	Mar. 21	*The Steve Allen Show*, NBC Television
	Oct 27	CBC Television, Montréal, Quebec, Canada
	Nov. 30	Rockefeller Institute, New York City
1961		
	Jan 27–29	Henry Street Playhouse
	Feb. 3–5, 10–12	Henry Street Playhouse
	Mar. 5	Loeb Student Center, New York University, New York City
	Mar. 14	University of Illinois, Urbana-Champaign

Note: The company name changed to Alwin Nikolais Dance Company, although "Playhouse Dance Company" continued to be used for some bookings.

	Mar. 19	Goodman Theatre, Chicago, IL
	May 8	Kaufmann Concert Hall, New York City
	June 25, July 2	CBC Television, Montréal, Quebec, Canada
	Aug. 5	Music and Dance Festival, Montréal, Quebec, Canada
	Aug. 7	Comedia Canadienne, Montréal, Quebec, Canada

1962

June 11, 12, 14,   Spoleto Festival of Two Worlds, Spoleto, Italy
    15, 19, 21, 22
Three dancers of the company performed excerpts from the repertory in
other concerts July 23, 24, 28, 29 and Aug. 5, 7, 8, 14

June (day not   Granada Television, London, U.K.
    available)

1963

Feb. 24   Hartford Jewish Community Center, Hartford, CT
Mar. 1–Apr. 7   Henry Street Playhouse
May 5   McMillan Theater of Columbia University, New
                   York City
May 8–June 10   Henry Street Playhouse
Oct. 3–7   Henry Street Playhouse

1964

Jan. 10   MacMillan Theatre, Toronto, Ontario, Canada
Feb. 20–Mar. 22   Henry Street Playhouse
May 14   (venue not given) Lausanne, Switzerland

1965

Mar. 2, 6   State Theater, Lincoln Center, New York City
Mar. 19–21   Henry Street Playhouse
Apr. 4   Wesleyan University, Middletown, CT
Apr. 23   Florida State University, Tallahassee
May 1   Southampton College, Southhampton, NY
Aug 2–4   Colorado College, Colorado Springs
Dec. 10, 11   Tyrone Guthrie Theater, Minneapolis, MN
Dec. 15   University of Illinois, Urbana-Champaign

1966

Jan. 28, 29   Hunter College, New York City
Feb 4   Pennsylvania State University, Pittsburg, PA
Feb. 6   Goucher College, Towson, MD
Apr. 28   University of Wisconsin, Madison
May 11   Trenton State College, Trenton, NJ
Sept. 2   Delacorte Theater, Central Park, New York City

1967

Jan. 20   The Cooper Union, New York City
Jan 28   Hunter College, New York City
Jan. 30   Brandeis University, Waltham, MA
Feb. 9   Guggenheim Museum, New York City

Feb. 26	Spencer Church, Brooklyn Heights, NY
Mar. 18	Middletown High School, Middletown, NY

Note: The company name became Alwin Nikolais Dance Theatre, although "Alwin Nikolais Dance Company" continued to be used for some performances. Personnel of the company increased to ten dancers, five women and five men.

Mar. 22	Detroit Institute of Arts, Detroit, MI
Mar. 28	George Abbot Theatre, New York City
Apr. 10	Kiel Opera House, St. Louis, MO
Apr. 17	University of California, Santa Barbara
Apr. 20–22	California State College, Los Angeles
Apr. 26	Irvine Auditorium, Philadelphia, PA
May 6	University of South Florida, Tampa
Nov. 7, 10–12	Harper Theater, Chicago, IL
Nov. 14, 15	Illinois State University, Normal
Nov. 19	Southern Illinois University, Carbondale
Nov. 21	State University College, Cortland, NY
Nov. 30–Dec. 24	Henry Street Playhouse

1968

July 5–7	University of South Florida, Tampa
Aug. 12–17	Guild Hall, East Hampton, NY
Sept. 13	Teatro la Fenice, Venice, Italy
Sept. 16	Opera House, Ljubljana, Yugoslavia
Sept. 19, 20	Atelier 212 Bitel, Belgrade, Yugoslavia
Sept. 23	People's University Workers Theater, Sarajevo, Yugoslavia
Sept. 25	Opera House, Skoplje, Yugoslavia
Oct. 2	Fort Revelin, Dubrovnik, Yugoslavia
Oct. 4–7	People's Theatre, Belgrade, Yugoslavia
Oct. 9, 10	Freie Volksbuhne, West Berlin, West Germany
Oct. 16, 17	Circus, Stockholm, Sweden
Oct. 20	Teatro Regio, Parma, Italy
Oct. 22, 23	Teatro Olimpico, Parma, Italy
Oct. 25	Palais de la Méditerranée, Nice, France
Oct. 29, 30	Piccolo Teatro, Milan, Italy
Nov. 1	Théâtre Beaulieu, Lausanne, Switzerland
Nov. 3	Grand Théâtre, Geneva, Switzerland
Nov. 5, 7–9	Théâtre des Champs-Élysées, Paris, France
Nov. 19	Mitchell College, New London, CT

Nov. 23	Danbury High School, Danbury, CT
Nov. 25	Queensborough Community College, Bayside, NY
Nov. 29	Brooklyn Academy of Music, Brooklyn, NY
Dec. 7	Cortland College, Cortland, NY
Dec. 15	Kiel Opera House, St. Louis, MO

1969

Feb. 10, 11	Allan Hancock College, Santa Maria, CA
Mar. 2	University of Nebraska, Omaha
Mar. 4	Culver Military Academy, Culver IN
Mar. 8	University of Wisconsin, Green Bay
Mar. 10	University of Wisconsin, Madison
Mar. 18–23	Harper Theater, Chicago, IL
Mar. 26	Ohio University, Athens
Mar. 28	Albert Magnus College, New Haven, CT
Mar. 29	Southern Connecticut State University, New Haven
Mar. 30	New Haven Jewish Community Center, New Haven, CT
Apr. 10	University of Rhode Island, Kingston
Apr. 18	University of New Hampshire, Durham
Apr. 20	Princeton University, Princeton, NJ
Apr. 22	Smithsonian Associations, Washington, DC
Apr. 27	University of North Carolina, Chapel Hill
Apr. 29	Duke University, Durham, NC
May 8, 9	Osaka International Festival, Osaka, Japan
May 17	State Opera, Hamburg, West Germany
May 20, 21	Bayerische Staatoper, Munich, West Germany
May 23	Wurttembergische Staatstheater, Stuttgart, West Germany
May 27–29	Théâtre Royal de la Monnaie, Brussels, Belgium
May 31–June 1	Theatre an der Wien, Vienna, Austria
June 3, 4	Magyar Allami Operhaz, Budapest, Hungary
June 6–8	Chatillon Festival, Chatillon-sous-Bagneux, France
June 10, 11	Théâtre du Capitole, Toulouse, France
June 13, 14	Grand Théâtre, Geneva, Switzerland
June 18–28	Sadler's Wells Theatre, London, UK
June 30–July 1	Holland Festival, Amsterdam, The Netherlands
July 2	Stadsschouwburg, Groningen, The Netherlands

July 3,	Rotterdanse Schouwburg, Rotterdam, The Netherlands
July 4	Stadsschouwburg, Groningen, The Netherlands
July 5, 6	Koninklijke Schouwburg, The Hague, The Netherlands
July 8	Grand Casino, Aix-les-Bains, France
July 10–13	International Ballet Festival, Nervi, Italy
July 15–17	Teatro dei Giardini di Palazzo Reale, Turin, Italy
July 20, 21	Temple of Bacchus, Baalbeck, Lebanon
July 26–28	Baalbeck Festival, Baalbeck, Lebanon
July 29	Herod Atticus Theatre, Athens, Greece
Aug. 4–15	ZDF-TV, Munich, West Germany
Sept. 2, 3	Opera House, Lodz, Poland
Sept. 5, 6	Congress Hall, Warsaw, Poland
Oct. 30	Western Michigan University, Kalamazoo
Nov. 1	Queensborough Community College, Bayside, NY
Nov. 4	State University of New York, Binghamton
Nov. 8	Nazareth College, Rochester, NY
Nov. 11	State University of New York, Buffalo
Nov. 15	Brooklyn College of the City of New York
Nov. 19, 20	University of Massachusetts, Amherst
Nov. 22, 23	Boston University, Boston, MA
Dec. 10	Hillhouse High School, New Haven, CT
Dec. 12	Lisner Auditorium, Philadelphia, PA

Note: Company name became Nikolais Dance Theatre.

1970

Jan. 9	Goucher College, Towson, MD
Jan. 11	Rider College, Trenton, NJ
Jan. 13	Trenton State College, Trenton, NJ
Jan. 17	Ohio State University, Columbus
Jan. 21	University of Michigan, Ann Arbor
Jan. 25	University of Minnesota, Minneapolis
Feb. 4	University of California, Riverside
Feb 2–15	University of California, Los Angeles
Feb. 10, 11	Allen Hancock Jr. College, Santa Maria, CA
Feb. 14, 15	University of California, Berkeley
Feb. 17, 18	University of California, Davis
Feb. 26, 27	San Jose State College, San Jose, CA
Mar. 4	Tulsa Municipal Theatre, Tulsa, OK

Mar. 7	Oklahoma City University, Oklahoma City
Mar. 11, 13, 14	University of Oklahoma, Norman
Mar. 20	University of Utah, Salt Lake City
Apr. 28–May 3	New York City Center of Music and Drama
May 6–10	Harper Civic Theater, Chicago, IL
May 13, 14	University of Connecticut, Storrs
Oct. 8	McAllen Civic Center, McAllen, TX
Oct. 12	University of Texas, Austin
Oct. 16	Texas Christian University, Fort Worth
Oct. 20	University of New Mexico, Albuquerque
Oct. 23	Arizona State University, Tempe
Oct. 30, 31	University of California, Los Angeles
Nov. 4–7	University of Hawaii, Honolulu
Nov. 9	Memorial Convention Hall, Kauai, HI
Nov. 13	Maui Community College, Maui, HI
Nov. 13	Hilo High School, Hilo, HI
Nov. 19	Michigan State University, East Lansing
Nov. 25	Kiel Opera House, St. Louis, MO
Dec. 2, 3	Dartmouth College, Hanover, NH
Dec. 6	Academy of Music, Philadelphia, PA
Dec. 8, 9	Lisner Auditorium, Washington, DC

1971

Jan 25–31	Harper Civic Theater, Chicago, IL
Feb. 3–7	University of Puerto Rico, Rio Piedras
Feb 19, 20	Virginia Museum Theater, Richmond
Mar. 1–6,	ANTA Theater, New York City
Apr. 10–12	Casino de Monte Carlo Théâtre, Monte Carlo, Monaco
Apr. 15–19	Rudaki Hall, Tehran, Iran
Apr. 21 24	BBC-TV filming, London, UK
Apr. 26–May 1	Gaumont Theatre, Southhampton, UK
May 3–29	Théâtre de la Ville, Paris, France
May 31–June 2	Hessiches Staatstheater, Weisbaden, West Germany
June 3	Teatro Rivoli, Porto, Portugal
June 5	Teatro Gil Vivente, Coimbra, Portugal
June 6–9	Fundacão Gulbenkian Auditorium, Lisbon, Portugal
June 12, 13	Gulbenkian Festival, Lausanne, Switzerland

June 15, 16	Theater au der Wien, Vienna, Austria
June 18	Rotterdamse Schouwburg, Rotterdam, The Netherlands
June 19	Stadsschouwburg, Eindhoven, The Netherlands
June 20, 21	Koninklijke Schoubrug, The Hague, The Netherlands
June 22	Stadsschouburg, Amsterdam, The Netherlands
June 23	Stadsschouburg, Nijmegen, The Netherlands
June 28–July 17	Sadler's Wells Theatre, London, UK
July 21, 22	Tunis Festival, Hammamet, Tunisia
July 24, 25	Tunis Festival, Carthage, Tunisia
July 28–31	Dubrovnik Festival, Dubrovnik, Yugoslavia
Aug. 1	Splitsko Ljeto, Split, Yugoslavia
Nov. 13	Henry Hudson High School, Hudson, NY
Nov. 17	Ohio University, Athens
Nov. 20, 21	Boston University, Boston, MA
Nov. 26, 27	Carleton College, Northfield, MN
Nov. 30–Dec. 1	Florida Atlantic University, Boca Raton
Dec 7	Hope College, Holland, MI
Dec. 11	Bushnell Memorial Hall, Hartford, CT

1972

Jan. 18–23	Brooklyn Academy of Music, Brooklyn, NY
Feb. 9	Ovens Auditorium, Charlotte, NC
Feb. 12	University of North Carolina, Greensboro
Mar. 2	State University of New York, Plattsburg
Mar. 4	Nazareth College, Rochester, NY
Mar. 7	State University College of New York, Geneseo
Mar. 14	Niagara University, Niagara, NY
Mar. 16	State University College, Potsdam, NY
Mar. 18	Staten Island Community College, Staten Island, NY
Mar. 24, 25	Tulsa Municipal Theatre, Tulsa, OK
Mar 26, 27	Kansas City Music Hall, Kansas City, MO
Mar. 28	William Jewell College, Liberty, MO
Apr. 1	Oklahoma City University, Oklahoma City
Apr. 4, 5	University of California, Berkeley
Apr. 7–9	Queen Elizabeth Theatre, Vancouver, British Columbia, Canada
Apr. 13–16	Moore Theatre, Seattle, WA

Sept. 16–22	Mann Auditorium, Tel Aviv, Israel
Sept. 23–26	Binyanei Ha'Uman Theatre, Jerusalem, Israel
Sept. 27	Mann Auditorium, Tel Aviv, Israel
Sept. 29	Amphitheatre, Ein Gev, Israel
Sept. 30, Oct. 1	Mann Auditorium, Tel Aviv, Israel
Oct. 5–7	Opera House, Bucharest, Romania
Oct. 10–12	Teatro de la Zarzuela, Madrid, Spain
Oct. 13–15	Teatre Arriaga, Bilbao, Spain
Oct. 17, 18	Maison de la Culture, Rennes, France
Oct 20–23	Théâtre d'Angers, Angers, France
Oct. 25	Opera House, Strasbourg, France
Oct. 27	Maison des Jeunes et de la Culture, Sochaux, France
Oct. 28–30	Operhaus Zurich, Zurich, Switzerland
Oct. 31–Nov. 2	Grand Théâtre, Geneva, Switzerland
Nov. 3, 4	Théâtre Beaulieu, Lausanne, Switzerland
Nov. 6–8	Théâtre National Mohammed V, Rabat, Morocco
Nov. 11, 12	Grand Théâtre Municipal, Casablanca, Morocco
Nov. 28	University of Colorado, Boulder
Dec. 1	Drake University, Des Moines, IA
Dec. 6–9	College of St. Benedict, St. Joseph, MN
Dec. 10–13	Southwest Missouri State University, Springfield

1973

Jan. 19, 20	University of Connecticut, Storrs
Jan. 24–28	Kiel Auditorium, St. Louis, MO
Jan. 30–Feb. 1	University of North Carolina, Greensboro
Feb. 3, 4	Duke University, Durham, NC
Feb. 15–25	Brooklyn Academy of Music, Brooklyn, NY (programs shared with Murray Louis Dance Company)
Mar. 20–25	Walnut Street Theater, Philadelphia, PA
Mar. 26–28	Kennedy Center for the Performing Arts, Washington, DC
Apr. 1–8	Teatro Municipal, Caracas, Venezuela
Apr. 10, 11	Martin Peña Teatro, Brasilia, Brazil
Apr. 13–16	Teatro Municipal, Rio de Janeiro, Brazil
Apr. 20–22	Teatro Guaira, Curitiba, Brazil
Apr. 25–30	Teatro Colón, Buenos Aires, Argentina

May 2–6	Teatro Municipal, Santiago, Chile
May 8–10	Teatro Municipal, Lima, Peru
June 29	American Dance Festival, New London, CT
July 20, 21	Broadmore International Theatre, Colorado Springs, CO
Oct. 23	University of Indiana, Bloomington
Oct. 30	Ohio State University, Columbus
Nov. 2, 3	Williams College, Williamstown, MA
Nov. 10	Queensborough Community College, Bayside, NY
Dec. 8	University of Wisconsin, Madison
Dec. 13–15	Wesleyan University, Middletown, CT

1974

Jan 8, 9	University of South Florida, Tampa
Jan 11	Whitney Museum of American Art, New York City
Jan 25, 26	Brandeis University, Waltham, MA
Feb. 2	Middletown High School, Middletown, NY
Feb 5, 6, 8–10, 13, 14–17	Lyceum Theatre, New York City
Feb. 22, 23	University of Massachusetts, Amherst, MA
Feb. 27	University of North Carolina, Wilmington
Mar. 4	Municipal Auditorium, Austin, TX
Mar. 13	University of California, Santa Barbara
Mar. 15, 16	University of California, Irvine
Mar. 22	El Camino College, Torrance, CA
Mar. 25, 26, 28	Palacio de Bellas Artes, Mexico City, Mexico
Apr. 1, 2	Teatro Degollado, Guadalajara, Mexico
Apr. 6	Kent State University, Kent, OH
Apr. 13	Palace Theatre, Waterbury, CT
Apr. 18	University of Michigan, Ann Arbor
Apr. 30–May 1	State University of New York, Albany
Apr. 26, 27	Prelude Theatre, Toronto, Ontario, Canada
June 26, 27	Wolf Trap Farm, Vienna, VA
July 1, 2	Temple Music Festival, Ambler, PA
July 5, 6	American Dance Festival, New London, CT
July 8	University of Delaware, Newark
July 17–20	Jacob's Pillow Dance Festival, Lee, MA
Sept. 2, 3	Artpark Theater, Lewiston, NY
Sept. 14, 15	Feire Volksbuhne, West Berlin, West Germany

3. *Nikolais Dance Theatre on tour, 1974. From left: Steven Iannacone, Rob Esposito. Bill Groves, Janet Katzenberg, Jessica Sayre, Suzanne McDermaid, Alwin Nikolais, David Williams (stage technician), Gladys Roman, Elizabeth Bagnold, James Teeters. A tenth dancer, Gerald Otte, was injured. The company traveled with three stage technicians and was accompanied by a tour manager provided by the booking agent. Courtesy of the Nikolais/Louis Foundation for Dance.*

Sept. 17–19	Teatro de la Zarzuela, Madrid, Spain
Sept. 24–29	Teatro Lycéo, Barcelona, Spain
Oct. 1–13	Théâtre de la Ville, Paris, France
Oct. 16, 17	Théâtre d'Angers, Angers, France
Oct. 19	Théâtre de Sochaux, Sochaux, France
Oct. 20	Farbwerke Höchst, Frankfurt am Main, West Germany
Oct. 21	Kulturabteilung, Leverkusen, West Germany
Oct. 23, 24	Wurtembergische Staatstheater, Stuttgart, West Germany
Nov. 1	Bergen Community College, Paramus, NJ
Nov. 6	Coker College, Hartsville, SC

Nov. 8, 9	Lisner Auditorium, Washington, DC
Nov, 15, 16	Grand Valley State College, Allendale, MI
Nov. 23	University of Minnesota, Minneapolis
Nov. 26	Central Michigan University, Mt. Pleasant
Nov. 29–Dec. 1	Music Hall Center for the Performing Arts, Detroit, MI
Dec. 2, 4	Hamilton Place, Hamilton, Ontario, Canada
Dec. 6, 7	Dartmouth College, Hanover, NH

1975

Jan. 7, 8	University of California, Berkeley
Jan 10, 11	Civic Auditorium, Portland, OR
Jan 13,	Opera House, Seattle, WA
Jan. 15, 16	Queen Elizabeth Theatre, Vancouver, British Columbia, Canada
Jan. 21, 22	San Diego State University, San Diego, CA
Jan. 24, 25	Colorado State University, Fort Collins
Mar. 11	College of William and Mary, Williamsburg, VA
Mar. 15	Center College, Danville, KY
Mar. 18, 19	University of Illinois, Urbana-Champaign
Mar. 20, 21	University of Iowa, Iowa City
Apr. 1–6,	Teatro Municipal, Caracas, Venezuela
Apr. 9–13	Teatro Municipal, Rio de Janeiro, Brazil
Apr. 15	Teatro Martin Peña, Brasillia, Brazil
Apr. 17–20	Teatro Municipal, São Paulo, Brazil
Apr. 22, 23	Teatro Guaira, Curitiba, Brazil
Apr. 25, 27	Teatro Leopoldina, Porto Alegre, Brazil
Apr. 29	Teatro Colón, Buenos Aires, Argentina
Apr. 30	Teatro Argentino, La Plata, Argentina
May 2–4	Teatro Colón, Buenos Aires, Argentina
May 6–9	Teatro Municipal, Santiago, Chile
May 12–14	Teatro Municipal, Lima, Peru
May 16, 17	Teatro Municipal, Cali, Columbia
May 20–22	Teatro Jorge Gaitan, Bogotá, Columbia
May 23	Teatro Municipal, Panama City, Panama
May 26, 27	Teatro Nacional, San José, Costa Rica
May 29–31	Teatro Ruben Dario, Managua, Nicaragua
June 2–9	Palacio de Bellas Artes, Mexico City, Mexico
June 10, 11	Teatro Degollado, Guadalajara, Mexico
June 18–29	Frederick Lowe Theatre, New York City

Aug. 21–23	Persepolis, Teheran, Iran
Aug. 26–30	Opera House, Monte Carlo, Monaco
Sept. 1	Opera House, Ghent, Belgium
Sept. 3	Municipal Theatre, Leuven, Belgium
Sept. 4	Royal Flemish Theater, Brussels, Belgium
Sept. 8–13	Royal Lyceum Theatre, Edinburgh, Scotland, UK
Nov. 3, 4	Seattle Opera House, Seattle, WA
Nov. 7, 8	Civic Auditorium, Portland, OR
Nov. 11	Opera House, Spokane, WA
Nov. 14, 15	University of California, Los Angeles
Nov. 18, 19	Flint Center, Santa Clara/Cupertino, CA
Nov. 21	Merritt College, Oakland, CA

1976

Mar. 2, 3	Civic Center of Onondaga County, Syracuse, NY
Mar. 5–7	Brandeis University, Waltham, MA
Mar. 11	Indiana University, Indiana, PA
Mar. 12	Pennsylvania State University, University Park
Mar. 16, 17	Barat College, Lake Forest, IL
Mar. 26, 27	Washington University, St. Louis, MO
Mar. 30	Iowa State University, Ames
May 15–17	(venue unknown) Taipei, Taiwan
May 22, 23	(venue unknown) Taichung, Taiwan
May 26–29	City Hall Concert Hall, Hong Kong
June 1	National Theatre, Bangkok, Thailand
June 3	(venue unknown) Singapore
June 8–10	Cultural Center of the Philippines, Manila
June 13	West High School, Anchorage, AK
July 15–17	American Dance Festival, New London, CT
July 20, 23	Jacob's Pillow Dance Festival, Lee, MA
Aug. 3–15	Beacon Theater, New York City
Oct. 5	Théâtre de l'Hexagone, L'Agora, Evry, France
Oct. 7	Théâtre Municipal, Besançon, France
Oct. 9	Théâtre Municipal de Dijon, Dijon, France
Oct. 12	Théâtre Municipal, Annecy, France
Oct. 14	Maison des Arts et Loisirs, Thônon-les-Bains, France
Oct. 16	Théâtre Charles Dullin, Chambéry, France
Oct. 18	Théâtre Municipal, Veillefranche-sur-Saône, France

Oct. 20	Théâtre du 8ᵉ, Lyon, France
Oct. 22	Théâtre Municipal de Mâcon, Mâcon, France
Oct. 23	Maison des Arts et des Loisirs, Le Creusot, France
Oct. 26, 27	Palais de la Méditerranée, Nice, France
Oct. 30	Théâtre d'Istres, Istres, France
Nov. 3	Théâtre Jean Vilar, Vitry-sur-Seine
Nov. 4	Maison des Arts, Créteil, France
Nov. 5	Centre d'Action Culturelle, Douai, France
Nov. 7	Théâtre Municipal, St. Quentin, France
Nov. 9–12	Maison de la Culture, Grenoble, France
Nov. 14	Théâtre de la Ville de Montpellier, Montpellier, France
Nov. 29, 30	Performing Arts Center, Milwaukee, WI
Dec. 3, 4	University of Minnesota, Minneapolis
Dec. 7	University of Nebraska, Lincoln
Dec. 10, 11	Nazareth College, Rochester, NY

1977

Feb. 8–Mar. 6	Beacon Theater, New York City (season shared with Murray Louis Dance Company)
Mar. 4	Walnut Street Theater, Philadelphia, PA
Mar. 9	Salem State College, Salem, MA
Mar. 11, 12	University of Massachusetts, Amherst
Mar. 15–20	Lisner Auditorium, Washington, DC
Mar. 22	Heinz Hall for the Performing Arts, Pittsburgh, PA
Mar. 26	Atlanta Memorial Arts Center, Atlanta, GA
Mar. 30	Brockton Community College, Brockton, GA
Apr. 1, 2	Virginia Museum Theatre, Richmond
Apr. 19, 20	Teatro Castro Alves, Salvador, Brazil
Apr. 27, 30	Palácio des Artes, Belo Horizonte, Brazil
May 4, 5	Teatro Juáres, Guanajuato City, Mexico
May 11	Teatro Solis, Montevideo, Uruguay
May 13, 15	Teatro Colón, Buenos Aires, Argentina
May 21, 22	Teatro Municipal, Lima, Peru
May 28, 29	El Teatro National, Costa Rica
June 3, 4	Teatro National Ruben Dario, Managua, Nicaragua
June 9, 10	Teatro Degollado, Guadalajara, Mexico

June 13–18	Teatro de Bellas Artes, Mexico City, Mexico
July 15, 17	American Dance Festival, New London, CT
July 25	Temple University, Philadelphia, PA
July 30	Southern Illinois University, Edwardsville
Sept. 19–21	University of North Carolina, Greensboro
Sept. 23, 24	University of Iowa, Iowa City
Sept. 26	Millikin University, Decator, IL
Sept. 29, 30	Arizona State University, Tempe
Oct. 3–5	Colorado State University, Fort Collins
Oct. 8	University of Denver, Denver, CO
Oct. 14–29	(in residence) Portland Public Schools, Portland, OR
Nov. 11, 12	University of Montana, Missoula
Nov. 16	Ohio University, Athens
Nov. 18, 19	Southwest Missouri State University, Springfield
Nov. 27	Theatre for the Performing Arts, Miami, FL
Dec. 2, 3	Lisner Auditorium, Washington, DC

1978

Jan. 29–Feb. 1	University of Northern Iowa, Cedar Falls
Feb. 2–4	Corning Glass Center, Corning, NY
Mar. 2–5	Florida State University, Tallahassee
Mar. 7, 8	University of Tennessee, Knoxville
Mar. 10, 11	Moody Civic Center, Galveston, TX
Mar. 20–22	University of Michigan, Ann Arbor
Apr. 19–29	Beacon Theater, New York City (Murray Louis Dance Company performs on three programs.)
May 5, 6	Annenberg Center, Philadelphia, PA
May 13–16	Teatro Comunale di Firenze, Florence, Italy
May 18	Théâtre de Beaulieu, Lausanne, Switzerland
May 23–June 10	Théâtre de la Ville, Paris, France
June 11–18	Grande Auditorio Gulbenkian, Lisbon, Portugal
June 25, 26	Lycabettus Theatre, Athens, Greece
June 28–July 1	(no venue recorded), Istanbul, Turkey
July 4–22	Sadler's Wells Theatre, London, UK
Aug. 2–7	Cour d'honneur, Palais des Papes, Avignon, France
Aug. 9, 10	(no venue given), Hammamet, Tunisia
Aug. 12, 13	(no venue given), Carthage, Tunisia
Oct. 28	Monmouth Art Center, Red Bank, NJ

Oct. 31	Bowdon College, Brunswick, ME
Nov. 3, 4	University of Minnesota, Minneapolis
Dec. 7–9	University of Wisconsin, Madison (in residence from Nov. 6)
Dec. 10	WHA-TV Madison

1979

Feb. 12–14	Township Auditorium, Columbia, SC
Feb. 17	Fox Theater, Atlanta, GA
Feb. 19	Heinz Hall for the Performing Arts, Pittsburgh, PA
Feb. 23, 24	Kiel Opera House, St. Louis, MO
Mar. 10	Freeport High School, Freeport, NY
Mar. 16, 17	Nazareth College, Rochester, NY
Mar. 21–25	Detroit Music Hall, Detroit, MI
May 3–8	Palacio de Bellas Artes, Mexico City, Mexico
May 13, 14	Teatro Manuel Bonilla, Tegucigalpa, Honduras
May 16, 17	Teatro National, Panama City, Panama
May 19, 20	Teatro Sucre, Quito, Ecuador
May 24, 27	Teatro Municipal, Santiago, Chile
May 29, 30	Teatro Solis, Montevideo, Uruguay
June 2, 3	Teatro Municipal, Asunción, Paraguay
June 6–9	Teatro Colón, Buenos Aires, Argentina
June 12–17	Teatro Municipal, São Paulo, Brazil
June 19, 20, 22–24	Teatro Municipal, Rio de Janeiro, Brazil
June 26, 27	Palacio des Artes, Belo Horizonte, Brazil
June 29	Nueavo Teatro, Brasilia, Brazil
July 1, 2	Teatro Castro Alves, Salvador, Brazil
July 6, 7, 9	Teatro Municipal, Caracas, Venezuela
Aug. 13–18	Jacob's Pillow Dance Festival, Lee, MA
Aug. 22–26	Ravinia Festival, Chicago, IL
Sept. 14, 15	Roger Sherman Theatre, New Haven, CT
Sept. 23	Dr. Sun Yat-Sen Memorial Hall, Taipei, Taiwan
Sept. 25	Chung-Hsin Hall, Taichung, Taiwan
Set. 26–29	Dr. Sun Yat-Sen Memorial Hall, Taipei, Taiwan
Oct. 1–4	City Hall Theatre, Hong Kong
Oct. 7	(venue not known) Kuala Lumpur, Malaysia
Oct. 9	(venue not known) Singapore
Oct. 12	ASTI (college-level arts institute), Den Pasar, Bali, Indonesia

	Oct 15–17	ASTI, Jogyakarta, Java, Indonesia
	Oct. 23, 24	Culture Center, Manila, Philippines
	Oct 30, 31	University of Puerto Rico, Rio Pierdas
	Dec. 27–31	City Center Theater, New York City
1980		
	Jan. 2–6	City Center Theater, New York City
	Jan. 11, 12	Iowa State University, Ames
	Jan 15, 16	University of California, Santa Barbara
	Jan. 17, 19	University of California, Los Angeles
	Jan. 21, 22	University of California, Berkeley
	Jan. 24, 25	Portland Civic Auditorium, Portland, OR
	Jan. 28	Oregon College of Education, Monmouth, OR
	Feb. 1, 2	University of Hawaii, Honolulu
	Feb 23, 24	University of Missouri, Columbia
	Mar. 8	Kingsborough Community College, Brooklyn, NY
	Mar. 15	Goucher College, Towson, MD
	Mar. 27–29	Dartmouth College, Hanover, NH
	May 12, 13	Teatro Juárez, Guanajuato, Mexico
	May 15–17	Teatro Juan Ruíz de Alarecón, Acapulco, Mexico
	June 4–6	Spoleto Festival, Charleston, SC
	June 16, 17	Colorado College, Colorado Springs
	June 19, 20	American Dance Festival, Durham, NC
	Sept 5–9	Stockholm Stadsteater, Stockholm, Sweden
	Sept. 12. 13	Den Nationale Scene, Bergen, Norway
	Sept 16, 17	Grand Casino, Geneva, Switzerland
	Sept 18, 19	Théâtre du Capitale, Bienne, Switzerland
	Sept. 22–Oct. 5	Théâtre Jean Vilar, Louvain, Belgium
	Oct. 12	Teatro Regio, Torino, Italy
	Oct. 13–20	(venue not given) Milan, Italy
	Oct. 22, 23	Teatro Olimpico, Rome, Italy
	Oct. 26–31	(venue not given) Salonika, Greece
	Nov. 4, 5	University of New Hampshire, Durham
	Nov. 7–9	Brandeis University, Waltham, MA
	Nov. 21	Michigan State University, East Lansing
	Nov. 24	Arkansas Art Center, Little Rock
	Nov. 28, 29	University of Virgin Island, St. Thomas, Virgin Islands
	Dec. 2, 3	University of Chattanooga, Chattanooga, TN
	Dec. 6	Fine Arts Center, Stony Brook, NY

1981

Feb. 11–22	City Center Theater, New York City
Mar. 5, 6	Stanford University, Palo Alto, CA
Mar. 13–15	Jefferson Performing Arts Center, Portland, OR
Mar. 19–21	University of Washington, Seattle
Mar. 23, 24	Orpheum Theatre, Omaha, NE
Mar. 26–28	Washington University, St. Louis, MO
Apr. 9, 10	Théâtre Municipal d'Angers, Angers, France
July 29–Aug. 1	Saratoga Performing Arts Center, Saratoga Springs, NY
Aug. 18–21	MacEwan Community College, Edmonton, Alberta, Canada
Oct. 19, 20	Opera House, Ottawa, Ontario, Canada
Oct. 22, 23	Glassboro State College, Glassboro, NJ
Oct. 26–28	Purdue University, West Lafayette, IN
Oct. 30, 31	John Carrol University, Cleveland, OH
Nov. 3	Kansas State University, Manhattan
Nov. 6–8	University of Nebraska, Lincoln
Nov. 10, 11	University of New Mexico, Albuquerque
Nov. 13, 14	University of California, Berkeley
Nov. 16, 17`	Arizona State University, Tempe
Nov. 20, 21	Vanderbilt University, Nashville, TN
Nov. 24	Rhode Island College, Providence
Nov. 27, 28	Eastman Theater, Rochester, NY
Dec. 8–10	Jesse H. Jones Hall, Houston, TX
Dec. 12, 13	Center for the Performing Arts, San Antonio, TX
Dec. 15	Van Wezel Performing Arts Hall, Sarasota, FL
Dec. 18, 19	West Palm Beach Auditorium, West Palm Beach, FL

1982

Mar. 12, 13	Wilbur Theatre, Boston, MA
Mar. 19, 20	Moorehead State University, Moorehead, MN
Apr. 26–28	Choreospace, New York City (programs shared with Murray Louis Dance Company)
May 8	Samuel Clemens Performing Arts Center, Elmira, NY
May 10	State University of New York, Binghamton
May 18–21	Grand Auditório Gulbenkian, Lisbon, Portugal

May 23, 24	Auditório Nacional Carlos Alberto, Oporto, Portugal
May 28, 29	Teatro Municipal, Funchal, Madeira
June 3–5	Sala Olimpia, Madrid, Spain
June 8	Basler Stadttheater, Basel, Switzerland
June 10	(no venue given) Vesoul, France
June 12	Centre d'Animation Culturelle, Mulhouse, France
June 15–27	Théâtre de la Ville au Théâtre de Paris, Paris, France
June 29, 30	Palais de Justice, Rouen, France
July 2	(no venue given) Pau, France
July 3	(no venue given) Biarritz, France
July 16, 17	American Dance Festival, Durham, NC
Sept. 10, 11	Arkell Pavilion, Manchester, VT
Sept 24, 25	Midland Center, Kansas City, MO
Oct. 6–24	City Center Theater, New York City
Nov. 5, 6	University of Texas, Austin
Nov. 11, 12	(no venue given) Fort Worth, TX
Nov. 14	Southern Methodist University, Dallas, TX
Nov. 17, 18	Madison Civic Center, Madison, WI

1983

Feb. 26	Lehman College, Bronx, NY
Mar. 5, 6	Northwestern University, Chicago, IL
Mar. 10, 12	Paramount Arts Centre, Aurora, IL
Mar. 29, 30, 31, Apr. 3	Teatro Municipal, Caracas, Venezuela
Apr. 5–7	Queens Hall St. Anne's, Trinidad, West Indies
Apr. 8, 9	Island Center, Sunny Isle, St. Croix
Apr. 13, 14	Florida Music Festival, Fort Lauderdale
Sept. 23, 25	Long Island University, Brooklyn, NY
Oct. 1	Amarillo Civic Center, Amarillo, TX
Oct. 11, 12	University of Minnesota, Minneapolis
Oct. 18–23	Maison de la Danse, Lyon, France
Nov, 8–12	Grand Opera, Belfast, Northern Ireland
Dec. 12	Association Bourguignonne Culturelle, Dijon, France
Dec. 13	Téâtre d'Annecy, Annecy, France
Dec. 16	Maison de la danse Lyon, France

1984

Jan. 6, 7	Zellerbach Theatre, Philadelphia, PA
Jan. 14–16	University of North Carolina, Greensboro
Feb. 3	Indiana University, Bloomington
Feb. 16–26	City Center Theater, New York City
Mar. 7	University of Texas, Austin
Mar. 9	Jackson Community College, Wayne, NJ
Mar. 24	Fine Arts Center, Greensboro, NC
Apr. 9–18	University of North Carolina, Greensboro
Apr. 24–28	Ryerson Theatre, Toronto, Ontario, Canada
Apr. 30	Heinz Hall for the Performing Arts, Pittsburgh, PA
May 2	University of Iowa, Iowa City
May 30	Virginia Center for the Performing Arts, Richmond
June 9	Midland Center for the Arts, Midland, MI
June 30	University of Iowa, Iowa City
July 7	Anamosa Junior High Auditorium, Iowa City, IA
July 16	Pasadena Civic Auditorium, Los Angeles, CA
July 19, 20	American Dance Festival, Durham, NC
July 25	Paper Mill Playhouse, Milburn, NJ
Aug. 19	Artpark, Lewiston, NY
Aug. 29	(venue not known) Terminal, Italy
Sept. 2	Teatro Antico, Taormina, Sicily
Sept. 18	Saenger Theatre, New Orleans, LA
Sept. 21	University of Florida, Gainesville
Oct. 2	Wright State University, Dayton, OH
Oct. 3	University of Colorado, Boulder
Oct. 7	Portland Civic Auditorium, Portland, OR
Oct. 24	Arizona State University, Tempe
Nov. 2, 3	Ohio Theatre, Cleveland
Nov. 9, 10	Iowa State University, Ames
Nov. 12	University of Missouri, Columbia
Nov. 16, 17	McFarlin Memorial Auditorium, Dallas, TX
Nov. 23	Nazareth College, Rochester, NY
Nov. 30, Dec. 1	Capitol Theatre, Salt Lake City, UT (programs shared with Ririe-Woodbury Dance Company)
Dec. 4, 5	Jesse H. Jones Hall, Houston, TX
Dec. 7–9	Spreckels Theatre, San Diego, CA
Dec. 14–16	University of California, Los Angeles

1985

Feb. 25–28	Western Michigan University, Kalamazoo
Mar. 1	Flynn Theatre, Burlington, VT
Mar. 2	Lyndon Institute, Lyndon, VT
Mar. 9	Jackson Community College, Jackson, MI
Mar. 12, 13	Ordway Music Theater, St. Paul, MN
Mar. 19,	Florida Theatre, Jacksonville
Mar. 23	Proctor Theater, Schenectady, NY
Apr. 23–26	Teatro Cardoza, São Paulo, Brazil
May. 27, 28	Teatro National, Brazilia, Brasil
June 5–9	Teatro Teresa Carreño, Caracas, Venezuela
June 12–14	American Dance Festival, Durham, NC
June 23, 24	University of Illinois, Urbana-Champaign
July 1–3	Cours Mirabeau, Aix-en-Provence, France
July 9, 10	Pavillon Vendome, Aix-en-Provence, France
July 12	Théâtre de la Mer, Nice, France
July 14	Sala d'Conciertos, Vigo, Spain
July 16	Teatro Garcia Barbon, Vigo, Spain
July 18	Fort de Champigny, Champigny, France
July 20, 21	(venue not known) Barcelona, Spain
July 23–25	Jardine de Viveros, Valencia, Spain
July 27	Teatro Dos Hermanas, Dos Hermanas, Spain
July 30, 31	Teatro Italica, Seville, Spain
Aug. 2	Teatro Osuna, Osuna, Spain
Aug. 4	Teatro Alcala, Alcala de Guadix, Spain
Aug. 6	(venue not known) San Javier, Spain
Aug. 8	Plaza Porticada, Santander, Spain
Aug. 10	Castillo de Olite, Olite, Spain
Aug. 12	Teatro Avenida, Burgos, Spain
Aug. 13	Teatro Rey Don Sancho, Valencia, Spain
Aug. 14	Calderon, Valladolid, Spain
Aug. 15	Teatro Leon, Leon, Spain
Aug. 19–22	Amphitheatre, Heraklion, Crete
Aug. 27, 28	The Amphitheatre, Athens, Greece
Oct. 3, 4	Dr. Sun Yat-Sen Memorial Hall, Taipei, Taiwan
Oct. 5	Chung-Hsing Hall, Taichung, Taiwan
Oct. 6, 7	Tainan Municipal Center, Tainan, Taiwan
Oct. 8	Hung-Cheng Cultural Center, Kaoshiung, Taiwan
Oct. 9–Nov. 3	Wacoal Arts Center, Minoto-ku Tokyo, Japan

Nov. 19	Arizona State University, Tempe
Nov. 23	University of Delaware, Newark

1986

Feb. 19	University of Massachusetts, Amherst
Feb. 20	Palace Performing Arts Center, New Haven, CT
Feb. 24	College of William and Mary, Williamsburg, VA
Mar. 15, 16	West Palm Beach Auditorium, West Palm Beach, FL
Mar. 18, 19	University of Illinois, Urbana-Champaign
Mar. 25, 26	Stamford Center for the Arts, Stamford, CT
July 21–26	Saratoga Performing Arts Center, Saratoga Springs, NY
Aug. 31–Sept. 13	University of Hawaii, Honolulu
Sept. 16–23	Spoleto Festival Melbourne, Melbourne, Australia
Sept. 27, 28	Freie Volksbühne, Berlin, West Germany
Oct. 1–4	Théâtre du 8e, Lyon, France
Oct. 7, 8	Maison de la Culture, Grenoble, France
Oct. 10	(venue not given) St. Quentin, France
Oct. 11	(venue not given) Montluçon, France
Oct. 14	(venue not given) Douai, France
Oct. 15	Théâtre de Sartrouville, Sartrouville, France
Oct. 16	(venue not given) Cergy-Poutoise, France
Oct. 17	Théâtre Des Sources, Fontenay-aux-Roses, France
Oct. 18	Nouveau Théâtre de Belfort, Belfort, France
Oct. 21–26	Festival Otoño, Madrid, Spain, with other festival performances in Móstoles, Alcorcón, San Sebastian de los Reyes, Alcalá de Henares, and Aranjuez
Oct. 28	Teatro Pérez Galdós, Las Palmas, Canary Islands, Spain
Oct. 30, 31	(venue not given) Tenerife, Canary Islands, Spain
Nov. 3	(venue not given) Lecce, Italy
Nov. 4	Teatro Petruzzeli, Bari, Italy
Nov. 6	(venue not given) Pescara, Italy
Nov. 22	Long Island University, Brookville, NY
Dec. 12–24, 26–30	Joyce Theater, New York City (joint programs with Murray Louis Dance Company)

1987

Jan. 2 – 4	Joyce Theater, New York City
Jan. 9, 10	Stanford University, Palo Alto, CA
Jan. 17, 18	Florida State University, Tallahassee
Mar. 6, 7	(venue not given) Dallas, TX
Mar. 20	Val-de-Marne Biennale Nationale de Danse, Fontenay-sous-Bois, France
Mar 23, 24	Kultur der Landeshaupt Stadt, Munich, Germany
Mar 27	Texas Tech University College, Lubbock
May 21	Forum Theatre, Leverkusen, West Germany
May 23, 24	Bergen International Festival, Bergen, Norway
May 29 – 31	New York State Museum, Albany
July 16 – 18	Town Square Vignale Festival, Vignale, Italy
July 20 – 23	(venue not given) Arles, France
Sept. 10 – 12	Whitney Hall, Louisville, KY
Sept. 15	Lafayette College, Easton, PA
Sept. 17	Keene State College, Keene, NH
Sept. 19	Bartlesville Community College, Bartlesville, OK
Sept. 22	Texas A&M University, College Station
Sept. 26	University of Arizona, Tucson
Oct. 9, 10	Montclair State University, Montclair, NJ
Oct. 24	(venue not given) Aranjuez, Spain
Oct. 26	(venue not given) Madrid, Spain
Oct. 27	Teatro Péres Galdós, Las Palmas, Canary Islands
Oct. 30	(venue not given) Tenerife, Canary Islands
Nov. 30	Great Valley High School, Malvern, PA
Dec. 7	Kennedy Center, Washington, DC
Dec. 15 – 17	Joyce Theater, New York City (joint programs with Murray Louis Dance Company)

1988

Jan. 6 – 10	Zellenbach Theatre, Philadelphia, PA
Jan. 29	State University of New York, Binghamton
Jan. 30	State University of New York, Purchase
Mar. 3, 4	Great Valley High School, Malvern, PA
Apr. 17, 18	Appalachian State University, Boone, NC
Apr. 29, 30	(venue not given) Los Angeles, CA
May 17, 18	'Spreckels Theatre, San Diego, CA
May 19, 20	University of California, Los Angeles
June 1	Midland Center for the Arts, Midland, MI

Sept. 14, 15	Miller Theater at Columbia University, New York City
Sept. 16	Pennsylvania State College, Lamar
Sept. 18–24	Kennedy Center for the Performing Arts, Washington, DC
Oct. 1	William Patterson University, Wayne, NJ
Oct. 2	Queensborough Community College, Bayside, NY
Oct. 10, 11	Portland State University, Portland, OR
Oct. 13–18	(venues not given) Fairbanks and Anchorage, Alaska
Oct. 19–22	University of Washington, Seattle, WA
Oct. 24, 25	Kimo Theatre, Albuquerque, NM
Nov. 9	Relais Culturel Régional, Wissenbourg, France
Nov. 10	Relais Culturel Régional, Thann, France
Nov. 12	La Malmaison, Cannes, France
Nov. 15	Centre d'Action Culturelle, Niort, France
Nov. 16	Centre de Beaulieu, Poiters, France
Nov. 17	Théâtre Municipal, Angoulême, France
Nov. 18, 19	Maison de la Culture, Nantes, France
Nov. 22	Théâtre Municipal, Bourg-en-Bresse, France
Nov. 23	Espace Culturel André Malraux, Chambéry, France
Nov. 24	Théâtre d'Annecy, Annecy, France
Nov. 25	Maison des Arts et Loisirs, Thônon-les-Bains, France
Nov. 26	Maison des Jeunes et de la Culture, Annemasse, France
Nov. 29	Centre d'Action Culturelle, Saint-Médard-en-Jalles, France
Dec. 1	Théâtre Municipal de Privas, Privas, France
Dec. 2	Centre Culturel Léonard de Vinci, Lyon, France
Dec. 6	Centre Culturel Odyssud, Blagnac, France
Dec. 8	Centre Culturel Le Parvis, Tarbes, France
Dec. 10	Maison de la Culture, La Rochelle, France
Dec. 13	Centre d'Action Culturelle Jean Renoir, Dieppe, France
Dec. 15	Palais des Congres et de la Culture du Mans, Le Mans, France
Dec. 17	Palais des Beaux-Arts, Brussels, Belgium

	Dec. 19	Teatro Noveli, Rimini, Italy
	Dec. 21	Teatro Kursal, Lugano, Switzerland
1989	Feb. 1, 2	(venue not given) New Haven, CT
	Feb. 3	Connecticut College, New London,
	Apr. 12, 13	University of Utah, Salt Lake City
	May 12, 13	State University of New York, Stony Brook
	May 19, 20	Wells Theater, Norfolk, VA
	May 23	Le Quartz de Brest, Brest, France
	May 25	Théâtre Municipal, Strasbourg, France
	May 27	Arsenal, Metz, France
	May 29–June 4	Teatro Olimpico, Rome, Italy
	June 6–13	Théâtre de la Ville, Paris, France
	June 15, 16	Nouveau Théâtre d'Angers, Angers, France
	July 4–6	Dos Hermanas, Seville, Spain
	July 8, 9	Teatro Municipal Miguel de Cervantes, Malaga, Spain
	July 10–15	Italica Festival, Seville, Spain. Additional performances in Ecija and Utrera
	July 19	Herod Atticus Theatre, Athens, Greece
	Aug. 2	Stockton State College, Pomona, NJ
	Sept. 8–11	Teatro Zandonai di Roverto, Roverto, Italy
	Sept. 23	Long Island University, Brookville, NY
	Sept 25, 25	Civic Center, Des Moines, IA
	Oct. 17–Nov. 5	Joyce Theater, New York City

In 1990, as Nikolais' health failed, his company combined with the Murray Louis Dance Company to form the Nikolais and Murray Louis Dance Company, which performed repertory of both choreographers. Later renamed Murray Louis and Nikolais Dance, the company toured nationally and internationally at almost the same pace as had the Nikolais Dance Theatre. Louis disbanded the company in 1999.

Contributors

PHILIP AUSLANDER is a professor in the School of Literature, Communication, and Culture of the Georgia Institute of Technology. He holds the Ph.D. in Theatre from Cornell University. At Georgia Tech, Prof. Auslander teaches in the areas of Performance Studies, Cultural Studies, and Media Studies. He is a contributing editor to the US-based *TDR: The Journal of Performance Studies*, the UK-based *Performance Research*, and the newly established *International Journal of Performance and Digital Technology*, also based in the United Kingdom. He contributes regularly to these and other journals and has published four books, including *Presence and Resistance: Postmodernism and Cultural Politics in Contemporary American Performance* (University of Michigan Press, 1992), *From Acting to Performance: Essays in Modernism and Postmodernism* (Routledge, 1997), and *Liveness: Performance in a Mediatized Culture* (Routledge, 1999). He received the prestigious Callaway Prize for the Best Book in Theatre or Drama for *Liveness*. Prof. Auslander is the editor of *Performance: Critical Concepts*, a reference collection of eighty-nine essays in four volumes published by Routledge in 2003 and, with Carrie Sandahl, co-editor of *Bodies in Commotion: Performance and Disability* (University of Michigan Press, 2005). His next book project as an author will be *All the Young Dudes: Performing Glam Rock*, also for the University of Michigan Press. In addition to his scholarly work on performance, Prof. Auslander writes art criticism for *ArtForum* in New York City and *Art Papers* in Atlanta.

HERBERT BLAU is Byron W. and Alice L. Lockwood Professor of the Humanities at the University of Washington. He has also had a distinguished career in the theater, as co-founder and co-director of the Actor's Workshop of San Francisco, then co-director of the Repertory Theater of Lincoln Center in New York, and as artistic director of the experimental group KRAKEN, the groundwork for which was laid at California Institute of the Arts, of which he was founding provost and dean of the School of Theater and Dance. Among his books are *Take Up the Bodies: Theater at the Vanishing Point* (University of Illinois Press, 1982), *The Audience* (John Hopkins University Press, 1993), *To All Appearances: Ideology and Performance* (Routledge, 1992), and recently, *Sails of the Herring Fleet: Essays on Beckett* (University of Michigan Press, 2000). He has also published a book recently on fashion,

Nothing in Itself: Complexions of Fashion (Indiana University Press, 1999), and a new collection of essays, *The Dubious Spectacle: Extremities of Theater, 1976–2000* (University of Minnesota Press, 2002).

JANA FEINMAN is the director of the Hunter College Dance Program of the City University of New York. In this position she has inaugurated an outreach program for public schools, New York State certification in dance education, and the "Sharing the Legacy" conference and concert series at Hunter College. The "Legacy" events have brought together students from around the country to honor such prominent dance figures as Erick Hawkins, Katherine Dunham, and Alwin Nikolais and to perform reconstructions of historic dance works. During Feinman's thirty-year career as a dancer, choreographer, and educator she has served on the boards of many dance organizations, established and participated in national conferences, and adjudicated major national projects. Feinman holds an EdD from Temple University where her interest in the creative process led her to investigate Alwin Nikolais' philosophy, methodology, and artistry in her doctoral dissertation, *Alwin Nikolais, a New Philosophy of Dance: The Process and the Product 1948–1968.*

MARK FRANKO is a professor at the Theater Arts Department at the University of California, Santa Cruz. He is the author of *The Work of Dance: Labor, Movement, and Identity in the 1930s* (Wesleyan University Press, 2002), *Dancing Modernism/Performing Politics* (Indiana University Press, 1995), *Dance as Text: Ideologies of the Baroque Body* (Cambridge University Press, 1993) *The Dancing Body in Renaissance Choreography* (Summa Publications, 1986), and most recently, *Excursions for Miracles: Paul Sanasardo, Donya Feuer, and Studio for Dance (1955–1964)* (University Press of New England, 2005). He is the co-editor, with Annette Richards, of *Acting on the Past: Historical Performances Across the Disciplines* (Wesleyan University Press, 2000). His articles on dance and performance have appeared in *Discourse, PMLA, The Drama Review, Res: Anthropology and Aesthetics, Theatre Journal,* and in numerous anthologies.

BOB GILMORE is a musicologist specializing in the study of contemporary music. He studied at York University in England and, on a Fulbright Scholarship, at the University of California, San Diego. He has taught at Queen's University, Belfast, and has been teaching at Dartington College of Arts in England since 1994. He is the author of *Harry Partch: A Biography* (Yale University Press, 1998), which won an ASCAP-Deems Taylor Award in 1999, and is presently writing a biography of the French-Canadian composer Claude Vivier. His writings on contemporary music have appeared in a variety of international media.

Dance artist, educator, and historian CLAUDIA GITELMAN is a veteran of the concert stage and Broadway. She was on the faculty of the Nikolais-Louis Dance Theatre Lab in New York City over a period of twenty-four years and a guest teacher and performer in universities and dance centers on four continents. She is the author of articles in encyclopedia and dance journals, and of two books, *Dancing with Principle: Hanya Holm in Colorado, 1941–1983* (University of Colorado Press, 2001), and *Liebe Hanya: Mary Wigman's Letters to Hanya Holm* (Wisconsin University Press, 2003). Gitelman is a professor emerita at Rutgers University.

YVONNE HARDT is a dancer and choreographer as well as a historian and dance scholar. She received her formation in Berlin, Germany, at the Free University and in Montreal at Concordia University. She is interested in combining dance practice and theory. One of her central topics is the relationship between dance and politics, most prominently seen in her Ph.D. thesis "*Politische KörperAusdruckstanz und politische Identität in der Weimarer Republik*" ("Political Bodies: German Dance and Political Identity in the Weimar Republic") (Münster, 2004). Currently she is working at the Free University of Berlin with the purpose of setting up a master's program in Dance Studies. She is creating dance theater pieces for her company, Body-AttacksWord.

REBEKAH KOWAL teaches dance history and theory at the University of Iowa. Prior to joining the UI faculty she held a Mellon Foundation Fellowship in Performance Studies at Haverford College and a Regional Faculty Research and Cultural Fellowship at the University of Pennsylvania Humanities Forum. Kowal holds a B.A. in English from Barnard College/Columbia University, a C.M.A. from the Laban/Bartenieff Institute of Movement Studies, and a Ph.D. in American Studies from New York University. Prior to attending graduate school, she danced professionally in New York City. Her book-length project, *Visible Difference: Modern Dance in Cold War America*, will be published by Wesleyan University Press. Currently she serves as reviews editor for *Dance Research Journal*.

RANDY MARTIN is a professor of Art and Public Policy at the Tisch School of the Arts, New York University, where he directs the graduate program in arts politics. He studied dance with Alwin Nikolais, Murray Louis, and Hanya Holm, and performed with Claudia Gitelman, among others. He is author of *Performance as Political Act: The Embodied Self* (Bergin & Garvey, 1990), *Socialist Ensembles: Theater and State in Cuba and Nicaragua* (University of Minnesota Press, 1994), *Critical Moves: Dance Studies in Theory and Politics* (Duke University Press, 1998), *On Your Marx: Relinking Socialism and the Left* (University of Minnesota Press, 2001); *Financialization of Daily Life* (Temple University Press, 2002), and *Empire of Indifference: American War and the Financial Logic of Risk Management* (Duke University Press, 2007).

NAIMA PREVOTS studied English and History at Brandeis and Brooklyn College before taking her M.S. in Dance at the University of Wisconsin and her Ph.D. in Performance Studies at the University of Southern California. She has danced and choreographed for many companies, co-produced the film *Children Dance* (1971), served as director of the Hollywood Bowl Museum, and was instrumental in starting the Department of a performing arts and the dance program at American University in Washington, D.C. where she is now a professor emerita of Dance. Her books include *Dancing the Sun: Hollywood Choreographers, 1915–1937* (UMI Research Press, 1987), *American Pageantry: A Movement for Art and Democracy* (UMI Research Press, 1990), and most recently, *Dance for Export: Cultural Diplomacy and the Cold War* (University Press of New England, 1998).

MARCIA B. SIEGEL is an internationally known dance critic, historian, and teacher. She is the author of *The Shapes of Change: Images of American Dance* (University of California Press, 1985), *Days on Earth* (Yale University Press, 1987), a biography of choreographer Doris Humphrey, as well as three collections of reviews and commentary. Her work is a subject of *First We Take Manhattan: Four American Women and the New York School of Dance Criticism*, by Diana Theodores. Over the past thirty-five years Siegel has reviewed dance regularly for major American newspapers and magazines, including the *Christian Science Monitor, New York Magazine*, the *Soho Weekly News*, and the *Boston Phoenix*. Her essays have appeared in reference works, books, general publications, and journals, including the *Hudson Review*, where she has been a contributing editor since 1973. In 1971 Siegel received a certificate in Laban Movement Analysis (CMA). From 1983 to 1999 she was a member of the resident faculty of the Department of Performance Studies, Tisch School of the Arts, New York University. Most recently, Siegel published *Howling Near Heaven: Twyla Tharp and the Re-invention of Modern Dance*, (Palgrave/St. Martin's Press, 2006).

Index

Numbers in *italics* represent illustrations.

Nikolais, Alwin, *continued*
auteur, 20–21, 206; awards, vii–viii; Balanchine and, 26, 36, 37, 161; break with traditional modern dance, 37–39; choreographic process of, 43; choreography of, chronological list, 228–48; classroom/studio process, 31–36, *34*, 49–50, 146, 194; Clement Greenberg and the aesthetics of, 154–66, 167n3; Clive Barnes on the art of, 5, 10–11, 205–6, 218–19; cold war gender anxiety and, 97–101; company name changes and mergers, 249, 254, 256, 258, 277; company replacements chosen by, 36; critical responses to, 1–5, 22n2, 31, 39–40, 50, 72, 75, 82–83, 101–2; and the dance canon, 3; dances documented, xi; debordering, 65, 71; decentralization esthetics of, 10, 15–16, 17, 29–31, 39, 69–70, 87–88, 101; "dehumanization" of dancers in work of, 3–4, 10, 12–13, 22n2, 30–31, 61–62, 77, 82, 101–2, 142, 164–66, 208, 213, 218, 227; documentation of the work of, xi–xii; electronic music used by, 51, 142–46, *145*, 212, 238; emotion/empathy in the choreography, 71–75, 85–86, 103n18, 200, 213–14; ethnic music used by, 138–40; Federal Theater Project work, 134; formalism of, 156–66, 167n2; in France, 144, 146; grants obtained by, 14; on the human body in dance, 73–75, 76–80, 159–62, 164–66, 224; improvisation technique, 66–67; individuality deconstructed by, 68–69; intellectual influences, 9–10; John Cage and, 89–91, 93–94, 142; Laban and, 60, 69, 192; lighting effects by, xi, 48, 51–52, *78*, 124, 161, 162–63, 204, 207–8, 212, 213, 214, *235*; log of all performance of works by, 249–77; memoir, postwar, 191–93; modernism and, 34–35, 42, 44n8, 72; movement style, 208; music composition/collaboration of, 20–21, 46, 51, 140–48, 149, 151n10; music synthesizers used by, 51, 142–46, *145*, 212, 238; as non-dancer, 3–4, 12–13, 22n2; objectivity, 86–93, 101–2; photos of, *4, 34, 78, 124, 145, 263*; as pianist for silent movies, 133–34; politics of, 77–80; post–World War II culture and, 42; props used by, 38, 94–97; as puppeteer, 5, 33–34, 62, 75, 77, 110–11, 218–19; recorded music borrowed by, 136–40; reel-to-reel tape recording technique, 140, 141; rehearsal process, 32, 40, 49, 192, 194; relationality in dances of, 69–70, 78–79, 119; Sasha Waltz and, 64–65; on sculpture, 159; sexuality and, 20, 84, 97–101, 160; sound scores by, 132, 135, 136–40, 142–46, 204–5, 209, 238; spatial flexibility, 207; spoken text (recorded "samples") used by, 144; students, 194–95; successors to, 62–63, 277; technology embraced by, 42, 142–46; theatricality of, 162, 198, 205–6, 211, 219; twenty-first century music anticipated by, 149; unisex costumes used by, 160; warm-up/stretching routine, 32, 49, 194. *See also titles of particular Nikolais works*
Nikolais and Murray Louis Dance Company, 135, 136, 277
Nikolais Dance Theatre, 218, 224, 263, *263*; log of performances, 258–77; merged with Murray Louis Dance Co., 277

292 : *Index*